PATTON VERSUS THE PANZERS

PATTON VERSUS THE PANZERS

THE BATTLE OF ARRACOURT, SEPTEMBER 1944

Steven Zaloga

STACKPOLE
BOOKS

STACKPOLE BOOKS
Copyright © 2016 by Steven Zaloga

Published by STACKPOLE BOOKS
An imprint of Rowman & Littlefield
Distributed by NATIONAL BOOK NETWORK

Printed in the United States

10 9 8 7 6 5 4 3 2 1

FIRST EDITION

Cover design by Wendy Reynolds

Library of Congress Cataloging-in-Publication Data Available

ISBN 978-0-8117-1789-2 (hardback)
ISBN 978-0-8117-6535-0 (e-book)

Contents

Introduction

THE RECENT HOLLYWOOD FILM *Fury,* about an American Sherman tank crew in 1945, starts with the statement that: "In WW2 American tanks were outgunned and out armored by the more advanced German tanks. U.S. tank crewmen suffered staggering losses against the superior enemy vehicles." Was the Sherman tank of World War II a "death trap" as claimed on many TV documentaries? Was the Sherman tank so bad that it cost five Shermans on average to knock out one German Panther tank? These urban legends have seeped into popular perceptions of the history of World War II, reinforced by television and movie sensationalism. While containing a grain of truth, this viewpoint is historical baloney.

In an earlier book in this series, *Armored Thunderbolt,* I examined the development of the Sherman tank in World War II from the technical perspective. Popular views of tank warfare are strongly shaped by technological determinism: "If Tank A is technically superior to Tank B, then Tank A will prevail on the battlefield." This viewpoint is simply not true. There are far more important criteria for battlefield success than technological advantages. As I will argue in this book, battlefield dynamics and crew quality trump technical advantages as the basis for battlefield success.

Having already explored the technical aspects of the U.S. Army's Sherman tank in *Armored Thunderbolt,* I take a different approach in this book. Rather than look at tank combat from the technical perspective, I take a look at it from the battlefield perspective. How did the Sherman tank perform against German tanks in actual battlefield conditions? In order to provide a reasonable level of detail, I have chosen the tank battles in Lorraine in September 1944 between Patton's Third U.S. Army and Manteuffel's 5.Panzer-Armee that culminated in the fighting around Arracourt.

I have chosen these battles for several reasons. To begin with, they were the first large-scale tank-vs.-tank clashes between the U.S. Army and the Wehrmacht in the European Theater of Operations (ETO) in 1944–1945. Although there were several large-scale tank battles between the British and German armies in Normandy in the summer of 1944, the U.S. Army had very few large tank-vs.-tank clashes in June–August 1944. The Lorraine battles are also interesting because they were a classic "meeting engagement" where both sides were offensively oriented and neither side had any particular defensive advantage. The Lorraine fighting is also a useful historical example since neither side enjoyed excessively large numerical advantages in most of the engagements.

Another reason that I selected the Lorraine tank battles was for the simple reason that there were not very many large-scale tank-vs.-tank battles between the American and German armies in the ETO. In fact, there were really only two: Lorraine and the Ardennes. After the heavy panzer losses in Normandy, the German tank force in the ETO after September 1944 was quite modest since Hitler was holding back the panzers for the surprise Ardennes offensive. German tank strength after the Battle of the Bulge was very small due to the Ardennes losses and the need to concentrate the panzers against the Red Army on the approaches to Berlin. I chose Lorraine over the Ardennes since I have already written about the Ardennes tank fighting, and the Lorraine tank battles occurred in a more limited expanse of space and time that makes them easier to explore in a fine level of detail.[1]

The Lorraine tank battles are also intriguing because they are not as well known as the Ardennes battles. If you ask the average military history buff about Hitler's "Vosges Panzer Offensive," you will probably be met with a blank stare. Unlike some earlier German panzer offensives such as the Operation Lüttich attacks at Mortain in August 1944, and the Ardennes offensive, the U.S. Army never really understood Hitler's intentions for the Lorraine tank battles. The battle plans for the Vosges Panzer Offensive were not intercepted by the Ultra signals intelligence services while the Mortain plans were decrypted. Nor did the U.S. Army scrutinize the Lorraine battles to the extent of the Ardennes panzer attack. The reasons for this will become more apparent in the subsequent chapters.

I would like to acknowledge the help of numerous individuals in the writing of this book. When I was a teenager and first became interested in tank history, a friend of my dad, Sliver Lapine, patiently answered my many questions about tank warfare. Sliver had served as a M4 medium tank gunner in the 8th Tank Battalion, 4th Armored Division. He lent me his copy of the 4th Armored Division history, which started my interest in this unit and in this battle. My mentor on military technology, the late Lt. Col. Jim Loop, had served as executive officer for Col. James Leach during the Vietnam War, and would recall the many conversations they had with Creighton Abrams about their wartime experiences. After his retirement, Jimmie Leach worked for the tank engine manufacturer Teledyne Continental. Back in the 1980s, I would see Jimmie every year at the Association for the U.S. Army convention in Washington, D.C. Jimmie would patiently answer my many questions about the 37th Tank Battalion and his experiences as the Company B, 37th Tank Battalion commander during World War II. Many other friends have helped on various aspects of this book, including David Isby, David Glantz, Tom Jentz, Joe DeMarco, Pierre-Olivier Buan, and Kevin Hymel.

Technical Notes

A FEW TECHNICAL NOTES are worth clarifying at the start of this book. I have left most German unit designations in their original German form since they are easy for an English-reading audience to understand, and they help to distinguish between German and American units. For example, I have used 21.Panzer-Division rather than 21st Tank Division. I have made a few exceptions for the sake of clarity, using the simple form 84.Korps instead of the cumbersome LXXXIV.Korps, and using Army Group G instead of Heeresgruppe G. I have used English spelling for the German ranks even if they are not entirely equivalent, so "Lt. Col." rather than "Oberstleutnant." Likewise, I have used the more familiar contemporary style of "mm" for gun calibers rather than the German cm, so 75mm gun rather than 7.5cm gun.

For brevity, the traditional conventions have been used when referring to units. In the case of U.S. units, A/37th Tank Battalion refers to Company A, 37th Tank Battalion. In the case of regimental formations, 2/16th Infantry refers to the 2nd Battalion, 16th Infantry Regiment. The U.S. Army traditionally uses Arabic numerals for divisions and smaller independent formations (4th Armored Division, 37th Tank Battalion); Roman numerals for corps (XV Corps), and spelled numbers for field armies (Third U.S. Army). I have used the nickname "Sherman" for the M4 medium tank in this book. In fact, "Sherman" was the British name for the M4 medium tank, and this name was rarely used by the U.S. Army in World War II. However, it became common practice in the United States after World War II, and so I have used it here.

In the case of German regiments, an Arabic numeral is used for the smaller formation (company or battery) and a Roman numeral for the battalion. So 2./Panzer Regiment.16 refers to the 2nd Company, Panzer Regiment.16; II./Panzer Regiment.16 refers to the 2nd Battalion, Panzer Regiment.16. The Germans usually followed the practice of indicating divisional numbers as a prefix, for example 21.Panzer-Division, while smaller formations were usually written as a suffix, for example Panzer Regiment.16. German field armies are contracted in the simple fashion (1.Armee for First Army) rather than the common style used in most German military documents of using the headquarters designation such as 1.AOK (1.Armee Oberkommando). Also, I have used the term "Wehrmacht" here to refer in a general sense to the German army. In fact, "Wehrmacht" refers to the German Armed Forces, and "Heer" refers to the army. However, this distinction is not well known to most English speakers. In addition, "Wehrmacht" is a useful abbreviation rather than having to use "Heer, Waffen-SS, and Luftwaffe" when referring to the varied German ground force formations. The German army frequently used the term "Kampfgruppe" for a temporary combat formation, but other terms such as "Gruppe" or "Stossgruppe" were also used in the Lorraine battles. I have used these as appropriate, or their English equivalent, "battle-group."

In this book, I have used the term "AFV" (armored fighting vehicle) to refer to armored vehicles roughly equivalent to tanks. So in the

German case, the AFV category includes the Sturmgeschütz (assault gun) and Panzerjäger (tank destroyer). In the American case, it includes GMC (gun motor carriage) tank destroyers. The AFV category in this book does not include light armored vehicles such as armored cars, armored half-tracks, or armored self-propelled field artillery.

When providing data on German tank strength, I have generally used the term "operational strength," which is equivalent to "Einsatzbereit" in wartime German documents. This is due to the complicated and irregular methods of strength reporting in the German army in 1944. Strength was reported in various forms with various abbreviations. "Soll" (s) was the intended strength under the KStN (Kriegsstärkenachweisungen, the German equivalent of U.S. Army Tables of Organization and Equipment—TO&E). The more common reporting standard was "Ist" or "Istbestand" (actual strength), which included all tanks on hand including operational tanks, battle damaged tanks, and tanks under short- and long-term repair. The problem with using the Istbestand as the basis for cataloging German tank strength is that the German army suffered from poor tank reliability and so the Istbestand is often considerably higher than actual strength that a unit could put into the field. For example, average German readiness rates for all tanks and assault guns in 1944 was 58 percent.[2] Secondly, for reasons that remain unclear, German strength-reporting practices in 1944–1945 tended to include knocked-out tanks that had been recovered, regardless of whether there were any realistic chances they would be put back into service. These were not written off until they were shipped back to Germany or, more often, abandoned during a retreat.

As a result, the most useful reporting category was "Einsatzbereit," which counted tanks ready for combat. This was the standard usually used by divisions when reporting to corps of field army headquarters since it provided a clear picture of potential combat strength without the murkiness of the Istbestand status that included derelict vehicles and vehicles under repair. This is the category used in this book when identified as "operational strength" since it is the only category that accurately reflects battlefield strength. There were several other categories sometimes included in longer reports such as Instandhaltung (in repair) and Zugänge (new deliveries) but these are of little relevance to the subject at hand.

The German army listed tanks as lost only when they met the criteria of "Totalverlust," which corresponds to "total unredeemable loss" as used by other armies. This often meant a tank that had been burned out and so of no use for rebuilding since its armor had been compromised by the fire. The other criteria for Totalverlust was if a tank had been left behind in enemy hands after the battle. Tanks that had been knocked out in combat but recovered were still considered to be on unit strength until shipped back to Germany for rebuilding. As a result, German wartime reports on monthly tank losses create a deceptive picture since they continue to list knocked-out tanks as still on strength even though the chances for their eventual return to service use were small or nonexistent. The clearest case of this was German reporting on tank losses in France in the summer of 1944 where the tank loss figures for June–August are clearly too low, only to be corrected in September in acknowledgment of the wholesale abandonment of knocked-out and damaged vehicles left behind in France.

On the accompanying maps in this book, the tactical map symbols are in white for American and French units while the map symbols for German units are in black. The French roads indentified in the text by their route numbers refer to the contemporary route numbers, not the wartime designations.

Unit Size		Arm-of-Service	
xxxx ▢	Army	⊠	Infantry
xxx ▢	Corps	▭⬭	Tank
xx ▢	Division	⊗	Armored Infantry
x ▢	Brigade	⊘	Mechanized Cavalry
III ▢	Regiment	▢●	Artillery
II ▢	Battalion	⬭●	Armored Artillery
I ▢	Company	TD	Tank Destroyer
••• ▢	Platoon	E	Engineer

Tactical Map Symbols

Glossary

AAR	After-Action Report
Abt.	Abteilung: German unit between battalion and regiment in size
AFV	Armored fighting vehicle; in this book, tank-based vehicles such as tank destroyers and assault guns
AHEC	U.S. Army Heritage and Education Center, Carlisle Barracks, Pennsylvania
AOK	Armee Oberkommando (Army high command): German field army headquarters
Armee	German field army
Army	Military formation of several corps
Army Group	Heeresgruppe: German army formation of several field armies
Army Group B	German headquarters commanding forces in Netherlands, Belgium, and northern France as far as Luxembourg border
Army Group G	German headquarters commanding forces in southern France; after September 1944 in Lorraine-Alsace sector
CCA	Combat Command A: brigade-size combined-arms formation in a U.S. armored division
CCB	Combat Command B: brigade-size combined-arms formation in a U.S. armored division
CCR	Combat Command R: headquarters for reserve units in a U.S. armored division
Co.	Company: unit consisting of several platoons
Co-axial	Typically a machine gun mounted in parallel to the main tank gun
CP	Command post
Ersatzheer	Replacement Army: German organization for raising and rebuilding army units inside Germany
ETO	European Theater of Operations
FHH	Feldherrnhalle: honorific designation for a German army unit with ties to the SA/Sturm Abteilungen
Flak	Flugabwehrkanone: Antiaircraft gun
Forêt	Forest (French)
G-2	U.S. Army intelligence at divisional or higher level
GMC	Gun motor carriage; typically a self-propelled tank destroyer
Gothic Line	German defense line in Italy in 1943–1944
GTL	Groupement Tactique Langlade: Combat Command Langlade of the 2e DB
HMC	Howitzer motor carriage; typically a self-propelled artillery vehicle
Jagdpanzer (JgPz)	Tank destroyer
KG	Kampfgruppe: Battle group; an improvised German formation ranging in size from a company to a regiment

Kompanie	German army company
Korps	German for Corps, a formation consisting of several divisions and supporting units
KTB	Kriegstagebuch: War diary
Marder	German tank destroyer, typically the Marder III with a 75mm gun on a PzKpfw 38(t) chassis
Mecz	U.S. Army abbreviation for "mechanized"
MTO	Mediterranean Theater of Operations
NARA	National Archives and Records Administration II, College Park, Maryland
NATO	North African Theater of Operations
OB West	Oberbefelshaber-West: Supreme Command West
OKH	Oberkommando der Heeres: Army High Command, in charge of Russian front
OKW	Oberkommando der Wehrmacht: Armed Forces High Command, in charge of western front
Operation Cobra	First U.S. Army operation starting 25 July 1944 to break out from Normandy
Operation Lüttich	German panzer attack to cut off U.S. Army by reaching Avranches starting night of 6/7 August 1944
Operation Market-Garden	Allied combined airborne-ground operation to seize Rhine bridge in the Netherlands starting 17 September 1944
Operation Nordwind	Army Group G offensive starting on 1 January 1945 in Alsace
Panzergrenadier	German equivalent of U.S. armored infantry
Panzerjäger	Tank destroyer
Pioner	German engineer unit
PzKpfw	Panzerkampfwagen: Tank
RBFM	Régiment Blindée de Fusiliers Marins: Tank destroyer battalion of the 2e DB

RVK	Reichsverteidigungskomissare: Reichs Defense Comissar: Nazi party official in charge of Homeland defense
s.Pz.Abt.	schwere Panzer Abteilung: Heavy tank battalion, usually a Tiger battalion
SCR	Signal Corps Radio: U.S. Army radio designation
SdKfz	Sonderkraftfahrzeug: Special vehicle; a designation for a specialized German military vehicle
SHAEF	Supreme Headquarters Allied Expeditionary Force: Eisenhower's headquarters
Stab	German headquarters unit
Stoßgrupe	Shock group; a variant of the term "Kampfgruppe"
StuG	Sturmgeschütz: German assault gun, typically the StuG III on PzKpfw III chassis with 75mm gun
TAC	Tactical Air Command
TALO	Tactical Air Liaison Officer
Volksgrenadier	Peoples Grenadier, typically a reduced-scale 1944 army division for defensive missions
Wehrkreis	German regional military district for raising and training troops
Zug	German army platoon
2e DB	2e Division Blindée: French 2nd Armored Division
6th Army Group	Gen. Jacob Devers' command in southern France and Alsace
12th Army Group	Gen. Omar Bradley's command in northwest Europe
21st Army Group	Field Marshal Bernard Montgomery's command in northwest Europe

Patton and
the Panzers

THIS INTRODUCTORY CHAPTER is intended to set the stage for the Lorraine tank battles. It provides a quick snapshot of Patton's previous experience with German panzer forces during World War II and a brief overview of the U.S. Army's engagement with German panzer divisions during the summer fighting in Normandy.

Gen. George S. Patton Jr. had about as much experience fighting the German panzer forces as any American field army commander of World War II. The first large-scale encounter between the U.S. Army and the German panzer divisions was during the Kasserine Pass battles in February 1943. At the time, Patton was commanding the I Armored Corps in Morocco, and so he was not involved in these battles. Due to the poor performance of the senior American commander at Kasserine, Maj. Gen. Lloyd Fredendall, Patton was transferred to Tunisia to take command of II Corps. One of his first combat actions in this new post was the defeat of the German panzer attack at El Guettar on 23 March 1943.

Following the campaign in Tunisia, Patton led the Seventh U.S. Army during Operation Husky, the amphibious landings on Sicily in July 1943. The combined German and Italian forces launched a tank counterattack on the American landing beaches at Gela that was soundly defeated.

During the subsequent campaign on mainland Italy from September 1943 to January 1944, German tank use was on a very small scale. Patton was no longer in a combat command position at this time after the controversial incident on Sicily where he had slapped two soldiers with combat fatigue for dereliction of duty. The mountain terrain

The U.S. tank force got a rude awakening at Kasserine Pass in February 1943. This is a pair of M4 medium tanks of Company F, 1st Armored Regiment, 1st Armored Division, knocked out during the 15 February counterattack by Combat Command C southwest of Sidi Salem. This company was virtually wiped out in a short engagement with Pz.Kpfw III and Pz.Kpfw IV tanks with the tank in the foreground, #19, knocked out by a 75mm round from a Pz.Kpfw IV, and the tank in the background, #3, knocked out by a 50mm round from a Pz.Kpfw III.

Although the German panzer forces gave the U.S. Army a thorough drubbing in the opening phases of the Kasserine Pass battle, the attack was eventually repulsed. This is a PzKpfw IV Ausf. F2 of Panzer-Regiment.8, 15.Panzer-Division left behind in Kasserine Pass late in February 1943. This division would fight Patton in Lorraine after having been reconstituted as the 15.Panzergrenadier-Division on Sicily.

Patton was brought in to redeem the performance of II Corps after Kasserine Pass. His first victory was at El Guettar against the 10.Panzer-Division in late March 1943. This is a view of a German motorized column of Panzergrenadier-Regiment.69 left behind after the German attack failed to penetrate U.S. defenses.

The U.S. II Corps under Patton's command eventually recovered from the Kasserine defeat. This is an M3 medium tank of the 751st Tank Battalion, supporting the 34th Division during the fighting for Bizerte on 7 May 1943.

Patton's old command, the 2nd Armored Division, played a prominent role in Operation Husky, the Allied invasion of Sicily on 11 July 1943. Here, an M4A1 of the HQ Company, 3/67th Armored, 2nd Armored Division comes ashore from a pontoon.

The combat debut of the Panther in the west was in Italy when a regiment was deployed near Anzio. However, the Panther saw little if any combat in Italy until the fighting on the approaches to Rome in May 1944, by which time the German army was in desperate condition.

during the autumn–winter 1943 campaign in Italy was not conducive to panzer operations. At the time of the Anzio amphibious landings in January 1944, the German tank force in Italy had been reinforced compared to 1943, but it still was quite modest with only 475 tanks and AFVs in theater, of which 358 were operational.[3] The next large-scale German panzer offensive in the Mediterranean Theater of Operations (MTO) was Operation Fischfang, the counterattack against the Anzio beachhead on 16 February 1944 involving several panzer and panzergrenadier divisions. By early 1944, Patton had been transferred from the Mediterranean theater to Britain to take part in the campaign in France.

Patton was assigned to lead the Third U.S. Army in the campaign in France. This formation remained in Britain for the first month of the Normandy

campaign. Bradley's First U.S. Army landed at Omaha and Utah beaches on D-Day and constituted the only U.S. Army field army in France until July 1944 when elements of Patton's Third U.S. Army began to arrive.

Bradley's First U.S. Army had frequent contact with German tanks and armored fighting vehicles in the Normandy fighting, but not on a particularly large scale. At the time of the D-Day landings in June 1944, there were no panzer divisions in the American sector, only a single panzergrenadier (mechanized infantry) division. All of the German panzer divisions were in the British/Canadian sector around Caen. The only other armored formations in the American sector were panzer training battalions, assault gun battalions, and infantry division antitank companies. During the fighting on the Cotentin peninsula in June 1944, the First U.S. Army fought against the 17.SS-Panzergrenadier-Division that had a single regiment of StuG IV assault guns. There were also two panzer replacement and training battalions, equipped with obsolete war-booty French tanks. The better German infantry divisions had a panzerjäger company typically equipped with 14 Marder III tank destroyers and 14 StuG III assault guns. Although some fighting did take place during the Cherbourg campaign between U.S. tanks and German AFVs, it was infrequent and on a very small scale. As can be seen in the accompanying table, tank fighting was much more pronounced in the British sector of the Normandy campaign. On average, U.S. forces claimed to have knocked out on about 3 German tanks per day while in the British/Canadian sector it was more than 14 per day, nearly five times as many. U.S. tank losses during this period were 647, though most of these losses were to antitank guns and infantry antitank rocket launchers.[4]

The initial fighting in the hedgerow country on the approaches to St. Lô in June–July 1944 followed much the same pattern, with occasional encounters between U.S. tanks and the occasional StuG III or Marder III from one of the infantry divisions, or StuG III from the assault-gun battalions attached to German corps. The success of the First U.S. Army in pushing through the hedgerow country to the road-junction at St. Lô prompted the Wehrmacht to begin to shift panzer divisions to the American sector for the first time.

Two divisions, the Panzer-Lehr Division and 2.SS-Panzer-Division "Das Reich" began to enter combat along the Vire River front in mid-July 1944. The first large-scale panzer attack against the U.S. Army in Normandy was by a Kampfgruppe (battle group) of Panzer-Lehr Division near Le Dezert on 11 July 1944 against elements of the 9th and 30th Infantry Divisions. The attack was a failure and cost Panzer-Lehr Division about thirty tanks. It is also worth noting that this was the first U.S. Army encounter with the Panther tank in the ETO. A regiment of Panther tanks had been deployed to Italy at the time of the Anzio battles, but for a variety of reasons they did not see significant combat use there until the early summer of 1944.[6] The Panther was not very successful in its combat debut against U.S. troops in the ETO, and the Panzer-Lehr Division commander later complained that it was not especially suitable for use in the confined hedgerow country of lower Normandy.

The First U.S. Army deployed its first two armored divisions to Normandy in July 1944, but they did not see extensive use until Operation Cobra on 24 July 1944. Cobra was the plan to break through the German defenses around St. Lô and then conduct a fast breakout operation using the 2nd and 3rd Armored Divisions. The 2nd Armored Division overran the badly weakened Panzer-Lehr Division in the opening days of Operation Cobra, but there was little tank fighting due to the small number of surviving German tanks in this division.[7] The attack trapped the 2.SS-Panzer-Division and the

ALLIED CLAIMS OF GERMAN TANK LOSSES IN NORMANDY, D-DAY TO AUGUST 1944[5]						
	Pz III	Pz IV	Panther	Tiger	Unidentified	Total
First Canadian Army		16	13	10		39
Second British Army	12	211	249	122	260	854
First U.S. Army		82	34	27	52	195
Total	**12**	**309**	**296**	**159**	**312**	**1,088**

U.S. claims thru 6 Aug, Canadian thru 11 Aug, British thru 12 Aug

The first large-scale panzer attack against the U.S. Army in Normandy took place on 11 July 1944 when a battle group of Panzer-Lehr Division attacked elements of the 9th and 30th Infantry Divisions along the Vire River near Le Dezert. The attack was beat off with heavy losses, and the German divisional commander later complained that the Panther was not well suited to use in the confines of the Norman hedgerow country. This Panther has taken several hits on the front-left corner of the hull, where the armor was much weaker than the front.

A pair of Panther Ausf. A tanks of Panzer-Regiment.130 of Panzer-Lehr Division knocked out in the hedgerow country along the Vire River during the failed 11 July 1944 attack.

Operation Cobra began on 25 July 1944 with the carpet bombing of the forward lines of the Panzer-Lehr Division. The few remaining Panther tanks of the division were smothered with bombs, many of the tanks ending up destroyed or collapsed into craters such as this one.

remnants of the 17.SS-Panzergrenadier-Division in the Roncey pocket. There were several nighttime battles as the Germans tried to escape the trap. Curiously enough, the biggest panzer killers were the M7 105mm self-propelled howitzers of the armored field artillery battalions that happened to be on the scene of several chaotic breakout attempts.

Tank-vs.-panzer fighting in early August 1944 was on a very small scale. Panzergruppe West dispatched two more panzer divisions against the First U.S. Army hoping to stop the Cobra breakout. There was small-scale skirmishing on a daily basis as the First U.S. Army gradually pushed the Wehrmacht back. So, for example, the 116.Panzer-Division lost seventeen Panther tanks in the first week of August 1944 while fighting against the First U.S. Army, less than half to bazookas and antitank guns and the rest in tank duels. The U.S. tank units lost twelve Sherman tanks in these skirmishes with the Panther.[8] The northern wing of Patton's Third U.S. Army, the XV Corps, encountered portions of the 9.Panzer-Division on the approaches to the Seine.[9]

One reason that the "five Shermans for every Panther" myth is so dubious is the lack of any supporting data. The U.S. and German after-action reports for most of the 1944–1945 fighting are not especially detailed, and there was practically no operational research conducted afterwards to fill in the data. The case of the 116.Panzer-Division's Panther tank losses is an interesting exception. The French researcher Frédéric Deprun was able to compile a detailed account decades later after making an interesting discovery. The French government required local municipalities in Normandy to catalog wrecked military vehicles in their villages to facilitate an organized salvage operation after the war. By combining these long-forgotten records with German and American after-action reports, he was able to provide a fine-grained account of the August tank fighting involving the division's

Panther tank battalion. As quickly becomes apparent in reading these accounts, the skirmishes were on a very small scale, seldom involving more than a few tanks on both sides. In most cases, victory or defeat depended on the battlefield dynamics. A tank lying in wait, whether a Sherman or Panther, would spot an enemy tank and knock it out before the other side was even aware of the threat. This adds further evidence to the work of operational researchers in the late 1940s and early 1950s who concluded that the secret of battlefield victory in tank fighting was "see first, shoot first, hit first."[10] Tank fighting in World War II was not a noble encounter of armored knights engaged in a fair contest on the open fields of battle. Most often tank-vs.-tank combat consisted of a few tanks ambushing a few other tanks that were unlucky or imprudent enough to stumble into them. It was closer in texture to the "skulking way of war" rather than grand encounters of cavalry or armored knights.

The largest German tank action against the U.S. Army in Normandy was Operation Lüttich, launched on 7 August 1944. This attack by four panzer divisions was intended to push across the Operation Cobra advance route all the way to the sea at Avranches, thereby cutting off the armored

There were frequent small-scale encounters between U.S. and German tanks in the wake of the Operation Cobra breakout from Normandy in late July 1944. Here an M4 passes a knocked-out Panther near La Chapelle on 2 August 1944.

spearheads of both the First U.S. Army and Third U.S. Army. This involved about 120 tanks and 32 assault guns and tank destroyers. The US Army became aware of the plans for this attack by the Ultra intelligence decryptions of German Enigma encyphered radio communications. The German attack became immediately bogged down when it ran into the stout defense of the 30th Infantry Division at Mortain. The 30th Infantry Division claimed to have knocked out 69 German tanks during the battle.[11] The most important consequence of this ill-conceived attack was that it weakened the panzer defenses facing the British and Canadian forces in the Caen sector. After having been stymied all summer by the determined resistance of Panzergruppe West, the British and Canadian forces launched Operation Totalize on 8 August 1944, starting a second Allied breakout operation aimed at Falaise.

The largest German panzer offensive prior to the Lorraine fighting was Operation Lüttich near Mortain. The intention was to cut off the spearhead of Patton's Third U.S. Army by reaching Avranches and the sea. These are two Panther Ausf. A tanks and a SdKfz.251 half-track of 3./SS-Pz.Abt.1, 1-SS-Panzer-Division Leibstandarte Adolf Hitler knocked out during the fighting with the 117th Infantry, 30th Infantry Division near St. Barthelemy.

The Mortain offensive was stopped by the 30th Infantry backed by heavy doses of field artillery. This is a view of some Panther Ausf. A of SS-Pz.Abt.1, 1-SS-Panzer-Division knocked out during the fighting.

The defeat of the panzer attack at Mortain so weakened the Wehrmacht that the front near Caen collapsed under relentless British and Canadian pressure, leading to the encirclement battle around Falaise. Here, U.S. troops of the 359th Infantry, 90th Division look over a Panther tank of I./Panzer-Regiment.33 of the 9.Panzer-Division knocked out on 20 August between Argentan and Chambois during the Falaise encirclement battles. The officer to the left, Capt. Henry Baushausen, was killed in action in Lorraine on 11 November 1944 and was awarded the Distinguished Service Cross for his actions that day.

PATTON ARRIVES

The success of the initial phase of Operation Cobra led to the introduction of Patton's Third U.S. Army in Normandy at the end of July 1944. The combat debut of Patton's Third U.S. Army was spectacular. Two of his spearhead units, the 4th and 6th Armored Divisions, took part in the second phase of the Operation Cobra breakout from Normandy. They had raced down along the coast past Avranches. Patton's operational mission had been to secure Brittany and its numerous ports. Against weak opposition, the Third U.S. Army rapidly advanced westward into Brittany, securing most of the peninsula in two weeks time. The port of Brest held out and it would take nearly two months of fighting to reduce this heavily fortified bastion. Patton's forces mainly faced German infantry divisions, and so there was little tank-vs.-tank fighting in early August.

Patton became convinced that the Brittany mission was fundamentally mistaken. He was egged on by his old friend Maj. Gen. John S. Wood, commander of the 4th Armored Division, who argued that the Brittany campaign was an insignificant distraction. While ports were certainly needed, the Germans had shown at Cherbourg in late June that they would demolish the ports before their capture, rendering them useless for months. The port of Cherbourg had been captured by VII Corps at the end of June. The Germans demolished the harbor facilities before their capture, undermining their value as alternative supply points. Several ports in Brittany had already been captured, but the main port and naval base at Brest was still resisting. Brest intact was priceless; Brest in shambles had little immediate value. The prospects for capturing Brest intact were slim in spite of the lightning speed of Patton's advance. The Brittany ports were away from the main direction of the Allied advance, adding precious miles to every ounce of supplies that would be delivered through these harbors. If Brittany was an irrelevant objective, Patton at the same time sensed the real opportunity. The German army in France was trapped and on the run after Cobra, and there was a void in German defenses on the approaches to the Seine River and Paris. A rapid rush to the Seine River could help bag German forces in a deep envelopment, while at the same time securing the Normandy lodgment area months earlier than anticipated.

Patton argued that the ultimate objective of the summer fighting could be a bold advance over the Seine River. After the Normandy battles, no significant German forces stood in his path. Eisenhower began to appreciate the opportunities for a rapid dash towards the Seine that would complete a deep envelopment of the German Seventh Army and precipitate its rout. The top British commander in Normandy, Field Marshal Bernard Montgomery, also agreed with Patton's plan.

The reorientation east was authorized on 3 August; Patton left behind one corps in Brittany to finish the mission against the Breton ports. His three other corps began the great mechanized race across France. Patton later referred to the August campaign as "Touring France with an Army."

The Wehrmacht was deeply alarmed by the threat posed by this new drive and attempted to split Lt. Gen. Courtney Hodge's First U.S. Army and Patton's Third U.S. Army by a panzer counteroffensive towards Avranches as described earlier. While this drama played itself out around Mortain, Patton's forces were racing eastward against weak German resistance. Hitler had forbidden the construction of secondary defense lines behind Normandy, and there were no major German formations in Patton's path. The tactical situation was ripe for exploitation, and Patton's bold cavalry style was ideally suited to the mission. Patton urged on his motorized and mechanized spearheads and told them to ignore their flanks. The northern flanks were covered by the advance of Hodge's First U.S. Army, while the Loire River offered a defensive shoulder that could be patrolled by Weyland's XIX Tactical Air Force acting as an airborne cavalry flank guard. The cities west of Paris fell in rapid succession, including the cathedral cities of Chartres and Orléans. Paris itself beckoned.

By 15 August, Patton's three corps were on their way towards Dreux (XV Corps), Chartres (XX Corps), and Orléans (XII Corps). Their tactical aim was to reach the Seine River and establish what was called the "D-Day lodgment area," the section of northwest France up to the Seine River that would be the base for further Allied operations in the autumn and winter of 1944 on the approaches to Germany. There were no orders to cross the Seine River, only to clear the western bank.

Major General Wade Haislip's XV Corps encountered modest resistance and established a bridgehead over the Eure River on the afternoon of August 16, placing it only thirty-seven miles (sixty km) from Paris. One infantry regiment advanced past one of the bends in the Seine River, where they found a catwalk over a dam. Since the mission was simply to hold the left bank of the Seine, the regiment was ordered to destroy the catwalk. The regimental commander took his time executing the order since he had sent a platoon across and didn't have enough explosives for such a mission. Patton had visited their headquarters while searching the area for future crossing sites.

The timing of this unauthorized Seine River crossing was fortuitous. The same day, Eisenhower had met with his two senior commanders, Montgomery and Bradley, to discuss future objectives. The original D-Day plans had not expected Allied forces to reach the outer boundary of the D-Day lodgment area until D+90, when in fact it had been reached on D+74. This had created significant logistics challenges that slowed the advance of Patton's Third US Army. All three commanders agreed to ignore earlier plans and to exploit the current German predicament. Montgomery had long been a proponent of a deep envelopment on the Seine since it might trap as many as 75,000 German troops on the western bank. All three commanders agreed to disregard previous planning and encourage Patton to push on beyond the Seine. Patton's staff had already begun to plan such a mission, and Bradley authorized him to begin the crossing operation later that day.

Patton ordered General Wyche of the 79th Division to begin crossing the Seine that evening. Further crossing sites were added, including a treadway bridge on August 20. The attack was so unexpected that the main German headquarters in northern France, Field Marshal Walter Model's

Army Group B underground bunker complex at Roche-Guyon, was hurriedly abandoned and a new command post hastily established at Soissons. Model quickly appreciated the threat posed by the bridgehead, but lacking ground forces, he attempted to stop the expansion of the bridgehead with heavy air attacks. In one of the largest showings of strength that month, several Luftwaffe squadrons began incessant air attacks using strafing, bombs, and rockets to stifle the bridgehead. The XV Corps moved all available antiaircraft defenses around the bridge and the US antiaircraft gunners claimed about fifty aircraft shot down in four days of fighting. The Luftwaffe attacks failed to inflict significant damage on any of the bridges.[12]

Delayed by the German defense at Chartres, Maj. Gen. Walton Walker's XX Corps reached the Seine on 22–23 August. The 5th Infantry Division reached the heights overlooking Fontainebleau in the early morning hours on August 23 and rushed the river at dawn. By the end of the day, XX Corps had five bridgeheads over the river, and corps engineers began constructing four treadway bridges. This permitted a rapid push out of the bridgeheads the following day, speeded along by the extensive use of captured German trucks. Some wags wanted to dub Walker's force the "20th Panzer Korps" for all their German motor vehicles.

Patton was concerned that the Germans might push units up from the south against his undefended southern flank, and Maj. Gen. Manton Eddy's XII Corps mission was to preempt this threat. Due to the enormous amount of ground to be covered, a major role in this operation was assigned to the XIX Tactical Air Command, which conducted repeated sorties along the Loire to look for German activity. In addition, the U.S. Army Air Force systematically destroyed bridges over the Loire to prevent any German flank attacks. As a result of the bold actions of Patton's three corps, by August 24 the Seine had been breached both north and south of Paris.

Eisenhower had not planned to liberate Paris, but simply to isolate it and await for the surrender of the German garrison there. When the French resistance staged an uprising there on 19 August, it forced his hand. On 22 August, Bradley and Eisenhower agreed that they would have to intervene in Paris regardless of previous planning. To permit Patton to continue his spectacular advance eastward, Bradley transferred Haislip's XV Corps from Patton to Hodge's First U.S. Army and assigned the Paris mission to Maj. Gen. Leonard Gerow's V Corps. While Patton would not enjoy the acclaim of the liberation of Paris, it was the Third U.S. Army that had placed the Allies in the suburbs of Paris. Ironically, on 24 August the BBC mistakenly announced that Patton's Third U.S. Army had taken Paris. Patton in his diary recalled that "This seemed to me poetic justice as I could have taken it had I not been told not to."

Patton's lightning advance to the Seine encountered few panzers since they were still concentrated farther north in Normandy. The convergence of Allied forces around Falaise trapped much of the Wehrmacht in Normandy. While some significant forces escaped and crossed the Seine River, the harried German forces were caught in successive Allied operations along the Seine, and then again across the Belgian border. For example,

in the case of I./Panzer-Regiment.24 of the 116. Panzer Division, 50 of its Panther tanks were lost in combat in Normandy from 30 July to 28 August. Of these, 26 were lost attempting to stem the American Cobra breakout from 30 July to 11 August. A further 12 were lost in counterattacks against the British/ Canadian/Polish breakout, and 12 were lost in the fighting around the Falaise pocket. Of the surviving 24 Panther tanks that crossed the Seine River on 25–27 August, 14 were lost during the retreat and only 10 escaped to Germany by early September.[13] Of the roughly 2,400 panzers and AFVs committed to Army Group B in Normandy during the summer of 1944, very few survived.[14]

In contrast to the German panzer predicament, the Allied tank forces retained their substantial numerical superiority. On 20 August 1944, the U.S. Army fielded 5,340 tanks and tank destroyers in France; the British force was a further 3,000.[15] In early September 1944, the Allies had a 100-to-1 superiority in tanks and AFVs over the Wehrmacht. It would take months to redress this imbalance.

The largest tank-vs.-tank battles between American and German forces took place in the Ardennes in December 1944. Here, an M4A3 (76mm) of Company C, 774th Tank Battalion, passes by a knocked-out Panther tank near Bovigny on 17 January 1945 while supporting the 83rd Division during the drive to seal the Bulge.

Manteuffel's 5.Panzer.Armee was routed beyond Bastogne near the Meuse River with large numbers of tanks trapped in a pocket near Celles by the onrushing 2nd Armored Division. These are an abandoned PzKpfw IV Ausf. J and Panther Ausf. G of the 2.Panzer Division.

The scale of tank fighting in the ETO decreased dramatically after the Ardennes campaign as the Wehrmacht rushed its tank force to the Russian front. This photo shows an M4A1 of Company F, 33rd Armored Regiment, Combat Command B, 3rd Armored Division passing by a knocked-out PzKpfw IV Ausf. G, probably from the 11.Panzer-Division, in Bad Marienburg on 28 March 1945 during the breakout from the Remagen bridgehead. By 10 April 1944, there were only eleven operational PzKpfw IV and twenty-four Panther tanks on the entire western front.

CHAPTER 2

Hitler's Plan

AT THE START OF SEPTEMBER 1944, the German army in the west had been defeated and was in full retreat. The situation was so dire that the German commanders later called the last week of August 1944 and the first few weeks of September "the Void." For senior Allied commanders such as Dwight Eisenhower and Bernard Montgomery, the situation was reminiscent of the state of the Kaiser's army in November 1918, on the verge of collapse and surrender. Many officers thought the war would be over within a few weeks, and that the Allied soldiers would be home by Christmas. This euphoria lasted until the middle of September when an ugly new reality emerged.

The Wehrmacht in the west suffered about 726,000 casualties in June–September 1944: about 55,000 killed in action, 339,000 missing, and 332,000 wounded. To make matter worse, Hitler ordered army and naval personnel in several key fortified French ports to remain in place, leaving a further quarter-million troops isolated and abandoned. By early September 1944, the German army in the west had only 13 infantry divisions, 3 panzer divisions, and 2 panzer brigades rated as combat effective. A further 42 infantry divisions and 13 panzer divisions were ineffective, and of the infantry divisions, 7 were simply disbanded.

Virtually all of the tanks and armored vehicles deployed in northern France in the summer of 1944 had been lost. This totaled more than 2,900 armored vehicles, including about 2,010 tanks, 590 assault guns, and more than 300 tank destroyers. A precise count of German tank losses in Normandy is difficult since many units kept damaged tanks on unit rosters even if battle damaged beyond repair. These weren't officially declared lost until September, distorting the actual situation.

GERMAN AFV LOSSES IN THE WEST, SUMMER 1944[16]

	Jun	Jul	Aug	Sep
Tanks	227	297	114	1,371
Assault guns	27	68	112	383
Tank destroyers	29	15	24	244
Total	283	380	250	1,998

Regardless of the precise numbers of tanks and AFVs lost in the summer campaign in France, by September 1944 the situation was extremely dire in the panzer divisions. As the chart here demonstrates, there were less than a hundred armored fighting vehicles still in operation on the western front; some panzer divisions had no functional tanks at all.

OPERATIONAL GERMAN TANK AND AFV STRENGTH, ARMY GROUP B, 12 SEPTEMBER 1944[17]

Type	Panther	PzKpfw IV	StuG	JgPz IV	Stu.Pz.IV
Report Code	D	CL	G1	G2	J
1.SS-Pz.Div.					
2.SS-Pz.Div.		2			
9.SS-Pz.Div.		2		8	
12.SS-Pz.Div.	1	2			
17.SS-Pz. Gren. Div.			2		
2.Pz.Div.				2	
9.Pz.Div.		2		5	
21.Pz.Div.					
116.Pz.Div.	19	2		4	
Pz.-Lehr Div.	11	18			
Stu.Pz.Abt.217					2

THE STRATEGIC SITUATION

Command of the German army in the west was the responsibility of OB West (*Oberbefelshaber-West*: Supreme Command West). This headquarters was led by General Field Marshal Gerd von Rundstedt until the beginning of July when he was replaced by Günther von Kluge because of his pessimistic assessments of German fortunes in Normandy. At peak strength in the summer of 1944, OB West commanded two army groups in France containing five field armies. The more important of the two army groups was Army Group B, which defended northern France including Normandy and Brittany as well as Belgium and the Netherlands. Its southern neighbor, Army Group G, defended central, western, and southern France.

Of Army Group B's three field armies, 7.Armee and 5.Panzer-Armee had been decimated in the Falaise Gap followed by further losses in the withdrawal over the Seine River in late August 1944 and in encirclements in Belgium in early September 1944. These formations lost most of the panzer strength in the west. The armies' best units were reduced to "torso divisions," so-called since they had lost the muscle of their close-combat strength, including infantry, panzer, engineer, and reconnaissance troops, but still retained an administrative and logistics core. They had little or no combat value until they could be rebuilt. Of the three field armies in Army Group B, only 15.Armee on the North Sea coast was still intact. Most of its best divisions had been shipped off to Normandy during the summer, and it was left with poor-quality static infantry divisions, suitable for coastal defense.

Hitler at a planning session with Gen. Theodor Busse, commander of the 9.Armee.

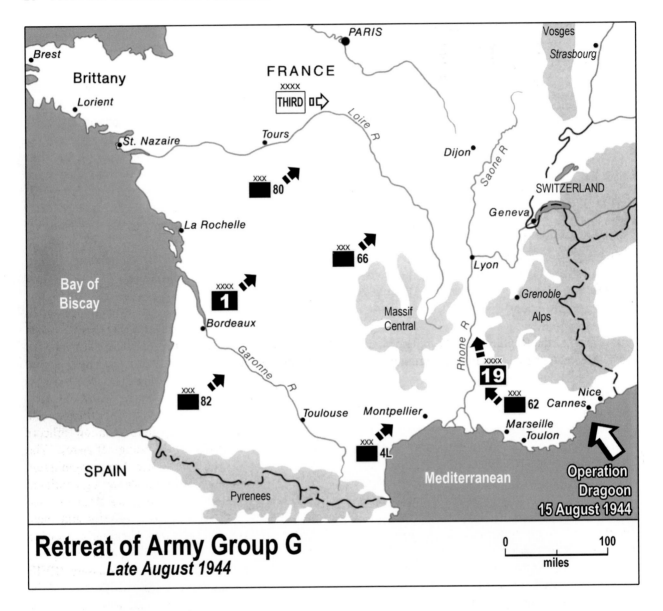

Retreat of Army Group G
Late August 1944

In the south, Army Group G had transferred most of its panzer forces and many of its better infantry divisions to Normandy during the summer, leaving it with ten infantry divisions and one panzer division to occupy all of central and southern France. When the Allies conducted the Operation Dragoon amphibious assault on the Mediterranean coast on 15 August 1944, Army Group G began to withdraw northward towards Germany rather than suffer encirclement by the rapidly advancing U.S. and French divisions. Hitler authorized the withdrawal on the night of 17/18 August.[18] Army Group G lost about 150,000 troops in the ensuing retreat. Equipment losses were heavy as well, with 1,316 field guns of the original 1,481 lost during the retreat.[19] It had only a single major tank unit, the 11.Panzer-Division, which conducted a costly but successful rearguard action as Army Group G withdrew.

Aside from the crippling defeats in Normandy and southern France, the most profound event of the summer was Operation Valkyrie, the attempted assassination of Adolf Hitler on 20 July 1944. Hitler was seriously injured by the bomb blast at his Wolf's Lair (Wolfsschanze) field headquarters

After the July 1944 military coup attempt against Hitler, SS chief Heinrich Himmler increasingly attempted to insert himself into army affairs, taking over the Replacement Army. Here he is seen awarding the Close-Combat Medal in Gold to army and Waffen-SS soldiers in late 1944.

in East Prussia. The conspiracy was centered in the senior ranks of the Replacement Army (Ersatzheer) that raised new army units inside Germany. Many senior commanders in France were implicated in the bomb plot, including OB West commander Günther von Kluge and Army Group B commander Erwin Rommel. Much of the senior staff of the military government of Paris was also complicit.

Hitler lost confidence in his military commanders, especially those in the west, and began to take an increasingly intrusive role in German military planning. He began by purging the senior commanders of the armies in western Europe at the slightest provocation. Hitler favored field commanders from the Russian front. The eastern-front commanders were often dismissive of the performance of their colleagues during the summer 1944 fighting. They mocked them as soft and lazy after comfortable years of French occupation duty. Yet the eastern-front commanders had little or no knowledge of the tactical differences between their familiar foe, the Red Army, and the much more modern Anglo-American armies in the west. Their condescending views of the U.S. Army tended to be based on cartoonish propaganda images. They would learn otherwise in the autumn 1944 fighting.

A far more malevolent role was played by Hitler's paladin, Reichsführer-SS Heinrich Himmler. He already controlled the state security apparatus and the SS, but Himmler also wanted greater control over the army. The bomb plot gave him the excuse to gradually take control of the regular army. He began by taking over the Replacement Army since it had been so central in the bomb plot. Nazi Party control within the army was further consolidated by the increasing role of the NFSO Nazi Party indoctrination officers (National Socialistische Führungsoffiziere). The NFSO were patterned after Red Army commissars and were intended to raise morale through political propaganda as well as keep a watchful eye for any signs of defeatism among officers and men. A further complication was Himmler's decision to expand the military role of regional Nazi party governors as Reich Defense Commissars (RVK: Reichsverteidigungskomissare). In August 1944, the RVK were assigned responsibility for the "Operational Zone" twenty kilometers behind the front, while the army controlled the "Combat Zone." They were also put in charge of a new military force, the Volkssturm militia. Party involvement in the autumn 1944 proved to be the source of endless aggravation for the senior army commanders.

The German army had long been famous for its agile battlefield performance due to its skilled and flexible command style, sometimes dubbed "Aufstragtaktik." This evaporated in the final months of 1944 when Hitler and Himmler took an increasingly intrusive role in directing the German war effort. Hasso von Manteuffel, the commander of 5.Panzer-Armee, described the change:

"The previous style of flexible and self-reliant German military leadership was paralyzed, shifting more and more to mechanical and perfunctory execution of orders issued as Führer Directives, concocted in a map room far away from the battlefield. That spelled death for the traditional German "Art of Command" in mobile warfare. Even the most outstanding senior commanders, raised under the traditional training regime, were compelled to follow these orders to the letter, and were not permitted to independently make decisions, even in small tactical matters involving single divisions."[20]

THE GENESIS OF THE VOSGES PANZER OFFENSIVE

In spite of the dire situation at the beginning of September 1944, Hitler began to think about possible offensive options to redeem the disaster.[21] The only large force that remained relatively intact was Army Group G, at the time retreating from cental and southern France. It was badly needed to help restore the defense along the German frontier in Lorraine and Alsace. Planning by the OKW (Oberkommando der Wehrmacht: Armed Forces High Command) began in late August to consider a variety of options for local counteroffensives to assist the retreat of Army Group G. Hitler began to speak about a "counter-offensive from the move," a euphemism for "counter-offensive during a retreat." The first scheme by the OKW in late August was to launch a panzer offensive from the Langres Plateau towards Reims to cut off and destroy Patton's Third U.S. Army to prevent it from interfering with the Army Group G retreat.[22] Curiously enough, Langres was the site of Patton's tank school in 1918.

Patton's forces were singled out for attention for several reasons. To begin with, they had engineered the boldest, most impressive offensive advance of the summer, charging across the breadth of France in little more than a week. Secondly, Patton's advance towards Lorraine posed a special threat. Army Group G had not yet completed its retreat from the Mediterranean and Atlantic coasts, and many of its units were still on the road. Not only might Patton's advance cut off these units, but their loss would make it very difficult to defend the entire German frontier from Luxembourg to Switzerland.

Army Group G consisted of two field armies, the 1.Armee and the 19.Armee. The 1.Armee had been stationed on France's Atlantic coast facing the Bay of Biscay. It had the longest distance to travel, more than 800 miles, but it was not being pursued by any Allied formations aside from French partisans. Nevertheless, it risked serious losses if Patton sealed off the approaches to Lorraine. The 19.Armee had been stationed on France's Mediterranean coast. It began retreating up the Rhone valley with the Seventh U.S. Army on its heels. Besides the threat posed to the 19.Armee, the advance of the Seventh U.S. Army also threatened to reach the vulnerable Belfort Gap. This area near the Swiss-German border offers quick access to the Upper Rhine and has been a traditional invasion route into southern Germany.

The problem facing German military planners at the end of August and early September was the lack of sufficient forces, and especially mobile forces. The heavy losses suffered both in France and on the Russian front left Germany largely bereft of reserve forces. To break this deadlock, in early September Hitler authorized the use of the new panzer brigades for this mission. These controversial new units had been formed in mid-summer at Hitler's instructions and were considered an untouchable Führer reserve. Their genesis will be described in more detail in a subsequent chapter. These would form the core element of the planned offensive.

Hitler's September 1944 panzer offensive never received a formal code name. It is usually called the Vosges Panzer Offensive in German accounts since its concentration points were in the western foreground of the Vosges mountains. Hitler began to further define the objectives of the attack, and he issued his first directive on the matter on 3 September 1944.[23] This initial scheme, sometimes called Plan 1 (Planung 1),

Gen. Johannes Blaskowitz led Army Group G through its precarious retreat in late August 1944, but he fell out of favor and was replaced in early September 1944.

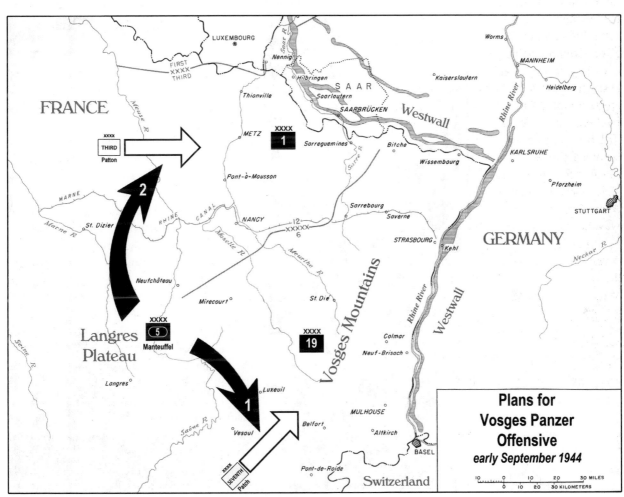

Plans for Vosges Panzer Offensive
early September 1944

was to thrust out of the Westwall-Moselle staging area west of the Vosges, across the Langres Plateau, and then pivot southwestward towards Pontarlier and the Swiss border. Unlike the first OKW plan mentioned above that was aimed northward at Patton's Third U.S. Army, the aim of Plan 1 was southward to cut off and destroy the spearhead of the Seventh U.S. Army, thereby shielding the retreat of 19.Armee from southern France. This would permit 19.Armee to create a new defense line in Alsace, and would help to shield the vulnerable Belfort Gap. The attack would take the direction of Vesoul-Gray-Pontarlier. Hitler intended to employ three panzergrenadier divisions and three of the new panzer brigades for the initial attack, and then add three more panzer divisions and three new panzer brigades as reinforcements.[24] Movement of the units was supposed to begin on 5 September 1944, but under the rapidly changing circumstances, this proved impossible.

Attack Force, Vosges Panzer Offensive Plan 1

Initial Force

3.Panzergrenadier-Division
15.Panzergrenadier-Division
17.SS-Panzergrenadier-Division
Panzer-Brigade.106
Panzer-Brigade.107
Panzer-Brigade.108

Reinforcements

Panzer-Lehr Division
11.Panzer-Division
21.Panzer-Division
Panzer-Brigade.111
Panzer-Brigade.112
Panzer-Brigade.113

The new panzer brigades were still scattered about in Germany and elsewhere and could not be concentrated in time. The panzer divisions were already committed to actions along the front and could not be quickly extracted without creating further havoc. The command structure up and down the western front was in chaos.

In order to coordinate the Vosges Panzer Offensive, Hitler decided to give it its own headquarters. The 5.Panzer-Armee headquarters at the time was based in the Netherlands but its main components, the battered Waffen-SS panzer divisions, had been ordered back to Germany for refitting.[25] The 5.Panzer-Armee headquarters was a redesignation of the previous Panzergruppe West headquarters that had directed the strategic panzer reserve in France before and after the D-Day landings. What was left of the headquarters after the summer retreat was ordered to move towards the Vosges. Hitler assigned the 5.Panzer-Armee a new commander, General of Panzer Troops Hasso von Manteuffel. At the time, Manteuffel was commanding one of the elite mechanized formations on the Russian front, Panzergrenadier-Division "Grossdeutschland," which was heavily involved in attempting to stem the Soviet attacks against the Kurland peninsula on the Baltic. Manteuffel was instructed to appear at Hitler's tactical headquarters, the Wolf's Lair in East Prussia. He arrived there on 5 September 1944.

Hitler intended to rejuvenate Germany's western armies using combat-hardened veterans from the Russian front who did not have the taint of any connection to the July bomb plot. Manteuffel was a typical example of this process. Hitler viewed him as one of Germany's most talented panzer commanders, and so an ideal leader for the Vosges Panzer Offensive. As a result, he leapfrogged the usual progression to a corps command, instead being appointed directly to command a field army. As a result, he was younger than his two subordinate corps commanders.[26]

Manteuffel arrived at the Wolf's Lair on the morning of 5 September 1944 in time to attend the daily situation report of the operations staff. He was subsequently brought to a private meeting with Hitler, who outlined his plans for the Vosges Panzer Offensive. Besides the new Panzer-Armee.5 headquarters, Hitler subordinated the 47.Panzer. Korps headquarters to his command.

Manteuffel left the Wolf's Lair and intended to travel to the new 5.Panzer-Armee headquarters in the village of Hochwald (French: Le Hohwald) outside the town of Barr, southwest of Strasbourg

Gen. Hasso von Manteuffel, on the left, is seen here in the late autumn of 1944 with Gen. Horst Stumpf, the General Inspector of the Panzer Force for Rundstedt's OB West headquarters, in the center, and Field Marshal Walter Model, commander of Army Group B.

in the Alsace region. What remained of the original 5.Panzer-Armee headquarters did not arrive from the Netherlands until 9 September 1944 and consisted of minimal operations staff and a small communications detachment.

Manteuffel was deeply skeptical of his new assignment. While traveling through the Vosges mountains outside Strasbourg on 9 September, he had a chance meeting with Col. Hans von Luck, a comrade-in-arms who had also fought alongside him in the 7.Panzer-Division in Russia in 1941. Luck at the time was commanding a battle group with the 21.Panzer-Division that would come under Manteuffel's command. He gave Luck his impression of the current situation and Hitler's new plans.

"I only got here yesterday from Belgium to take command of the 5.Panzer-Armee. Before I left, Montgomery had taken the offensive with his army group and had reached Brussels on 3 September and Antwerp on 4 September against weak resistance. Far more dangerous was the thrust of the Americans, Gen. Patton with his Third U.S. Army. It was Patton who managed to make the decisive breakthrough at Avranches and who then,

without regard for his open southern flank, pushed vigorously to the east. I would almost call him the American Rommel. . . . The worst of it is that Hitler is juggling with divisions that are divisions no more. And now, Hitler wants to launch a tank attack from the Dijon area to the north, in order, as he likes to put it, 'to seize Patton in the flank, cut his lines of communication and destroy him.' What a misjudgment of the situation and the possibilities open to us!"[27]

Manteuffel was called back to Hitler's command post again on 10 September due to the changing situation at the front. Allied forces were rapidly closing the gap between north and south. On 10 September, the spearheads of Patton's Third U.S. Army and Lt. Gen. Alexander Patch's Seventh U.S. Army had linked up at Autun, France. This created a solid Allied front line from the Mediterranean to the North Sea. Some retreating German units, mainly from Army Group G's 1.Armee, were still wandering back to Germany behind Allied lines. As a result of this linkup, the original mission of the Vosges Panzer Offensive, to cover the retreat of 19.Armee, was no longer meaningful.

The junction of Patton's Third U.S. Army and Patch's Seventh U.S. Army around Dijon in mid-September trapped the more distant German columns of 1.Armee. On 15 September, Gen. Maj. Botho Elster and his staff negotiated the surrender of the 20,000 troops trapped in a pocket near Romorantin on the Loire River. Elster had previously been the military governor of the Biarritz area on the Atlantic coast and was ordered by Berlin to head the withdrawal effort of the garrisons from Biarritz and Bordeaux.

During discussions at the Wolf's Lair on 10 September, Hitler reoriented the direction of the Vosges Panzer Offensive. It would emanate from the same area, but instead of heading southward, it would head northward. This variant of the plan was called Planung.2 as shown on the accompanying map on page 19. The 5.Panzer-Armee would attack out of the Langres Plateau, west of the Meuse River, and cut off Patton's Third U.S. Army.

The direction of the attack was based on new threat assessments in Berlin. In the last days of August 1944, Patton's Third U.S. Army had halted along the Meuse in the area of Verdun. German intelligence believed that Patton had stopped to regroup and resupply in preparation for a major new offensive thrust that would cross the Moselle River and push directly towards Frankfurt. This was indeed Patton's intention, but his halt was due to an unanticipated fuel shortage, not a deliberate pause. Another alarming development at the same time was the advance by Hodge's First U.S. Army over the German frontier near Aachen.[28]

From the broader perspective, these two advances suggested that the Americans were trying to envelope Germany's main industrial centers in the Ruhr and Saar. Both these areas were on Germany's western frontier, and the loss of the industrial resources would mean the end of the German war industries. These areas contained the main sources of German coal and steel, to say nothing of many of its weapons factories. The Ruhr was the more significant, and the loss of the Ruhr would eliminate 65 percent of German steel production and 56 percent of its coal production. In addition, the routes being taken by the Americans were two of the traditional invasion routes into Germany.

Some indication of sensitivity of these areas in German war planning can be seen on a map of German border fortifications. When Germany created the Westwall fortification line in the late 1930s, only two areas received double lines of fortification: the area around Aachen in the north and the area around Saarlautern-Saarbrücken facing Lorraine. Both of these heavily fortified sectors covered traditional invasion routes between Germany and France and these were the targets of the First U.S. Army and Third U.S. Army attacks.

Alsace-Lorraine had been a warpath between France and Germany for centuries. When Germany seized Alsace-Lorraine from France after the 1870 Franco-Prussian War, an extensive series of fortifications were erected along the Moselle River to shield Germany's new possessions. Germany's interest in Alsace-Lorraine was in no small measure to create a strategic buffer between France and Germany and to shield the vital Saar industrial region. This was an age-old preoccupation of German strategy, and one that Hitler in September 1944 clearly understood.

By 1944 the Westwall had been stripped of much of its armament, which had been sent off to reinforce the Atlantic Wall. The old Moselle River forts in Lorraine were similarly abandoned and ignored. While neither line was of major concern to the combatants in 1944, they do reveal the deeper concerns of traditional German strategic planning. It should come as no surprise that the Vosges Panzer Offensive eventually took place in much the same area as the Battle of the Charmes Gap in World War I, and countless battles in previous centuries.

In view of the deteriorating condition of German infantry divisions in late summer, Hitler ordered a rejuvenation of the old Westwall in September 1944 as the new West-Stellung (West Position). This consisted of the old Westwall bunkers but with a substantial array of new tactical defense lines added. Thousands of kilometers of antitank ditches, new defense lines, and new strongpoints were created. This new defense line was called the Siegfried Line by the Allies. It is often confused with the old Westwall, though it was in fact considerably more elaborate.[29]

The main obstacle to the Vosges Panzer Offensive was the weak state of the Wehrmacht in September 1944 and the tyranny of time. The new panzer brigades were barely ready for combat, and the existing panzer divisions were days away from the staging areas in Lorraine. Although Hitler had planned to start the offensive on 12 September 1944, Manteuffel's forces were not ready until nearly a week later. These delays would have crippling consequences on its prospects.

CHAPTER 3

Patton's Plans

ON 23 AUGUST 1944, Lt. Gen. Alphonse Juin visited Patton's headquarters in the field. Juin was an old acquaintance of Patton from the North African campaign, where he commanded Free French forces. Juin had an excellent reputation among other Allied commanders as a result of his leadership of the French expeditionary force in Italy that had been instrumental in overcoming the Gothic Line. Juin complimented Patton's drive across the Seine, describing it as "Napoleonic," a welcome compliment coming from a French general.

Patton was already thinking ahead about the future missions of the Third U.S. Army. His immediate objective was to reach and cross the Moselle River east of Paris. But the real objective was Germany. Patton hoped that the current offensive would push him through the Siegfried Line on Germany's western frontier, and on to the Rhine. With these goals in mind, he asked Juin his opinion about the best invasion route into Germany. Juin immediately identified the "Nancy Gap." In French, this is more commonly called "La Trouée de Charmes," the Charmes Gap, but it is sometimes named after the old provincial capital of Nancy because it is a much larger city in the area. The Charmes or Nancy Gap is an area east of these two cities that offers a relatively easy passage through the Vosges Mountains and to the Alsatian capital of Strasbourg on the Rhine River. It was a traditional invasion route between France and Germany, most recently in the 1914 border battles of the Great War. Patton recalled that "I had come to the same conclusion from a study of the map, because, if you find a large number of big roads leading through a place, that is the place to go regardless of enemy resistance. It is useless to capture an easy place that you can't move from."[30]

Patton is seen with some of his staff here at the Third U.S. Army headquarters in Étain, France, on 30 September 1944 with his English bull terrier, Willie, by his side. The pugnacious general in the right foreground is Walton Walker, commander of XX Corps; above him and right of Patton is his chief of staff, Brig. Gen. Hobart Gay. Left of Patton are his Deputy Chief of Staff for Operations Col. Paul Harkins, 5th Infantry Division commander Maj. Gen. Leroy Irwin, and Patton's "pirate and chief scrounger," Brig. Gen. Walter Muller (Third Army G-4); and in the foreground, commander of CCB, 7th Armored Division, Brig. Gen. John Thompson.

Patton had already had discussions with Bradley about the direction of the Third U.S Army in the upcoming weeks. His "Plan A" was to strike behind the Seine in the northerly direction with an aim towards trapping remaining German forces. During a meeting later on 23 August, Bradley pointed out that the problem with Plan A was that it drove the Third U.S. Army across the path of Hodge's First U.S. Army and into the zones allotted to Montgomery's 21st Army Group. Plan B was to continue advancing east into Lorraine towards the Charmes Gap. In view of Eisenhower's preference for a broad front strategy, this was the more plausible direction. On 25 August, Patton had a meeting with Bradley in Chartres, confirming Plan B. In his diary, Patton warmed to the idea of executing Plan B, now saying, "The direction is part of my plan . . . we still had seven good divisions going in the direction which Bradley and I always wanted to go.[31] Curiously enough, Patton had foreseen the likely direction of his advance and as early as March 1944 had told his intelligence staff to prepare for moving towards Metz.[32] For Patton, the advance through the Argonne region towards the German frontier presented a string of familiar sights; in 1918, his tank battalions had trained and fought in the area. But unlike 1918, the advance over the old battlefields was remarkably swift and the casualties light.

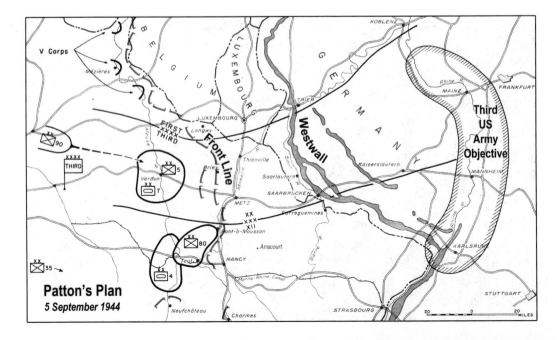

Patton's Plan
5 September 1944

THE SUPPLY PROBLEM

One of the major impediments that Patton would face in September 1944 was a continual supply of fuel and ammunition. The Allied advance through France in August 1944 had placed the Allied forces far beyond the pre-invasion planning. The logistics chain was not keeping up with the pace of the advance. The plans had expected the Allied forces to be on the Seine River in early September when in fact they were now 150 miles beyond. On 11 September 1944, the first day U.S. troops entered Germany, the Allies were along a phase line that the Operation Overlord plans did not expect to reach until D+330, 2 May 1945, some 233 days ahead of schedule. Patton's Third U.S. Army was at the phase line expected for April 1945.[33]

Supplies that were landed on the Normandy beaches had to be trucked forward as the French railroad network had been shattered by pre-invasion bombing. The port of Cherbourg had been captured, but the harbor had been sabotaged by the Germans before their surrender. Much the same occurred farther up the coast, including Le Havre and Boulogne. By early August, 8,500 tons of supply were arriving daily at Cherbourg, reaching 20,000 tons daily by the end of September 1944. Bradley's 12th Army Group and its associated forces were consuming more than 20,000 tons of supplies per day,

and Cherbourg also had to support Montgomery's 21st Army Group, which had similar requirements.[34] Even once Cherbourg began operating, it was even farther away from the front than the Normandy beaches. Ideally, a new port was needed closer to the front. Antwerp was the obvious solution since it had the greatest capacity of the ports along the North Sea and Atlantic coast and was closest to the front lines. The British 7th Armoured Division liberated Antwerp on 4 September 1944. However, in one of the more significant Allied blunders of 1944, the approaches to Antwerp along the Scheldt River were not cleared, and the Germans managed to block access to the port until November 1944.[35] Due to the supply shortages in September 1944, Gen. Dwight Eisenhower as Supreme Commander, Allied Expeditionary Force (SHAEF) had to decide which element of his forces would receive priority for supplies.

The Allied forces in the European Theater of Operations (ETO) under Eisenhower's command consisted of three army groups. Field Marshal Bernard Montgomery's 21st Army Group on the northern flank was advancing from the areas of Dieppe and Amiens along the North Sea coast of Belgium into the Netherlands. The 21st Army Group consisted of the First Canadian Army on

Gen. Manton Eddy, XII Corps commander, on the left, discusses plans with Gen. John "P" Wood, 4th Armored Division commander.

the extreme left and the Second British Army to its right. The largest American force under Eisenhower's command was Gen. Omar Bradley's 12th Army Group, consisting of Hodge's First U.S. Army moving through central Belgium towards the German frontier around Aachen, Gen. George S. Patton's Third U.S. Army moving through the Argonne into Lorraine, and the newly arrived Ninth U.S. Army. The most remote of the Allied forces was Gen. Jacob Devers' 6th Army Group, consisting of the Seventh U.S. Army and the First French Army. These forces had landed on the Mediterranean coast in southern France on 15 August 1944 and were advancing northward along the Swiss border towards the Belfort Gap and Alsace.

The controversy over supplies most greatly affected Montgomery's 21st Army Group and Bradley's 12th Army Group. Devers' 6th Army Group had captured the Mediterranean ports of Toulon and Marseilles largely intact, and the southern French railway network had not been smashed as badly as the railways in northern France and Belgium. They were not as badly affected by the supply crisis of September 1944.

Prior to the September supply shortage, the presumption had been that the campaign after Normandy would proceed along two axes. By May 1944, SHAEF plans included a northern assault through Belgium, north of the Ardennes forest, followed by a swing behind the Rhine River to eliminate Germany's industrial heart in the Ruhr. This would involve Montgomery's 21st Army Group and the First U.S. Army. The secondary axis of attack would be through Lorraine towards Frankfurt to take the Saar industrial region and win bridgeheads over the Rhine into central Germany. This would involve Patton's Third U.S. Army and the 6th Army Group.

The late-summer supply problems led to squabbles about these plans, especially from the commander of the British forces, Field Marshal Bernard Montgomery. In early September, Montgomery argued that the lack of sufficient supplies would make Eisenhower's broad front attack impossible. Instead, he urged that the resources be directed to his 21st Army Group, which would make a bold thrust through the Netherlands. Montgomery contended that Germany was on the brink of defeat

and that his forces could race to Berlin, bringing about a swift end of the war.

Montgomery's position was contested by U.S. Army leaders, especially his American counterpart, Gen. Omar Bradley. The U.S. Army commanders had lost confidence in Montgomery due to the repeated failures of his armored offensives to take Caen during the Normandy campaign, and they were skeptical of his ability to conduct the rapid offensive he proposed. The American leadership was suspicious of Montgomery's motives, feeling that they were prompted more by his desire for the British forces to play the predominant role in the European campaign rather than by realistic tactical opportunities. Bradley wanted Patton's advance through Lorraine to continue, in the hope of being able to seize Rhine crossings towards Frankfurt should German resistance continue to falter. Since Patton's forces were the most distant from the supply ports, Montgomery's plan would force the Third U.S. Army to halt before breaching the Moselle River line and before joining with Devers' 6th Army Group.

Eisenhower attempted to mediate, with little appreciation from either side. Montgomery was openly contemptuous of his ability as a field commander, while Bradley felt that Ike was overly solicitous to Montgomery's exorbitant demands. In a cable to Eisenhower on 4 September, Montgomery continued to urge "a powerful and full-blooded thrust towards Berlin." Due to the importance of seizing Antwerp, Eisenhower granted Montgomery priority in the allotment of supplies on 4 September. But arguments would continue through early September over how much priority the 21st Army Group would in fact receive.

The key issue was the Allies' assessment of the condition of the German forces. Was the Wehrmacht on the brink of collapse, or was it on the brink of recovery? In the case that the Germans were on the verge of collapse, then bold ventures were worth the risk. Many Allied leaders were convinced that Germany was facing a calamity every bit as dire as November 1918 and that the war would be over by Christmas. But if the Germans were on the verge of recovering, then more attention needed to be paid to the logistical dimensions of war making in preparation for a prolonged campaign along the

A column from the 8th Tank Battalion, 4th Armored Division pass through Coutances on 31 July 1944.

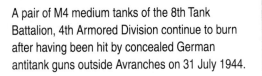

A pair of M4 medium tanks of the 8th Tank Battalion, 4th Armored Division continue to burn after having been hit by concealed German antitank guns outside Avranches on 31 July 1944.

German border into 1945. So, for example, more attention would need to be paid to clearing the Scheldt estuary to open up the port of Antwerp.

The issue finally came to a head at a 10 September meeting of the senior Allied commanders. Montgomery again demanded a thrust on Berlin, but it became evident that Eisenhower would not consider any such operation until the port of Antwerp was functioning. As a first step towards the Berlin operation, Montgomery proposed an airborne operation called Market-Garden with an aim towards seizing a bridgehead over the Rhine as the first stage of a northern Ruhr envelopment. Three Allied airborne divisions, one British and two American, would lay down an airborne carpet between Allied front lines and the Rhine bridge at Arnhem, clearing the way for a British armored assault along the corridor. Eisenhower was taken aback by the boldness of the plan, since Montgomery was usually a very conservative commander more prone to excessive preparation than risky gambles. Eisenhower approved Market-Garden as a less fanciful and less disruptive alternative than Montgomery's vague Berlin plan. Eisenhower, like many of the other senior Allied commanders, was caught up in the victory euphoria after the successful race over the Seine and the collapse of the Wehrmacht in France. Furthermore, he had been receiving pressure from senior Allied commanders including his boss, U.S. Army Chief of Staff George C. Marshall, who had been urging more use of the Allied airborne army that had been built up at such great effort and cost.

Eisenhower's decision to approve Market-Garden shaped the subsequent conduct of Allied operations in mid-September 1944. The broad front strategy had not been given up, but realistically the supply problem would limit the amount of offensive operations the Allies could conduct. Eisenhower gave priority to the northern thrust, including both the 21st Army Group's Market-Garden operation and a supporting drive by the U.S. First Army in Belgium to protect the British right flank. Patton's advance in Lorraine was not yet frozen, but Patton realized that his operations might be halted at any moment due to a cutoff in precious supplies.[36] Patton's Third U.S. Army ground to a halt around Verdun in the final days of August 1944 as fuel and ammunition supplies dried up.

CHAPTER 4

Opposing Forces

THIS CHAPTER EXAMINES THE TWO opposing forces in the Lorraine fighting. On the German side, this was primarily the 1.Armee and 5.Panzer-Armee of Army Group G, and on the American side, Patton's Third U.S. Army.

THE WEHRMACHT

The German army in Lorraine at the beginning of September 1944 was in a shambles, but it was beginning to coalesce around defense lines along the Moselle River. As the month went on, additional units were brought into the area from Germany to stabilize the front and to carry out Hitler's planned counteroffensive.

Until mid-August 1944, the 1.Armee was stationed on France's Atlantic coast facing the Bay of Biscay. Its primary mission was the defense of the coast against any potential Allied amphibious landing. Since the probability of an Allied attack in this area was low, the 1.Armee did not have a particularly impressive array of forces. Most of its units were static infantry divisions, a special type of division designed for coastal defense. These divisions had no mobility at all, lacking most of the horses and vehicles found in normal German infantry divisions. In addition, these units received a substandard selection of troops, usually older men, thirty-five to forty-five years old, or soldiers who had been wounded or who had medical problems. The 1.Armee was further weakened by the transfer of many of its better units to the Normandy front in June and July 1944. After the U.S. Army's Operation Cobra breakout from Normandy in late July to early August 1944, a rump element of the field army was dispatched in a vain effort to defend the Seine River line. These forces were overrun by Patton's Third U.S. Army in mid-August.

Army Group G was stationed along the Bay of Biscay and the Mediterranean coast as an anti-invasion force, and so was not well suited to mobile operations.

Army Group G was harassed during its retreat by French partisan units. This is a scene repeated many times in Provence in the summer of 1944. An isolated German soldier of the 19.Armee, hunted down by some young maquisards and brought to a U.S. Army post.

When the Operation Dragoon landings occurred on the French Riviera coast on 15 August 1944, the 1.Armee was threatened with isolation and capture. The Seventh U.S. Army made rapid progress up the Rhône valley, threatening the reach the Belfort Gap leading to the Rhine and the German frontier. There were no defenses along the western German border from Luxembourg to the Swiss border except for the derelict Westwall defense line. Hitler authorized both of the field armies of Army Group G, the 1.Armee and 19.Armee, to withdraw back to Germany in the hopes of creating a viable defense line before the arrival of American forces.

As a result, Army Group G spent the last week of August and first week of September in a headlong retreat back to the German frontier. This was a chaotic process, often using commandeered French civilian vehicles and horses. The railroad network in this section of France had not been as systematically bombed as in northern France; nevertheless, rail travel was very risky due to the frequent presence of Allied fighter-bombers and medium bombers. The 1.Armee was harassed along its retreat route by French partisans. However, it did not have to worry about encountering major Allied combat units until it neared the German frontier. In contrast, the 19.Armee had the Seventh U.S. Army on its heels all the way from the Mediterranean coast to Alsace.

By early September 1944, the 1.Armee had barely three weak infantry divisions along the Moselle River facing Patton's Third U.S. Army. Hitler wanted the 1.Armee to establish its defense lines on the western side of the Moselle River to create a buffer in front of the German frontier. In reality, 1.Armee was too weak and disorganized to accomplish this, and it was quickly pushed back to the east side of the Moselle River by Patton's advance. In an attempt to reinforce this sector, Berlin dispatched another corps headquarters and began to gradually feed new Volksgrenadier divisions into the area once they had been created in Germany by the Replacement Army.

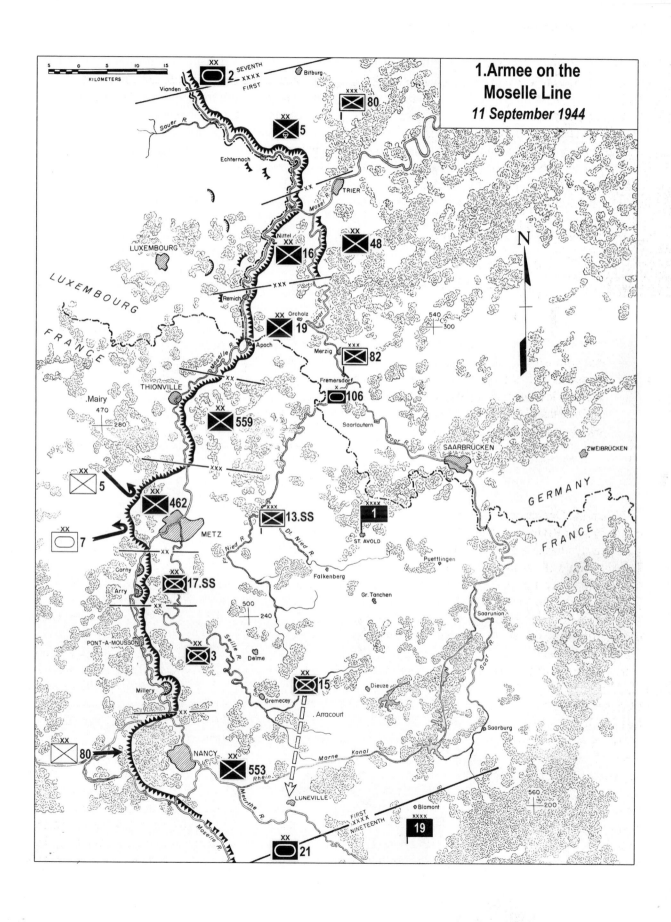

1. Armee on the Moselle Line
11 September 1944

The principal formations of the German army in Lorraine were infantry divisions of three types: divisions shattered in earlier fighting, new Volksgrenadier divisions that had been only recently raised, or divisions withdrawn more or less intact from southern France. As a result, the infantry formations were of very mixed quality. For example, the 16.Infanterie-Division was one of the better units. Earlier in 1944, it had been deployed for occupation duty near the Bay of Biscay and had retreated eastward in August, losing the equivalent of two infantry battalions in fighting with French partisans. By early September, it had a strength of about 7,000 men, above average for the units in Lorraine. Many of the other infantry divisions retained the names and numbers of earlier formations but were in fact nearly entirely new formations rebuilt from scratch. The Volksgrenadier divisions were a last-minute attempt by Hitler to mobilize every able-bodied man for a final, desperate effort to defend Germany. They were organized by scraping the bottom of the barrel: from schools, Luftwaffe units, naval units, static fortress units, and support formations. Some were better than others. For example, the 462.Volksgrenadier-Division contained a regiment drawn from a school for young lieutenants who had earned battlefield commissions on the eastern front. In nearly all cases, the infantry divisions were very weak in antitank guns and field artillery.

A hasty meeting by platoon leaders in Lorraine in the autumn of 1944 with a hauptfeldwebel (1st sergeant) on the left and a leutnant (2nd lieutenant) on the right. The sergeant is armed with one of the new Sturmgewehr StG 44 assault rifles that were intended for the new Volksgrenadier divisions.

The German infantry divisions remained dependent on horse transport throughout the war. This is a Grosser Gefechtswagen Hf. 7/11 (larger supply wagon), which had a carrying capacity of up to 1,700 kilograms.

15 CM SCHWERE
FELDHAUBITZE SFH 18

10.5 CM LEICHTE
FELDHAUBITZE LFH 18/40

German infantry division field artillery included three light battalions of the 105mm lFH 18/40 and one medium battalion of the 150mm sFH 18, with each battalion having twelve field guns.

The German forces in Lorraine were particularly weak in artillery. As mentioned earlier, 19.Armee had lost 1,316 of their 1,481 artillery pieces during the retreat from southern France. Although artillery was not as central to tactics as in World War I, artillery was still the dominant killing arm on the battlefield. One senior commander estimated that German field artillery bore 60 to 80 percent of the combat burden by 1943–1944 due to the declining combat power of the German infantry.[37] Most of the field artillery in German infantry divisions was horse drawn, and there were frequent shortages of ammunition due to transportation bottlenecks resulting from Allied fighter-bomber interdiction of the road and railways. The German lack of firepower was a decided disadvantage.

Army Group G suffered heavy equipment losses during the retreat back to Germany. This is a horse-drawn 105mm lFH 18/40 light field howitzer, the backbone of the German field artillery, lost in the Montelimar pocket in August 1944.

A 150mm sFH 18 heavy field howitzer, captured from 1.Armee by Patton's Third U.S. Army near Verdun. Patton's army suffered from ammunition shortages through the autumn of 1944, and some field artillery battalions added a so-called "Z battery" equipped with captured German guns to use up large stocks of German ammunition.

To reinforce the Moselle front, mechanized units were transferred both from Army Group B and from elsewhere in Army Group G. The 17.SS-Panzergrenadier-Division "Götz von Berlichingen" had served on the Normandy front before being transferred to the Metz area. It was largely destroyed in the Normandy fighting and was rebuilt in early August using the cadres of the partially formed 26.SS-Panzer-Division and 27.SS-Panzer-Division. However, by early September it was still significantly understrength at 56 percent, with 10,233 troops instead of its authorized strength of 18,354 troops. In spite of its name, it had very few tanks or armored half-tracks. Its panzer battalion had only 5 StuG IV assault guns and 2 old PzKpfw III tanks. The entire division had only 459 trucks instead of its authorized strength of 1,717 trucks.[38]

Two panzergrenadier divisions were transferred from Italy to southern France shortly before the Operation Dragoon landings. These were the best units in 1.Armee in September 1944. The 3.Panzergrenadier-Division was understrength, with 87 percent of its authorized strength: 12,750 troops instead of 14,700 troops. However, it was relatively well equipped with AFVs and vehicles. Its panzer battalion had 37 StuG III assault guns, 4 PzKpfw III tanks, and 1 PzKpfw IV tank. Its

tank destroyer battalion had 31 Jagdpanzer IV tank destroyers, though 10 were in repair. The division was reasonably well mechanized with 102 SdKfz 250 and 21 SdKfz 251 armored half-tracks out of an authorized strength of 143. The division had about half of its intended truck inventory, 956 instead of 1,765. Most important, the division was a hardened, combat-experienced formation.

The other veteran of the Italian campaign was the 15.Panzergrenadier-Division. This unit was also called the Division Sicilien after it was founded on Sicily in 1943 from the remnants of the 15.Panzer Division that had been destroyed in North Africa. Its personnel strength at the beginning of September was 83 percent, 13,408 troops of the intended 16,143. It had a significant AFV strength with 32 PzKpfw IV and 3 PzKpfw III tanks in its panzer battalion and a further 29 Jagdpanzer IV in its tank destroyer battalion. Unlike the 3.Panzergrenadier-Division, it had very few armored half-tracks and so was dependent on trucks for mobility. It was deficient in this respect, having 1,033 of the intended 1,853. However, it was especially deficient in military trucks with only 204, the majority being commandeered civilian trucks of various types. Like the 3.Panzergrenadier-Division, it was a combat-hardened, veteran formation.

AFV PEAK STRENGTH IN ARMY GROUP G, SEPTEMBER 1944							
	Panther	PzKpfw III	Pzkpfw IV	JagdPz IV	StuG III/IV	FlakPz IV	Total
PzBrig 106	36			11		4	51
PzBrig 111	45		45		10	8	108
PzBrig 112	45		46		10	8	109
PzBrig 113	45		45		10	8	108
11 Pz Div	30	4	16		1	7	58
21 Pz Div					5		5
3 PzGr Div				31	37		68
15 Pz Gr Div			42	34			76
17 SS PzGr				4	17	12	33
Total	201	4	194	80	90	47	616

As of 20 August 1944, there were only 184 panzers and assault guns on the entire western front. This would change by the middle of September as more armor was rushed forward. The plan was to increase the strength in the west to 712 tanks and assault guns by early September in order to carry out Hitler's directives for a Lorraine counteroffensive. Tank production in Germany reached record levels in 1944, thanks to the belated industrial rationalization of Albert Speer. But at the same time, fuel and manpower shortages meant that there were not enough trained crews or trained tank unit officers to replace the heavy losses in experienced troops. The quality of German tank crews fell steadily in 1944, especially after the summer of 1944 disasters.

The 1.Armee had no panzer divisions, though later in the Lorraine campaign it would receive elements of the battered 11.Panzer-Division and the 21.Panzer-Division. Of the two, the 11.Panzer-Division proved the more effective.

This unit, nicknamed the "Ghost Division," had belonged to the 19.Armee through the summer campaign.[39] It had served as the rearguard of the 19.Armee during the retreat up the Rhône valley and had performed an exemplary job at keeping the Seventh U.S. Army at bay. This had come at a significant cost in armored vehicles, though the division remained near full strength in personnel. At the beginning of September 1944, it was at 96 percent strength with 14,832 troops. Its tank and AFV strength was poor, with only 5 PzKpfw IV and 19 Panthers operational out of an intended strength of 170 tanks, and only 1 StuG III assault gun of the intended 21. Its armored half-track strength was about half the intended strength with 23 SdKfz 250 and 128 SdKfz 251 operational. Overall, this was one of the best divisions in Army Group G, and it saw combat for the first three weeks of September in the 19.Armee sector in Alsace.

The 21.Panzer-Division was largely destroyed in the Normandy fighting. It was withdrawn back into Germany for rebuilding but kept a Kampfgruppe in action in the 1.Armee sector. The division attracted unwanted attention due to its controversial commander. Lt. Gen. Edgar Feuchtinger was embroiled in a civil lawsuit involving insurance fraud, and he was suspected of diverting army fuel supplies for personal gain. He managed to avoid arrest through the autumn of 1944 but was convicted in early 1945 and sentenced to death. He narrowly escaped execution and survived the war, only to be arrested again in the 1950s as a Soviet spy. General Balck, the Army Group G commander in late September 1944, was very unhappy with

The only panzer division that remained in Army Group G at the end of August was 11.Panzer-Division. It served as a rearguard for the 19.Armee during their retreat towards Alsace. This is a Panther Ausf. A tank of the division lost in the battle for Meximieux, which took place from 31 August to 2 September. This rearguard action was intended to block the advance by the U.S. 45th Infantry Division on the city of Lyon.

Feuchtinger's shenanigans and felt that the division failed to carry its own weight during the September 1944 fighting.

One of the most significant differences between German and U.S. divisions in World War II was their practices of force regeneration. The Wehrmacht generally kept units in the field until they were no longer combat effective. They did not receive enough replacements to remain near their intended strength. As units suffered casualties, they were consolidated into Kampfgruppen (battle groups) of smaller and smaller size. In some cases, divisions would receive march battalions from their home Military District, but more often than not, they would be amalgamated with scraps of other units.

If not completely destroyed in combat, the division would be withdrawn back to the home Military District for disbandment or rebuilding. In contrast, U.S. Army divisions were kept close to their TO&E (Table of Organization and Equipment) through a continual supply of men and materiel. As a result, the respective Orders of Battle of the two sides can be very deceptive from a superficial glance, since it often appeared that the Germans had a substantial force advantage over the U.S. Army in terms of the number of divisions. In reality, the U.S. divisions were usually near full strength, while the German units were divisions in name only with a strength that was only a fraction of their official organization tables.

THE PANZER BRIGADES

Due to the shortage of panzer divisions in Lorraine, Hitler's Vosges Panzer Offensive would ultimately depend on the new panzer brigades. The panzer brigades were formed by diverting much of the summer production run of new Panther and PzKpfw IV tanks to the new units rather than shipping them to the front to re-equip existing panzer divisions. The German tank factories had not yet been subjected to any dedicated bombing raids by the Allied "Combined Bomber Offensive," and so summer production actually reached very high levels. August 1944 was the highest month on record, with 1,688 tanks delivered. Gen. Heinz Guderian, the legendary German panzer commander, wanted this production to rebuild the badly understrength panzer divisions on both fronts. As inspector general of the panzer forces, it was usually his responsibility to allot tank deliveries. However, Hitler demanded the creation of a new type of tank unit, the panzer brigade, specifically for use on the Russian front. This unit was patterned to some extent on Heavy Panzer Regiment Bäke, an improvised unit made up of Panther and Tiger tanks that was reported to have destroyed hundreds of Soviet tanks in early 1944 while suffering miniscule losses.

One of the tactical dilemmas on the Russian front was a better method to contain Soviet tank breakthroughs. German defenses in the east were so thin and had such weak reserves that once the Red Army secured a breakthrough, Soviet tanks were soon rampaging deep behind German lines. The panzer brigade was Hitler's solution to this problem. Rather than constructing a balanced combined-arms formation like a panzer division, the panzer brigades contained only the tank and panzergrenadier elements. They lacked sufficient artillery, reconnaissance, and engineer troops, and their command structure and logistics train were rudimentary. The panzer brigades were designed to stage fast and violent counterattacks of short duration, and they were not designed for prolonged campaigns.

The first ten of these brigades began their formation in July 1944, numbered as Panzer Brigade.101 to Panzer Brigade.110. The brigades of the first wave were fairly weak in tanks, with only a single battalion of thirty-six Panther tanks. However, they had a strong panzergrenadier component with large numbers of the SdKfz 251 armored half-tracks. While this strength level might seem rather puny by British or American standards, these brigades had as much armored strength as most panzer divisions of the time.

The Panther Ausf. G was the principal tank in the first wave of panzer brigades. In the second wave, a second battalion with the PzKpfw IV was added. This is a Panther Ausf. G of Panzer-Brigade.111 in Lorraine in September 1944.

The panzer brigades usually had a section of Flakpanzer IV antiaircraft tanks. In the case of Panzer-Brigade.111, it was the 20mm Vierling armed with the quad 20mm Flak Vierling 38. Although they possessed a fearsome amount of firepower, the fire-control systems of the day gave them a poor probability of hitting fast-moving aircraft.

Panzer-Brigade.105 was one of the first of the new panzer brigades to be committed to the fighting in the west. It was dispatched to the Aachen sector in early September 1944, and this is one of its Panther tanks knocked out in fighting with the 3rd Armored Division in the Stolberg corridor.

Panzer-Brigade.107 was sent into action in the Netherlands in mid-September 1944 to help stem Operation Market-Garden. This is the Panther command tank of Maj. Hans-Albrecht von Plüskow, the leader of Pz.Abt.2107, that was knocked out by a British Sherman of the 44 RTR during the fighting near the Erp road on 23 September.

The first-wave panzer brigades, organized under the 7 July 1944 table of organization, consisted of a headquarters and headquarters company, a panzer battalion, a panzergrenadier battalion, and brigade services. The headquarters company included a signal platoon, an engineer reconnaissance platoon, and an armored reconnaissance platoon. The panzer battalion had a staff component that included a flak section and an armored recovery and repair platoon, three panzer companies with Panther tanks, and a fourth company with Panzer IV/70 tank destroyers. The panzergrenadier battalion had a staff, two light panzergrenadier companies, one heavy panzergrenadier company, an armored engineer company, and a supply company. The brigade services included a transportation company. The revised 18 July table of organization somewhat changed the brigade structure, making the armored engineer company separate from the panzergrenadier battalion. There was yet another reorganization on 1 August 1944, mostly shifting the allotment of flak weapons within the brigade due to Hitler's insistence that the brigades receive large numbers of the SdKfz 251/17 with triple 20mm automatic cannon. There were six in each panzergrenadier company. This reorganization also increased the number of companies within the panzergrenadier battalion to five.[40] In practice, the actual organization often differed from the tables, with Panzer-Brigade.106 eventually having eight panzergrenadier companies in its battalion.[41]

The first wave of panzer brigades had a well-equipped panzer-grenadier regiment with large numbers of SdKfz 251 armored half-tracks. Among these were the SdKfz 251/9 "Kanonenwagen" armed with a short 75mm howitzer for direct fire support.

The early panzer brigades had a company of Panzer IV/70, a version of the earlier Jagdpanzer IV, but used as an expedient tank. It consisted of the same 75mm gun as the Panther, but in a fixed casemate on a PzKpfw IV chassis.

Guderian opposed the formation of the panzer brigades for two reasons. He argued that they were not a well-balanced formation. His biggest objection was that they would invariably be created using new and inexperienced tank crews. Guderian was well aware that it took months of combat experience before a panzer unit reached its prime performance. In the desperate circumstances of the late summer of 1944, he preferred to ship the new Panther tanks to existing panzer divisions that already knew how to use them. Regardless of Guderian's opinions, Hitler had his way and the ten new panzer brigades ate up about a quarter of the late-summer tank production.

Recognizing the shortcomings of the original units, the second wave of panzer brigades that were formed later in August 1944 were enlarged and had some significant organizational improvements. Instead of having a single panzer battalion, they received a battalion of Panther tanks and a battalion of PzKpfw IV tanks, more than doubling their overall tank strength. The panzergrenadier component was expanded from a battalion to a regiment consisting of two panzergrenadier battalions, each with three companies, plus a heavy weapon company. Several of the supporting elements were separated, including the escort company, armored reconnaissance company, assault gun company, and engineer company. On the negative side, there was a growing shortage of SdKfz 251 armored half-tracks, and therefore many of their panzergrenadier regiments had to make do with ordinary trucks. The second-wave brigades were more than double the size of the first-wave brigades, about 4,800 troops versus 2,100. The second-wave panzer brigades were numbered 111 to 119.

None of the senior panzer commanders were happy about the panzer brigade organization. Hasso von Manteuffel, 5.Panzer.Armee commander in Lorraine, was scathing about their shortcomings:

> The three independent Panzer brigades [111, 112, and 113] had been newly created by the General Inspector of Panzer Troops and had to be considered improvisations as a result of the general lack of men and materiel. Aside from their rather poor organization, the fighting qualifications of these Brigades was particularly handicapped by the fact that the brigades having been activated in different Wehrkreise (Military Districts), they did not have internal coherence whatsoever. Two of the brigade commanders became acquainted

The second wave of panzer brigades lacked half-tracks for the panzergrenadiers, and so expedient methods were often used, including tank riding. This is a Panther Ausf. G of Panzer-Brigade.111 during the September fighting around Arracourt.

with their subordinate commanders only in the railroad unloading area. In addition, there was a lack of all kinds of materiel and equipment, necessary for that type of organization. The brigades' organization in many respects showed signs of improvised measures. There was no artillery whatever nor was there a coordinating staff for the two armored battalions. The reconnaissance and engineer units were in no way adequate. There was a definite lack of radio equipment. In proportion to the general shortages, the strength and equipment of the armored recovery and repair services were altogether insufficient, although these services are as vitally necessary for the commitment of an armored unit as the very tank itself. The men could not be trained in the combined arms tactics, as they had been activated in several different localities. In spite of numerous examples of individual bravery on the part of men of all ranks, they were unable to live up to what had been expected of them. I had my justified doubts as to whether these units would be suitable for any offensive operation with a more far-reaching objective against an enemy such as the one in the Western Theater of Operation, especially so since the commanders had only limited practical experience in the command of combined arms units on the battlefield.[42]

General of Panzer Troops Walter Krüger, who led the 58.Panzer Korps in the Lorraine battles, had this to say about the new formations:

Panzer Brigades 111 and 113, like all the panzer brigades that had been formed, were a makeshift organization. Their combat value was slight. They had originally been intended for commitment in the East and had been organized in various garrisons and bases. Their training was just as incomplete as their equipment. They had been given no training as a unit and they had not become accustomed to coordinating their sub-units. They were composed by and large of young, inexperienced personnel, together with a small cadre of battle-tested junior officers and NCOs as well as some "barrel scrapings" of over-age men from rear area formations, supply units and administrative offices.[43]

THE LUFTWAFFE IN LORRAINE

The Luftwaffe would not prove to be of any use to the Wehrmacht in the Lorraine battles. The fighter and fighter-bomber force in France was under the control of Jagdkorps II, while fighters in neighboring Germany deployed for defense of the Reich were controlled by Jagdkorps I. On 29 August 1944, the advance of Allied forces had obliged Jagdkorps II to order all remaining fighter-bomber units out of France and into western Germany. At the beginning of September, there were about 420 fighters and fighter-bombers in this force, of which about 110 covered the Nancy-Metz area of Lorraine.

Unlike the U.S. Army, the Wehrmacht received very little air support during the Lorraine fighting. As in the case of tanks, this was not so much from lack of aircraft production as from lack of trained pilots. The Luftwaffe had suffered massive losses in air battles over the Reich since the spring of 1944, which was further accelerated by the summer fighting. To make matters worse, there was a fuel crisis in August, which further curtailed training. The main oil supply in Romania had been cut off by the Red Army, and the U.S. Army Air Force had begun a campaign against the synthetic fuel plants in Germany in May 1944. German aircraft production reached record levels in the summer of 1944, but this did not translate into a readily useful force. U.S. aircraft encountered the Luftwaffe in large numbers on only two occasions during the Lorraine fighting in September, and they found that the pilots were inexperienced and vulnerable. Besides the sheer lack of experienced pilots, the Luftwaffe's

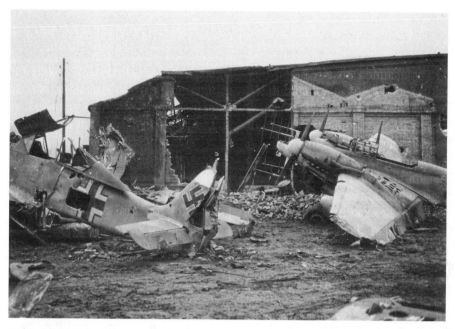

The Luftwaffe in Lorraine was shattered by Allied airpower. This is one of the airfields near Metz, with the wreckage of an FW-190 fighter to the left and Bf-110G night fighter to the right.

fighter-bomber force had atrophied badly by 1944, due in part to the heavy concentration on fighter aviation for defense of the Reich. There was no standardized means for ground direction of close air support, and despite frequent army calls for air support, none was forthcoming except for a few rare occasions when key bridges were attacked.

The Lorraine Battlefield

The geography of Lorraine held mixed opportunities for both sides. From the German perspective, the Moselle River valley formed a natural defense line since the river has a high rate of flow, many potential crossing sites were wooded, the river banks have a high gradient, and most crossing sites are covered by hills on the east bank. This area had been a traditional invasion route over the centuries, and the areas on both sides of the river were filled with ancient and modern fortifications. Patton's Third U.S. Army reached the Verdun area in late August, the site of the violent World War I battles. From the German perspective, the Moselle defenses were particularly formidable in the northern portion of the sector since likely river crossings were covered by the artillery in the Metz fortresses. Germany had controlled the area around Metz from 1870 to 1918, and again after 1940, so the most modern defenses faced westward. The Metz-Thionville Stellung was the major defensive obstacle in Lorraine. These forts were not as modern as the French Maginot Line or German Westwall. Nevertheless, they contained a substantial amount of fixed artillery batteries that would prove useful in defending the Moselle Line against American attempts at river crossing.[44] The traditional capital of Lorraine, Nancy, has not been fortified in modern times, but the river lines and the plateau of the Massif de Haye on its west bank serve as a significant natural obstacle. The ground most suitable for mobile operations was in the southern sector between Toul and Épinal. This region, known to French planners as the *Trouée de Charmes*, or the Charmes Gap, has been a traditional battlefield, most recently three decades before when the German army was defeated there in the opening phases of World War I. The weather slightly favored the Germans. September 1944 was unusually wet and foggy, and the weather often limited Allied close air support.

A typical example of the Moselle forts was Feste Obergentringen, part of the Thionville fortification belt built by Germany in the 1890s and located on the west bank of the Moselle. These armored cupolas are typical of the Schumann turrets used in other Metz-Diedenhofen forts, such as Fort Driant. The fort was captured by the 358th Infantry, 90th Division without a fight on 12 September 1944. Today, the fort is the site of a museum.

GERMAN ORDER OF BATTLE, 16 SEPTEMBER 1944

Army Group G	**Generaloberst Johannes Blaskowitz**
1.Armee	**General der Panzertruppe Otto von Knobelsdorff**
80.Armee Korps	**General der Infanterie Dr. Franz Bayer**
5.Fallschirmjäger Division	Generalmajor Ludwig Heilmann
82.Armee Korps	**General der Artillerie Johann Sinnhuber**
19.Volksgrenadier Division	Generalleutnant Karl Wissmath
36.Volksgrenadier Division	Generalmajor August Welln
559.Volksgrenadier Division	Generalmajor Baron Kurt von Muhlen
13.SS-Korps	**Generalleutnant der Waffen-SS Herman Priess**
3.Panzergrenadier-Division	Generalmajor Hans Hecker
15.Panzergrenadier-Division	Generalleutnant Eberhard Rodt
17.SS-Panzergrenadier-Division "Götz von Berlichingen"	Oberst Eduard Deisenhofer
462.Volksgrenadier Division	Generalleutnant Vollrath Lubbe
553.Volksgrenadier Division	Oberst Enrich von Lösch
Panzer-Brigade.106 "Feldherrnhalle"	Oberst Franz Bäke

(continued)

GERMAN ORDER OF BATTLE, 16 SEPTEMBER 1944 (*continued*)

5.Panzer Armee	**General der Panzertruppe Hasso von Manteuffel**
47.Panzer-Korps	**General der Panzertruppen Heinrich von Lüttwitz**
21.Panzer-Division	Generalleutnant Edgar Feuchtinger
Panzer-Brigade.111	Oberst Heinrich von Bronsart-Schellendorf
Panzer-Brigade.112	Oberst Horst von Usedom
Panzer-Brigade.113	Oberst Erich von Seckendorff
19.Armee	**General der Infanterie Friederich Weise**
66.Armee Korps	**General der Artillerie Walter Lucht**
16.Infanterie-Division	General der Infanterie Ernst Haechel
Kampfgruppe Ottenbacher	Generalleutnant Ernst Ottenbacher
64.Armee Korps	**General der Pionere Karl Sachs**
716.Infanterie-Division	Generalleutnant Wilhelm Richter
189.Infanterie-Division	Generalmajor Bogislav von Schwerin
85.Armee Korps	**Generalleutenant Baptist Kneiss**
11.Panzer-Division	Generalleutnant Wend von Wietersheim
4.Luftwaffe Feld Korps	**Generalleutenant Erich Petersen**
338.Infanterie-Division	Generalleutenant Folttmann
159.Infanterie-Division	Generalleutnant Albin Nake
198.Infanterie-Division	Generalmajor Otto Richter

THE U.S. ARMY IN LORRAINE

Patton's Third U.S. Army entered the Lorraine campaign with two corps, down from its peak strength of four corps in August 1944. The VIII Corps was laying siege to the fortified port of Brest on the coast of Brittany and was subsequently transferred to the Ninth U.S. Army. The XV Corps had been taken from Patton during the Paris operation, but it would be returned later in September to cover his southern flank.

In contrast to the German army, the U.S. Army in September 1944 was in excellent shape after a triumphant dash across France in August 1944.

The divisions in Patton's Third U.S. Army were generally in better condition than those in Hodge's First U.S. Army, which had experienced the brutal close-country bocage fighting in June–July 1944. In marked contrast to the German units, which were seldom at full organizational strength, the Third U.S. Army had not yet encountered the personnel shortages that would afflict the army in the late autumn of 1944. Unit cohesion, training, and morale were generally excellent.

Patton's Third U.S. Army often had three or four armored divisions on strength, as well as several separate tank and tank destroyer battalions. As a result, Patton's tank strength was usually significantly superior at the operational level. The intention of the Vosges Panzer Offensive was to counter Patton's overall tank superiority by concentrating Army Group G's modest panzer force in a limited sector.

Of the armored divisions under Patton's command, three of them were arguably among the best in the ETO. Two of these, the 4th Armored Division and the French 2nd Armored Division, will be described in detail in following chapters. The other exceptional armored division was the 6th Armored Division, but this division did not reach Lorraine until relatively late in the campaign and does not figure prominently in the battles described in this book. Patton regarded the 7th Armored Division as something of a problem child due to mediocre leadership. This division was involved in some of the early fighting in Lorraine but was taken away from the Third U.S. Army and sent to the Netherlands in the middle of the month.

All of the armored divisions in Patton's Third U.S. Army were the so-called "light" divisions of the 1943 Table of Organization and Equipment. The earlier 1942 "heavy" configuration was retained by only two divisions in the ETO, the 2nd and 3rd Armored Divisions serving in the First U.S. Army. The difference between these configurations was the relative balance of the tank, infantry, and artillery components. The 1943 light configuration had three battalions each of tanks, infantry, and artillery. The older 1942 heavy configuration was "tank-heavy" with six tank battalions but only three infantry and artillery battalions.[45] The technical balance between the two tank forces is described in more detail in the next section.

THIRD U.S. ARMY TANK STRENGTH, 6 SEPTEMBER 1944			
	M5A1 Light	M4 75mm	M4A3 76mm
4th Armored Division	77	148	18
7th Armored Division	50	94	24
2nd French Armored Division	77	164	34
702nd Tank Battalion	12	41	—
712th Tank Battalion	16	52	—
735th Tank Battalion	12	43	—
737th Tank Battalion	17	54	—
Total	261	596	76 (933 total)

THE 4TH ARMORED DIVISION

The principal unit facing the Vosges Panzer Offensive was the 4th Armored Division. The division served the whole war in Patton's Third U.S. Army and was regarded as Patton's favorite unit, frequently serving as the spearhead during offensive operations. The 4th Armored Division was one of the few U.S. armored divisions during the war not to receive an official nickname, although veterans of the unit sometimes called it "Patton's Best."

The division had been activated on 15 April 1941 at Pine Camp, New York, and arrived in Britain on 8 January 1944. It continued its training while in Britain, and tank veterans recall that one of the important aspects of their training there was the use of innovative British tank gunnery ranges.[46] Since it was assigned to Patton's Third U.S. Army, it deployed to France on D+37, 13 July 1944. The 4th

Armored Division was commanded by Maj. Gen. John S. Wood. He was nicknamed "Tiger Jack" by some in the press, but usually called "P Wood" for Professor Wood by his close associates. The noted British military historian Liddell Hart dubbed him "the Rommel of the American armored force."[47]

The U.S. armored divisions in Lorraine were far better equipped than their German counterparts, being close to establishment strength. On 15 September 1944, the 4th Armored Division had 143 M4 (75mm) Sherman tanks, 20 M4A3 (76mm) Sherman tanks, 18 M4 (105mm) assault guns, 82 M5A1 light tanks, 16 M8 75mm HMC assault guns, 3 M4 tanks with dozers, and 27 M31 tank-recovery vehicles. The nominal table of strength for an armored division was 168 medium tanks and the 4th Armored Division that day had 163 tanks, very slightly understrength.

An M4 medium tank of the 8th Tank Battalion, 4th Armored Division passing through Avranches in early August 1944 during the breakout from Normandy.

The commander of the 37th Tank Battalion, 4th Armored Division, Lt. Col. Creighton Abrams, named his M4 medium tank "Thunderbolt V," and it is seen here in Périers on 28 July 1944 during the beginning of Operation Cobra.

This illustration shows the M4 medium tank of Lt. Col. Creighton Abrams, commander of the 37th Tank Battalion, 4th Armored Division, at the time of the Arracourt battles.

Until the fighting in Lorraine, the 4th Armored Division encountered few if any Panther tanks on the battlefield. Tank-vs.-tank fighting by the division was quite limited until mid-September 1944 simply because the division had seldom faced any German panzer divisions. Tankers in the division were aware of the Panther tank due to intelligence briefings, but they had little or no practical experience with it.[48]

Aside from excellent, prolonged training, the 4th Armored Division was lucky enough to have a relatively slow introduction into combat. The first elements of the division entered combat on 17 July 1944, and the division as a whole was committed to action during Operation Cobra on 28 July 1944. They took part in the advance past Avranches and into Brittany against battered German infantry divisions. Some U.S. tank units suffered as many as half of their total casualties in their first month of combat due to inexperience. The 4th Armored Division's casualties in August 1944 were relatively modest, while at the same time the division was able to learn practical battlefield lessons without paying an inordinate price.

U.S. tank battalions equipped each Company D with M5A1 light tanks. This is one of the M5A1 light tanks of Company D, 37th Tank Battalion that took part in the Arracourt battles.

The M4A3 (76mm) began to appear in the Third U.S. Army in late August and early September 1944. This differed from the earlier versions of the Sherman in having a new 76mm gun in an enlarged turret that offered better antitank performance than the previous 75mm gun. This example served in the French 2nd Armored Division and is now a memorial in Ville-sur-Illon. (Pierre-Olivier Buan)

The headquarter companies in the tank battalions of the 4th Armored Division had a platoon of M4 (105mm) assault guns to provide fire support. These resembled the normal 75mm tanks, but with a 105mm howitzer instead. This is one of the assault-gun companies training in England in June 1944 before the division was shipped to France.

Sgt. Kenneth H. Boyer, a tank commander in the 1st Platoon, Company B, 37th Tank Battalion, photographed on the company's M4 (105mm) assault gun on 26 September 1944 after the battalion had been withdrawn south of Arracourt for recuperation.

4th Armored Division

8th Tank Battalion
35th Tank Battalion
37th Tank Battalion
10th Armored Infantry Battalion
51st Armored Infantry Battalion
53d Armored Infantry Battalion
25th Cavalry Reconnaissance Squadron (Mecz)
24th Armored Engineer Battalion
144th Armored Signal Company
22d Armored Field Artillery Battalion
66th Armored Field Artillery Battalion
94th Armored Field Artillery Battalion
126th Ordnance Maintenance Battalion
4th Armored Medical Battalion

The tactical employment of U.S. armored divisions was different from the German, British, or Soviet pattern. The primary combat unit was the combat command, essentially a brigade head-quarters. There were three combat commands in each division called CCA, CCB, and CCR, the "R" indicating reserve. Battle-weary battalions would be periodically cycled through the CCR to prevent the corrosive effects of battle exhaustion. The combat commands did not have a fixed composition. Each combat command was tailored to the day's tactical mission and often included a tank battalion, an armored infantry battalion, and an armored field artillery battalion. Other units could be added from division or corps. For example, during part of the Lorraine fighting, the 4th Armored Division's Combat Command A sometimes had three artillery battalions at its disposal.

The armored infantry battalions in U.S. armored divisions were entirely mechanized, relying on the M2 and M3 armored half-tracks. As mentioned earlier, most German panzer divisions and panzergrenadier divisions were short of armored half-tracks and so had to rely on ordinary trucks. The main advantage of the half-track versus truck was that it provided superior cross-country mobility. The German army tended to rely on converted civilian trucks for their army use, which offered poor cross-country mobility. American tactics saw the principal use of the half-track for transporting the infantry to the battlefield. The infantry usually dismounted for close combat. However, in pursuit operations or other fast-moving operations, the infantry could remain mounted for greater speed.

The armored infantry battalions in the armored division used the M3 armored half-track as their standard vehicle. This is a M3A1 half-track with the .50 cal machine-gun pulpit added on the forward right side.

A parade of the 4th Armored Division in Britain shortly before their departure to France. The M5A1 light tanks and M3A1 half-tracks seen here belonged to the divisional headquarters company.

U.S. armored divisions used mechanized artillery, while German panzer divisions mostly used towed artillery. The standard field artillery piece in the U.S. armored divisions was the M7 105mm howitzer motor carriage (HMC). This was essentially an M4 Sherman tank chassis mated to the standard 105mm howitzer. This allowed the armored field artillery battalion (AFAB) to keep up with the tank and armored infantry battalions in cross-country travel. The armored division lacked the heavier firepower of the 155mm howitzer found in U.S. infantry divisions, so it was not unusual for a tractor-drawn 155mm howitzer battalion to be attached to an armored division for offensive operations. So, for example, during the battle of Arracourt, CCA 4th Armored Division had the 191st Field Artillery Battalion attached from XII Corps.

The backbone of the armored field artillery battalions was the M7 105mm howitzer motor carriage (HMC), which combined the standard 105mm howitzer on the chassis of the M4 Sherman tank.

The backbone of the towed field artillery battalions was the M2 and M2A1 105mm howitzers. Each infantry division had three battalions of these, with each battalion having eighteen howitzers.

In addition to its organic battalions, armored divisions in Patton's Third U.S. Army tended to have a permanently attached tank destroyer battalion. These had been formed in 1940–1941 as the artillery branch's response to the Blitzkrieg. These battalions were supposed to be consolidated under tank destroyer groups at corps level to defend against massed panzer attack. Since 1943, it had become apparent that the massed panzer attacks of the Blitzkrieg era were no longer a major concern. As a result, the tank destroyer battalions were parceled out to provide additional antitank firepower to the divisions.[49] The infantry divisions in the ETO in 1944 generally received the towed 3-inch gun battalions, while armored divisions received self-propelled tank destroyers.

The 4th Armored Division had the 704th Tank Destroyer attached to it in France, and it played a very prominent role in the Arracourt fighting. The tank destroyer battalions were smaller than comparable tank battalions, with three companies each for a total of thirty-six tank destroyers. The 704th Tank Destroyer Battalion was equipped with the M18 76mm gun motor carriage (GMC).

Other units in the Third U.S. Army used the older M10 3-inch GMC. There were conflicting views of the relative merits of both types. The M18 was the fastest tracked armored vehicle in the U.S. Army in World War II, with road speeds up to fifty-five mph. On the negative side, the M18 was significantly smaller than the M10, and many veteran tank destroyer crews thought it was too small and cramped inside for prolonged campaigns. The M10 was based on the M4A2 Sherman but with a new superstructure and an open-topped turret. The 3-inch gun on the M10 was a different design than the 76mm gun on the M18, but both used the same projectiles and had essentially the same performance. The gun designations were different simply as a means to keep the two different types of ammunition separate in the supply chain; they used different propellant casings due to the difference in their bore configuration.

The U.S. Army had a larger and more robust ground reconnaissance capability than the Wehrmacht in 1944. The armored divisions had an organic mechanized cavalry reconnaissance squadron based around four reconnaissance troops, each with twelve M8 light armored cars and four M3 half-tracks with a total of fifty-two armored cars in the squadron. There were 145 personnel in each troop, and they were expected to fight both mounted and dismounted. These armored car troops were supported by an assault gun troop with eight M8 75mm howitzer motor carriages, and a light tank company with seventeen M5A1 light tanks.

Aside from the divisional reconnaissance units, each corps usually had an attached mechanized cavalry reconnaissance group. These headquarters usually controlled a pair of mechanized cavalry squadrons, but they could also serve as the basis for a larger task force with attached field artillery and other elements. Although primarily intended for the ground reconnaissance role, Patton tended to employ them for broader and more traditional cavalry missions, including flank security.

One of Patton's more innovative uses of the mechanized cavalry was his creation of the Army Information Service. This consisted of fifteen detachments created from one of the squadrons of the Third U.S. Army's 6th Cavalry Group. Each of these detachments, roughly a platoon in size, was attached to a corps or division to provide Patton with direct and frequent status reports. This circumvented and supplemented the usual chain of command and provided Patton with a separate and more timely source of information on the Third U.S. Army's main subordinate units.[50]

If there was one combat arm where the U.S. Army had unquestioned superiority over the Wehrmacht, it was the artillery. This was not simply a question of quantity. The U.S. field artillery battalions were more modern than their German counterparts in nearly all respects. While their cannons were not significantly different in capability, the U.S. field artillery battalions were entirely motorized, while German field artillery, especially infantry division units, was still horse drawn. U.S. heavy artillery was mechanized, using fully tracked high-speed tractors. The high level of motorization provided mobility for the batteries and also ensured supply.

As in the other branches, the U.S. field artillery enjoyed a broader and more modern assortment of communication equipment. Another U.S. innovation was the fire direction center (FDC). Located at battalion, division, and corps level, these FDC concentrated the analog computers and other calculation devices alongside the communication equipment, permitting prompt receipt of messages and prompt calculation of fire missions. The communication revolution allowed new tactics, the most lethal of which was TOT, or "time-on-target." Field artillery is most effective when the first few rounds catch the enemy out in the open. Once the first few rounds land, enemy troops take cover, and the rate of casualties to subsequent fire declines dramatically. The aim of TOT was to deliver the fire on the target simultaneously, even from separate batteries. Such TOT fire missions were more lethal and more economical of ammunition than traditional staggered fire strikes. Communication advantages allowed the batteries to switch targets rapidly as well.

Aside from indirect fire support from the field artillery battalions, each tank battalion had a platoon of M4 assault guns with 105mm howitzers in the headquarters company that could provide immediate fire support.

THE AIRPOWER ADVANTAGE

There is a popular perception of Patton as an archaic cavalier more comfortable in the wars of centuries past. This was fostered by the popular film *Patton*. Yet Patton made his reputation from 1943 to 1945 through his successful use of the most modern tools of war: amphibious landings, tanks, and tactical airpower. Patton's enthusiasm for airpower offered the Third U.S. Army a critical tactical advantage in the fighting in Lorraine.

Patton had been harshly critical of Allied air support in Tunisia and Sicily, so his relationship with the U.S. Army Air Force in 1944 in France might have started on a wrong foot. But by Normandy, many of the bugs in the close-air support system had been worked out, and Patton's judgment of the value of air support changed completely. The Third U.S. Army was supported by the XIX Tactical Air Command (TAC). The U.S. Army Air Force's tactical air commands were structured to operate in direct support of a single army. As a result, Patton's Third U.S. Army had Brig. Gen. Otto Weyland's XIX TAC directly attached to it.

Patton later dubbed the XIX TAC commander "the best damned general in the Air Force." In August 1944, Patton had used XIX TAC as a form of aerial cavalry. In the rapid thrust across France, Patton ignored his flanks. He used airpower to destroy bridges along his flanks as well as frequent air patrols to keep an eye on possible German threats to his exposed flanks. He regarded Weyland's XIX TAC as an essential element of the Third U.S. Army. By his personal interest, he fostered strong bonds between the air and ground elements. The successful collaboration of the Third U.S. Army and the XIX TAC in August–September 1944 started one of the most successful partnerships of the ETO campaign.[51]

U.S. tactical air units were more tightly integrated than in any other army, and Weyland's command was co-located with Patton's headquarters. The XIX TAC generally had about 400 aircraft available to it, usually organized into two fighter wings. The wings were organized into groups, each averaging about three fighter squadrons. A fighter squadron had twenty-five aircraft; a squadron mission typically employed twelve fighters, and a group mission used thirty-six. At the beginning of September 1944, XIX TAC had seven fighter groups and one photoreconnaissance group.

The majority of the XIX TAC squadrons were equipped with P-47 Thunderbolt fighter-bombers, which were used to provide close support and interdiction using heavy machine-gun fire, bombs, napalm, and rockets. There were also one or two squadrons of P-51s, used to provide tactical air cover as well as "fast reconnaissance," including spotting for the corps' heavy 240mm guns. The XIX TAC conducted a larger percent of close-air support missions out of their total combat missions than any other TAC in Europe.

The XIX TAC deployed twenty radio teams with the ground units: one team per corps and infantry division headquarters, two with each armored division (with each combat command), and one with each cavalry group when they were performing key screening or holding missions. The team was based around a radio crew that linked the division to the XIX TAC headquarters by means of an SCR-624 radio installed in the division's truck-mounted SCR-399 "doghouse." The tactical air liaison officers (TALO) operated from "veeps," jeeps with a rack-mounted SCR-522 VHF aircraft radio, or sometimes in specially adapted M4 Sherman tanks. They deployed forward with advancing units so that they could vector attacking fighter-bombers on to targets much in the same fashion as artillery forward observers.

The effectiveness of close air support in World War II remains controversial.[52] Both the Allied and German sides tended to exaggerate its power: the U.S. Air Force in its postwar struggle to become a separate service, the Germans as an excuse for poor battlefield performance. Wartime and postwar operational studies have concluded that the ability of fighter-bombers to knock out tanks on the battlefield was greatly exaggerated. In a post-battle survey after the Ardennes fighting in 1945 of a XIX TAC sector, it was found that aircraft had knocked out about six armored vehicles of the ninety claimed.

The munitions of the day, unguided rockets, bombs, and heavy machine guns, were not sufficiently accurate or sufficiently powerful to easily destroy tanks. On the other hand, fighter-bombers had an enormous psychological impact, bolstering the morale of GIs and terrifying the average German soldier. German field commanders spoke of the fear instilled by close air attack in much the same way as the "tank panic" of the 1939–1941 blitzkrieg years. This was a significant factor in the Lorraine fighting, since so many of the panzer crews in the new panzer brigades were completely inexperienced. As in the case of tank panic, the psychological effects of close air attack lessened quickly through experience.

The most effective employment of close air support was to attack supply columns, storage areas, and other soft targets. Even if not particularly effective against the tanks themselves, the fighter-bombers could be very effective at limiting the mobility of panzer units by forcing them to conduct road marches only at night. Furthermore, the avaricious demand for fuel and ammunition in modern armies made them very vulnerable to supply cutoffs. A panzer brigade could be rendered as ineffective by destroying its trucks and supply vehicles as it could by destroying the tanks themselves. The commander of CCA of the 4th Armored Division, Col. Bruce Clarke, later remarked, "We were certainly glad to have [close air support] but I would say their effect was certainly not decisive in any place."

Besides the fighter-bombers, the Third U.S. Army benefitted from a robust aerial reconnaissance capability provided by the 10th Photo Reconnaissance Group. So long as weather was clear, these converted fighter aircraft provided Patton's intelligence office with a steady stream of aerial photographs to support ground operations.[53]

Besides the U.S. Army Air Force units supporting the Third U.S. Army, U.S. divisions had organic aviation in the form of L-4 (Piper Cub) and other liaison aircraft. Popularly called "Flying Grasshoppers," these were primarily used to correct field artillery, conduct artillery reconnaissance, and perform basic liaison tasks.[54] Col. Bruce Clarke of the CCA of the 4th Armored Division flew ahead of his advancing tank columns in one, enabling him to direct the columns with precision.

Third U.S. Army	Lieutenant General George S. Patton Jr.
XX Corps	**Major General Walton Walker**
2nd Cavalry Reconnaissance Group (Mecz)	Colonel W. P. Withers
7th Armored Division	Major General Lindsay Silvester
5th Infantry Division	Major General Stafford Irwin
90th Infantry Division	Major General Raymond McClain
XII Corps	**Major General Manton S. Eddy**
106th Cavalry Reconnaissance Group (Mecz)	Colonel Vennard Wilson
4th Armored Division	Major General John Wood
6th Armored Division	Major General Robert Grow
35th Infantry Division	Major General Paul Baade
80th Infantry Division	Major General Horace McBride
XV Corps	**Major General Wade Haislip**
3rd Cavalry Reconnaissance Group (Mecz)	Colonel James Polk
79th Infantry Division	Major General Ira Wyche
2nd French Armored Division	Major General Jacques Leclerc

OPPOSING FORCES: THE TANK BALANCE

The principal tank types in the Wehrmacht in the late summer of 1944 were the PzKpfw IV Ausf H and the Panther Ausf G. On the American side, the predominant type was the M4 Sherman medium tank. There was also a significant number of M5A1 light tanks since each tank battalion consisted of three companies of medium tanks and one company of light tanks. By 1944, the M5A1 light tank was obsolete, having very weak armor and a 37mm gun. As a result, the light tank companies tended to be used for traditional cavalry missions such as reconnaissance and flank security.

The PzKpfw IV Ausf H used by the panzer brigades in Lorraine had a conventional layout with a three-man turret crew.

The Panther used the standard German tank layout with the gunner in the forward left section of the turret and the commander behind him.

There were two basic types of Sherman tanks in service in the late summer of 1944, the basic M4 or M4A1 tank and the newer M4A1 (76mm) and M4A3 (76mm). The M4 and M4A1 tanks were essentially identical except that the M4 used a welded upper hull while the M4A1 used a cast upper hull. The 4th Armored Division was equipped almost exclusively with the M4 version. In general, U.S. tank design had stagnated during 1943–1944 due to the failure of the Ordnance Department and the armored force to appreciate the dynamics of tank technology. As a result, the armored divisions in Lorraine were using essentially the same M4 medium tank as was standard in Tunisia two years before. New versions of the M4 medium tanks were becoming available with the newer 76mm gun, but they were not numerous, their armor was not improved sufficiently, and their armor penetration capability was inferior to the German tank guns. For example, the 4th Armored Division had only twenty M4A3 (76mm) tanks at the time of the Lorraine battles. The M4A3 (76mm) was disparaged by Patton and was not initially popular in the 4th Armored Division. Tankers felt that the older 75mm gun was more versatile than the 76mm gun, which was optimized for tank fighting only. The 75mm gun fired a more powerful high-explosive round than the 76mm gun, with 665 grams of high explosive versus only 390 grams in the 76mm projectile. Since the vast majority of targets engaged in the ETO were not tanks, this was a significant concern for tank crews.

Patton's views on tank tactics placed little emphasis on tank-vs.-tank fighting. Rule No. 1 in armor fighting was: "The primary mission of armored units is the attack of enemy infantry and artillery. The enemy's rear is the happy hunting ground for armor. Use every means to get it there."[55]

The standard, armor-piercing 76mm projectile for the 76mm gun could not penetrate the Panther's glacis armor at any range, and it could penetrate the turret mantlet reliably only at ranges of 250 yards or less. The 76mm gun could penetrate the Panther's side armor from more than 2,000 yards away; for the Sherman, typical combat ranges in the ETO were 890 yards.

In terms of weaponry, the German panzer force enjoyed a significant technological advantage in the form of its Panther tank. Even the old PzKpfw IV Ausf H tank was equal or superior to the Sherman, especially in terms of firepower.[56] Of the two German tanks, the Panther was the more significant in the Lorraine battles since the first-wave panzer

Commander
Loader
Gunner
Bow gunner
Driver

The Sherman tank layout was similar to the German layout except that the commander and gunner were on the right side of the turret rather than the left.

brigades were equipped exclusively with this type, while the second-wave brigades had a battalion of PzKpfw IV and a battalion of Panthers.

The Panther was a generation ahead of the Sherman in terms of firepower and armor. It was essentially a heavy tank by 1944 standards, although not designated as such. The Panther was half again as heavy as the Sherman, forty-five tons versus thirty tons. The Panther had been developed as an antidote to the Soviet T-34 and saw its introduction to combat the previous summer at the battle of Kursk. It was optimized for tank-vs.-tank fighting by an army on the strategic defensive. It was very well suited to the type of warfare fought on the Russian front in 1943–1944, but it was not durable enough to have waged the type of mobile blitzkrieg warfare as practiced by the Wehrmacht in 1939–1941.

The Panther's combat debut was disappointing. The new tank had serious technical problems, especially in regards to its power-train. During the course of its development, the Panther's armor weight continued to increase without suitable improvements in the design of the power-train. This led to very low reliability.

On the positive side, its frontal armor was extremely efficient and it was resistant to both the standard Soviet 76mm and American 75mm tank guns. Unlike the Tiger heavy tank, the side armor of the Panther was not especially formidable, and the Panther could be knocked out by standard Soviet and American tanks when engaged from the flanks. In terms of firepower, the Panther had an excellent 75mm gun with a length of L/70 and a new ammunition type with a substantially enlarged propellant casing. This gun was optimized for antitank performance; its high-explosive firepower was no better than the shorter L/48 gun used on the PzKpfw IV tank. Based on operational research during the war, the normal firing range for the Panther in combat was about 850 meters (930 yards), and it could easily penetrate the frontal armor of the Soviet T-34 or the American Sherman tank at this range, while neither opposing tank could penetrate the glacis plate or turret front.

COMPARATIVE TECHNICAL DATA: U.S. VERSUS GERMAN TANK GUNS 1944				
Caliber	75mm	76mm	75mm	75mm
Tank type	M4	M4A3 (76mm)	PzKpfw IV	Panther
Main gun	M3	M1	KwK 40	KwK 42
Tube length	L/40	L/52	L/48	L/70
Armor-piercing projectile	**M61**	**M62A1**	**Pz.Gr.39**	**Pz.Gr.39/42**
Type	APCBC	APCBC	APCBC	APCBC
Initial muzzle velocity (m/s)	617	792	790	925
Projectile weight (kg)	6.78	7.0	6.8	6.8
Propellant weight (kg)	0.98	1.64	2.4	3.67
Penetration (mm; @500m, 30 degree)	62–72	92–96	91–96	117–129
High-explosive projectile	**M48**	**M42A1**	**Spr.Gr.34**	**Spr.Gr.42**
Projectile weight (kg)	6.7	5.8	5.74	5.74
Explosive fill (g)	665	390	653	653

In a head-to-head tank fight at normal combat ranges, the Panther front armor was impervious to the M4 tank's 75mm gun, while the Panther could destroy the M4 tank frontally at any reasonable combat range. In order to knock out a Panther, a Sherman with 75mm gun had to maneuver to engage its thinner side armor.

The Panther held the greatest technical advantage when it could begin to engage the Sherman from long ranges of 1,000 yards or more. Its technical edge became less pronounced in close range. The M4 had several advantages in fire control that had important consequences in the close-range tank battles around Arracourt on 19–20 September. The Sherman gunner had two sights, a periscope and a more powerful coaxial telescopic sight. The gun could be aimed using either device. The main advantage of the periscopic sight was that it permitted the gunner to continuously observe the local terrain, giving him situational awareness. When ordered to engage a target, the Sherman gunner was already aware of the terrain ahead. In contrast, the Panther gunner only had the telescopic sight. Although this was an excellent sight for long-range engagements, it provided the gunner with only a narrow "soda-straw" view of the local terrain and could not be used comfortably during cross-country travel. The Panther gunner was essentially blind until the tank halted. As a result, the Panther gun lost precious seconds in any close-range tank duel in acquiring and engaging an opposing Sherman tank. A postwar French army report concluded that "Once the [Panther] commander has located a target, it takes between 20 and 30 seconds until the gunner can open fire. This delay, which is significantly greater than that of the Sherman, stems from the absence of a periscope for the gunner."

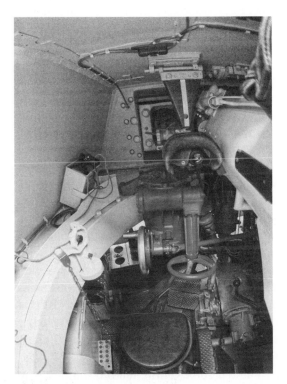

The gunner in the Panther had poor situational awareness in close-range tank duels since he only had the telescopic sight for viewing the surrounding terrain.

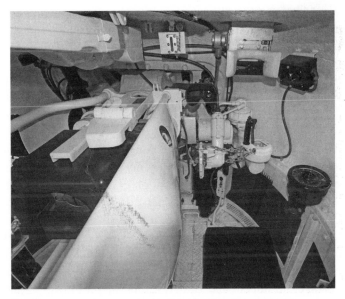

The Sherman tank gunner had better situational awareness in close-range tank duels since he could observe the terrain through a periscopic sight, seen here in the upper right, or use the telescopic sight, below and to the left, for fine adjustment.

Another advantage for the Sherman in a close-range duel was its hydraulic power traverse that permitted rapid slewing of the turret against an opposing tank. The Panther also had a power traverse system, but it was not an independent motor, but rather was driven off the main engine power train. This required coordination between the gunner and driver to make certain that power would be available. In addition, the Panther turret was not especially well balanced due to its long and heavy gun barrel, and this created issues when trying to use the manual turret traverse if the tank was on a slope. The Sherman turret traversed at about 25 degrees per second or a full 360 degree traverse in 15 seconds, while the Panther turret traversed at a maximum of about 15 degrees per second but only if the engine was at full power and the tank on level ground.

The combination of the Panther gunner's poor situational awareness and the turret traverse issues was a disadvantage in close-range tank duels, especially in the foggy conditions that prevailed around Arracourt in the September tank fighting. One U.S. tank company commander concluded that "Almost all our losses were to tanks or guns in emplaced positions. Unless our tanks ran directly into prepared fire, they could get off four or five rounds before the Germans could traverse their turrets."[57]

The main advantage enjoyed by U.S. tankers compared to German panzer crews in 1944 was superior training. By the summer of 1944, German fuel supplies were so low and training time so short that the quality of German tank crews had declined precipitously since the glory days of 1939–1942.

Innovative American tactics helped to reduce the Panther's formidable armor advantages. A popular tactic when encountering Panthers was to strike them first with white phosphorous smoke rounds.[58] Inexperienced German crews would sometimes mistake the impact and smoke for an internal fire, and then bale out. More determined crews would sometimes be forced out by the acrid smoke, drawn in through the tank's ventilator. Even if these tricks didn't work, the smoke prevented the Panthers from locating their opponents, giving the M4 tanks time to maneuver to the flanks or rear, where their 75mm gun could penetrate its armor. This tactic was standard operating procedure in some units, including the CCA of 4th Armored Division.[59] Some U.S. tank units preferred to fire high-explosive rounds at the Panther, finding that inexperienced German crews would simply abandon their tanks. When engaging the Panther frontally, the British discovered that the Achilles heel of the Panther was the lower surface of the curved gun mantlet. A 75mm round striking this tended to deflect downward into the thin hull roof armor. This tactic was only effective at close range where the chances of striking this area were reasonably high.

In terms of mobility, the Panther offered wider tracks for better floatation in mud, while the Sherman had better range. The Panther had a slightly better power-to-weight ratio on paper, though in practice the difference was smaller due to U.S. use of 80 octane gasoline while the Wehrmacht was obliged to use inferior fuel, which degraded engine performance. The Panther had wide steel track offering a ground pressure of 12.3 psi. The basic track used on the Sherman provided it with a 15.1 psi ground pressure, which was poor for operations in muddy conditions of the type encountered in late September in Lorraine. The Panther carried 190 gallons of gasoline, giving it an effective road range of about 60 to 80 miles (100 to 130 kilometers) and cross-country range of about 40 to 50 miles (70 to 80 kilometers). Its fuel consumption was so high and Wehrmacht supplies so low that in the summer of 1944, Gen. Heinz Guderian, the inspector general of the panzer force, sent a directive reminding commanders that "the large fuel consumption of Panthers makes it necessary to consider whether the mission is worth the cost." As a result, the Panther battalions were generally shipped by rail for any long distances. This proved to be a greater liability in the ETO than on the Russian front due to the vigorous Allied air interdiction campaign. As will be evident later in this book, most of the panzer brigades lost a part of their Panther force during the rail journey from Germany to the battlefield. The M4A3 (76mm) carried 168 gallons of gasoline, giving it better road range of about 100 miles and a cross-country range of about 65 miles.

COMPARATIVE TECHNICAL DATA: U.S. VERSUS GERMAN TANKS 1944			
	M4 (75mm)	M4A3 (76mm)	PzKpfw IV Ausf J	Panther Ausf. G
Crew	5	5	5	5
Dimensions: L x W x H (m)	5.84x2.61x2.74	6.27x2.61x2.74	7.02x2.88x2.68	8.86x3.42x2.98
Loaded weight (tons)	30.3	31.5	25.0	45.5
Main gun	75mm M3	76mm M1A1	75mm KwK40	75mm KwK42
Main gun ammo	90	71	87	79
Engine (hp)	350	450	300	600
Max. speed (km/h)	39	42	38	46
Fuel (liters)	662	635	470	720
Range (km)	195	160	210	200
Ground pressure (kg/cm^2)	0.96	1.0	0.91	.88
Armor**				
Mantlet (mm)	76*=>76	90@5=90	50*=>50	100*=>100
Turret front (mm)	76@30=88	51@30=59	50@10=51	110@5=110.5
Turret side (mm)	51@5=51.2	51@5=51	33@25=36	45@25=50
Upper hull front (mm)	51@56=91	63.5@47=93	80@8=81	80@55=139
Lower hull front (mm)	51–108*=>51–108	51–108*=>51–108	80@14=83	60@55=113
Upper hull side (mm)	38@0=38	38@0=38	30@0=30	40@40=52

*Curved

**Armor data provided as actual thickness in mm @ angle from vertical = effective thickness in mm

The reliability of the Panther improved from its combat debut in 1943 through 1944. During 1943, only about 37 percent of Panthers were operational at any given time, its nadir having been in August 1943 when its reliability rate was only 22 percent.[60] Panther reliability increased dramatically in 1944 both due to technical improvements in the new Ausf. A variant as well as the seasonal increase in the availability of spare parts in preparation for the summer campaign series. Reliability reached its peak in June 1944 at 80 percent, falling back to 51 percent in August due to the grinding effect of the summer tank battles. By September 1944, it was back up to about 60 percent. Data beyond this date is generally lacking, and as will become clear in the ensuing battle accounts, Panther reliability in Lorraine was poor.

The problems facing the Panther on the battlefield were a combination of declining production quality exacerbated by the declining quality of crew training. Hitler's emphasis on increasing panzer production in 1944 led to distortions in the manufacturing process. In order to increase tank production, the industry cut back on the supply of spare parts. Panzer units ended up with broken-down tanks that were sidelined due to a lack of essential replacement parts. In addition to the shortage of spare parts, reliability suffered from the decline in key alloys due to the Allied bombing campaigns and trade embargos. The Panther was typical of German tank designs and was optimized for manufacture in an industry that favored craftsmanship. As more and more skilled German workers were drafted, the workforce shifted to unskilled foreign forced labor. Not only did this impact quality control but it led to a growing problem of deliberate sabotage. These technical factors degraded the combat power of Panther battalions.

The Achilles heel of the Panther in terms of reliability was its transmission and final drives. Many of these problems could be mitigated by an experienced driver and crew, but in Lorraine in September 1944, experienced drivers were in short supply. The Panther's transmission was an elegant design, but it was badly overstressed and suffered from premature stripping of the third gear. A more serious problem was the final drive, which had a nominal life expectancy of 1,500 kilometers but which in practice was sometimes as low as 150 kilometers.[61] A postwar test of captured Panther tanks had to be prematurely curtailed due to the excessive break-down rate as well as a tendency to engine fires due to carburetor flooding.[62] Half of all abandoned Panther tanks found by the Allies in Normandy had faulty final drives. The final drive design was not adequate for a tank of this weight, and its single-teeth spur gears tended to strip more readily than the more robust double-herringbone design used in the Sherman. To make matters worse, the pivot turn feature of the transmission accelerated final drive failure in the hands of inexperienced drivers such as those in the panzer brigades in Lorraine, and so drivers were instructed to use skid steering to avoid these problems. While this situation was bad enough, the Panther transmission was fully enclosed by the front armor, meaning that to replace the final drive, the entire driver's compartment and transmission had to be disassembled to gain access to the faulty assembly. The combination of premature transmission failure, time-consuming repair, and shortage of spare parts meant that Panther units in Lorraine in September 1944 were usually understrength due to the significant number of tanks

sidelined with mechanical problems. For example, when Panzer-Brigade.106 saw its combat debut on 7–8 September as described in a following chapter, it had only twenty-two of its thirty-six tanks, with about a third of its brand-new tanks under repair after simply having driven from the railway road-head to its base at Audun-le-Roman.

In contrast to the Panther, the Sherman tank used a robust syncro-mesh transmission with controlled differential steering. This design was the product of nearly a decade of evolution. The U.S. tank industry, centered around automotive and locomotive plants, had abandoned the artisan approach to industrial manufacturing in favor of mass production techniques such as statistical process control that emphasized durability. The U.S. Army, after having suffered from poor reliability of it trucks in World War I, had adopted a policy of rigorous testing of vehicle designs to ensure durability. In the event of transmission problems, access to the transmission was straightforward since the transmission was behind a cast-armored cover that could be unbolted and quickly removed. U.S. tank units in Lorraine in September 1944 had availability rates of 90 percent or more. The poor reliability of the Panther meant decreased combat power in the panzer brigades; the excellent reliability of the Sherman meant enhanced combat power in U.S. Army armored divisions.

The PzKpfw IV had a better reliability than the Panther, though still less than the Sherman. In the last half of 1943, the PzKpfw IV had an availability rate of 48 percent, while in January–September 1944, it was 61 percent. The average tank status of the M4 Sherman in the 4th Armored Division in September 1944 was about 1 percent of the tanks under repair on a daily basis, or an availability rate of about 99 percent. The worst day for the 4th Armored Division in September 1944 in terms of availability was on 22 September when about 8 percent of the Shermans were under repair.[63] The American advantage was a combination of the greater durability of the American design, greater availability of spare parts, and a robust recovery and repair system. Another reason for the extreme difference between the Sherman and its German counterparts was that the U.S. Army wrote off damaged tanks much more quickly than in the German case.

U.S. tank units had a more modern command-and-control network than panzer units. U.S. tankers enjoyed communications advantages due to the use of more modern FM radios. The Panther tank still used the same AM radio in use since 1940. FM radios were less susceptible to interference than the older AM radios. Aside from better radios, the combat commands usually had tank-mounted artillery forward observers and, in some cases, tank-mounted air force liaison officers. This meant that the forward tank formations could call for artillery fire support, and, in some cases, close air support, to carry out their mission. This was often the case when a column was stopped by hidden German armor in defilade position that could not be easily eliminated by direct tank fire. Most combat commands had at least one battalion of self-propelled M7 105mm howitzer motor carriages for each tank battalion, sometimes more. Communications were a critical ingredient in combined-arms tactics, and the U.S. Army enjoyed significant advantages in this regard.

CHAPTER 5

False Start: The Battle of Mairy

EVEN THOUGH HITLER HAD ORDERED that the new panzer brigades should be reserved for the Vosges Panzer Offensive, the situation in Lorraine was so desperate that local commanders began to request their use for local missions. The threats of a major breakthrough by Patton's Third U.S. Army forced premature commitment of these precious resources. The first of the Lorraine panzer battles began in the predawn hours of 8 September 1944 with an attack by the newly arrived Panzer-Brigade.106 against Patton's XX Corps.

OPPOSING PLANS: THE WEHRMACHT

At the beginning of September 1944, the situation in Lorraine had reached a critical stage due to the weakness of the 1.Armee on the approaches to the fortified city of Metz. The advance of Gen. Walton Walker's XX Corps towards the Moselle River had been slowed more by American fuel shortages than by German resistance. The German infantry divisions in this sector were weak and battered, and so were unable to offer vigorous resistance to the American attacks.

Berlin was profoundly concerned that Patton's Third U.S. Army was on the verge of a major thrust to the Rhine River. When Patton's Third U.S. Army stalled around Verdun from 31 August to 6 September 1944 due to fuel shortages, this delay was misinterpreted in Berlin as a preparation for a major thrust through Luxembourg, across the German frontier by way of Trier and Hündsbruck to the Rhine River.[64] All that was standing in Patton's path was the badly mauled 1.Armee.

At this time, 1.Armee was commanded by General of Infantry Kurt von der Chevallerie. He was well aware of the precariousness of his army's defenses, and in early September he began to request the dispatch of additional reinforcements to strengthen this beleaguered front. To make matters worse, on 4 September 1944, 1.Armee was ordered to transfer one of its few mechanized units, the 15.Panzergrenadier-Division, to the neighboring 19.Armee to take part in the planned Vosges Panzer Offensive. The only consolation was that Berlin acquiesced to his temporary control over the new Panzer-Brigade.106 with the caveat that any operations by this unit would have to be directly approved by Hitler.[65]

Chevallerie convinced Berlin to let him use Panzer-Brigade.106 as the vanguard of a spoiling attack aimed at smashing into the assembly areas of Patton's forces north of Metz. The plan was to reinforce Panzer-Brigade.106 with elements of the 19.Volksgrenadier-Division and a regiment from 15.Panzergrenadier-Division. Berlin approved the use of Panzer-Brigade.106 on 5 September 1944 but warned Chevallerie that he could only employ the unit for forty-eight hours, at which point it would revert back to the strategic reserve for the planned Vosges Panzer Offensive. It remains a mystery why Hitler acquiesced to the use of Panzer-Brigade.106 for this mission after his earlier imprecations against the dilution of the new panzer forces prior to the Vosges Panzer Offensive. The most likely reason was his distraction on 4–5 September by larger matters. He was in the midst of reorganizing the command of the German army in the west, returning Field Marshal von Rundstedt to the leadership of OB West after having relieved him on 1 July due to his pessimistic assessment of German fortunes in Normandy. A further distraction was Hitler's insistence on personally briefing the newly arrived Hasso von Manteuffel on 5 September about his intentions for the Vosges Panzer Offensive.

In the midst of this command shake-up, Hitler decided to relieve Chevallerie from command of 1.Armee. The official rationale for the command shake-up at such an awkward moment was ill health.[66] The unofficial explanation was the failure of the rump 1.Armee to hold the Seine River in late August 1944. While this may have been the catalyst for the dismissal, there were contributing factors. Hitler was suspicious of German commanders in France since so many had been involved in the 20 July 1944 bomb plot against him. Another contributing factor was the malevolent involvement of SS-Reichsführer Heinrich Himmler. After the 20 July 1944 bomb plot against Hitler, Himmler took over control of the Replacement Army (Ersatzheer) that had been at the heart of the conspiracy and, along with it, the internal military districts (Wehrkreisen) in Germany that had a secondary defense function when enemy forces reached German soil. Until late August, Military District 11 was in charge of the defenses in the sector eventually taken over by the retreating 1.Armee. There was a sharp series of exchanges between Himmler's headquarters and Chevallerie's headquarters on 29 August 1944 over control of the units in this sector.[67] It was not wise to cross Himmler at so delicate a moment when there were grave suspicions about the loyalty of the generals in France. Chevallerie further alienated Himmler's minions when he complained to the Wehrmacht High Command about the inglorious departure of Gauleiter (regional governor) Gustav Simon from Luxembourg. Simon got revenge by sending lurid reports to Berlin about tens of thousands of stragglers congregating in the rear areas of Chevallerie's 1.Armee.[68] In the event, Chevallerie was formally relieved of command on 5 September, and command transferred to General of Panzer Troops Otto von Knobelsdorff. However, it would take several days for Knobelsdorff to reach 1.Armee headquarters in Lorraine, and so Chevallerie remained in command as a lame duck through 9 September.[69]

The attack against Patton's XX Corps was authorized by Berlin later on 5 September 1944. The Wehrmacht High Command daily log for 6 September 1944 summarized the mission as follows: "A separate attack is underway consisting of a third of 15.Pz. Gren. Div. and Pz. Brig. 106 from the Longwy-Aumetz area with the aim to penetrate into the Etain area and east in order to clarify the enemy situation, to crush enemy forces there and to secure the line Longuyon-Briey-Metz Bridgehead."[70] Panzer-Brigade.106 began moving from its staging area near Trier in Germany to its start position at Audun-le-Roman in Lorraine around 18:00 hours on 6 September 1944.[71]

The planning for the attack was haphazard at best. Aside from the command turmoil caused by Chevallerie's dismissal, the headquarters staff of 1.Armee was badly overstretched and of poor quality. "The officers, with the exception of some general staff officers and a few others, were not suitable for mobile warfare. Most were over forty years old and had been on active duty in Bordeaux only during the quiet years [of occupation], were often not fit for active service. In many cases, they were seriously war-disabled and had neither battle experience nor training for higher staff duties on a main defensive front. As a result, the work was left mainly to a small circle of men who consequently were badly overburdened."[72] To further complicate matters, the direction of this attack normally would have been managed by a corps headquarters subordinate to 1.Armee. However, in the chaos of early September, the corps headquarters were in flux and the 13.SS.Korps did not assume control in this sector until 7 September 1944, after the planning had already taken place.[73]

The 1.Armee was not aware of any details of the opposing American forces, except for the vaguest reports from front-line units about the extent of American penetrations into German defenses. Most importantly, there had been little or no reconnaissance of the battle area. This was a recipe for disaster.

OPPOSING PLANS: PATTON'S THIRD U.S. ARMY

At the beginning of September 1944, Patton's operational goal was to close on the Siegfried Line, the Allied nickname for the German Westwall fortifications along the western border. Patton was a consummate cavalryman, and nothing inspires the cavalry like the fast pursuit of a retreating enemy. He was convinced that the elements of the Wehrmacht in front of the Third U.S. Army were defeated and that he could plunge beyond the German border if given enough fuel and supplies. As mentioned earlier, fuel shortages began to cripple his advance in the last days of August and first days of September 1944. For example, the Third U.S. Army requested 4.7 million gallons of fuel for 1–7 September but received only 1.8 million gallons.[74] To put this in some perspective, it took 14,500 gallons of gasoline to move a U.S. infantry division one hundred miles; an armored division required 73,200 gallons.

In the case of the XX Corps facing Metz and the 1.Armee, the 7th Armored Division siphoned enough gas from all the vehicles in the division to keep a task force mobile for a few days; it was forced to halt on 3 September when its gas tanks went empty.[75] The 3rd Cavalry Group managed to capture 4,000 gallons of high-octane aviation fuel from Luftwaffe stores. Patton authorized the use of this precious fuel reserve to permit the 3rd Cavalry to continue their probes into German lines. The 1.Armee was shocked when patrols from the 3rd Cavalry appeared in the city of Thionville on 1–2 September. Probes were sent towards Metz, but operations along the XX Corps ground to a halt for lack of fuel. Patton's operational intentions were to conduct the campaign in two phases, first to reach the Moselle River, and then to press on to the Rhine. In discussions with Gen. Omar Bradley, commander of the 12th Army Group, the operational objective of Patton's Third U.S. Army was Frankfurt. This was seen as a critical gateway into Germany.

The fuel drought temporarily ended on 4 September 1944 when Bradley informed Patton that the Third U.S. Army would receive half of its normal supply. He suggested that it should be enough to force the Moselle River and begin moving on the Siegfried Line. The Third U.S. Army had a daily requirement of about 400,000 gallons per day, and on 4 September it received about 240,000 gallons. Some 110,000 gallons of fuel was flown into Reims in C-47 transport aircraft. This permitted a renewal of the offensive on 5–6 September 1944. It was this renewal of the attacks by the XX Corps that served as the catalyst for the 1.Armee counteroffensive planned for the night of 7–8 September.

The XX Corps attack towards the Moselle River consisted of the 90th Infantry Division attacking towards Thionville in the north near the Luxembourg border, the 7th Armored Division attacking on either side of Metz around Mondelange in the center, and the 5th Infantry Division attacking south of Metz.

OPPOSING FORCES: PANZER-BRIGADE.106

The core of the 1.Armee counterattack on Patton's XX Corps was Panzer-Brigade.106 "Feldherrn-halle." This was one of the new panzer brigades formed in late July 1944. It began to be assembled on 28 July 1944 at the Mielau Troop Training Grounds (now Mława, Poland). It was based on survivors from Panzergrenadier-Division "Feldherrnhalle" that had been encircled and destroyed in Belarus in July 1944 during the Red Army's summer offensive, Operation Bagration. The brigade's honorary name "Feldherrnhalle" (Field Marshal's Hall) was named after a monument on the Odeansplatz in Munich commissioned in 1841 by King Ludwig of Bavaria to honor the tradition of the Bavarian army. It became a symbol of the Nazi Party after it was the scene of a brief skirmish between the Nazi SA "brownshirts" (SA: Sturmabteiling) against local police and troops in November 1923 that ended Hitler's Beer Hall Putsch. At least on paper, units with the honorific Feldherrnhalle title were supposed to contain a high proportion of men with backgrounds in the SA movement.[76] In reality, the SA had long since been superseded by the SS, and reconstituted units in 1944 received whatever troops were available with little regard to their political past.

The brigade was commanded by one of the most distinguished Wehrmacht tank commanders, Col. Dr. Franz Bäke. Besides Bäke, the brigade had at least two other Knight's Cross holders, Erich Oberwöhrmann, commanding its Panther battalion, and Ewald Bartel, the brigade adjutant.

In spite of its association with Panzergrenadier-Division FHH, the newly formed panzer brigade in fact received few survivors from the original division. A cadre of 347 men from the original unit arrived at the training grounds on 28 July 1944 to start the formation process; this represented less than a fifth of its total strength of 2,135 men. Many of the remaining troops came from Luftwaffe ground crews made redundant by the fuel shortages that led to the disbandment of many Luftwaffe bomber units.

Panzer-Brigade.106 followed the early configuration for these brigades, with only a single tank battalion, Panzer-Abteilung.2106. This unit received thirty-six new Panther tanks on 9–12 August. The new crews had little opportunity to train on them due to fuel shortages. Other armored fighting vehicles operated by the brigade included 11 Pz IV/70(V). This vehicle was originally called the leichte Jagdpanzer IV (light tank destroyer), but a shortage of Panther tanks led to its adoption as an expedient tank. Nicknamed "Guderian's duck," it consisted of the PzKpfw IV tank hull with a fixed casemate armed with the same long 75mm gun as the Panther tank. These vehicles equipped the 4th Company in the tank battalion. Although well armed, the fixed superstructure made the vehicle less versatile than a tank in combat, and the forward location of the long gun led to frequent accidents due to the tendency of the gun barrel to become embedded in the ground when moving across rough terrain. The other armored fighting vehicle used by the brigade were four Flakpanzer IV, a version of the PzKpfw IV armed with a 37mm flak automatic cannon for protection of the brigade headquarters from air attack.

The most common armored vehicle in the brigade was the SdKfz 251 armored half-track, with an authorized strength of 157 vehicles. Of these, 116 were allotted to the Panzergrenadier-Batallion.2106, while most of the remainder belonged to the Pioner (combat engineer) company.[77]

The closest analog to the German panzer brigade was a combat command in a U.S. Army armored division. Although the panzer brigade might appear to be a balanced combined-arms force, its most glaring shortcoming was the lack of any field artillery component. This would become especially apparent when fighting enemy infantry. Another shortcoming was the lack of a dedicated reconnaissance unit. This was not considered to be a major issue in the field manual for the new panzer brigades issued on 26 July 1944, which indicated that the panzer battalion could perform this mission on its own without a specialized component.[78] As would become obvious in the forthcoming battle, this was not really the case.

During the fighting in early September, Panzer-Brigade.106 was supported by Grenadier-Regiment .59, part of the new 19.Grenadier-Division. This division had been created in Denmark in August 1944 from remaining elements of the 19. Luftwaffe-Sturm-Division. The division was at about 80 percent strength in September 1944 but was badly short of experienced noncommissioned officers, having only about 70 percent of the authorized strength.[79]

OPPOSING FORCES: 90TH INFANTRY DIVISION

The XX Corps unit facing the German counterattack was the 90th Infantry Division. This division was nicknamed the "Tough 'Ombres" after their divisional insignia, a superimposed "T and O" symbolizing their National Guard recruitment area in Texas and Oklahoma. The division had served in France in World War I and was re-activated in March 1942. Elements of the division landed on Utah Beach on D-Day, and the division was heavily engaged in the battles for the Cotentin peninsula leading up to the liberation of Cherbourg at the end of June 1944.

The division earned a bad reputation due to its poor combat performance in Normandy in its first weeks of combat. Indeed, its performance was so bad that some senior U.S. Army officers considered disbanding the division and using its troops to reinforce other divisions. More sober judgment prevailed, and it was recognized that poor leadership was the core problem. The division commander was relieved twice before Maj. Gen. Raymond McLain was assigned command in August 1944, finally putting the division on a sound footing.

The 90th Division paid a heavy price for its combat initiation. Within six weeks of the D-Day landings, it had lost the equivalent of 100 percent of its strength, and some rifle companies suffered casualties the equivalent of 400 percent of their establishment strength. By September 1944, it was at full strength and was a seasoned, combat-hardened unit.

Like most U.S. infantry divisions in the ETO, it received significant armored attachments for direct support. The 712th Tank Battalion was attached to the division starting from 28 June 1944, and at the time of the battle with Panzer-Brigade.106, it had fifty-six M4 Sherman medium tanks and eighteen M5A1 light tanks. While the 712th Tank Battalion had more tanks than Panzer-Brigade.106, the Panther was significantly superior to the Sherman tank in a head-to-head confrontation in terms of armor and firepower. The usual practice in 1944 was to attach a medium tank company to each of the division's three regiments. The 90th Division also had the support of the 607th Tank Destroyer Battalion, equipped with 3-inch, towed antitank guns.

THE PANZER ATTACK, 7–8 SEPTEMBER 1944

The attack against Patton's XX Corps was supposed to begin at 23:00 hours on the night of 6–7 September. Bäke formed his brigade into two shock groups (Stoßgruppen). Surviving documents provide no detail into the composition or leadership of the shock groups, though most likely they were led by the commanders of the brigade's panzer battalion and panzergrenadier regiment.

Panzer-Brigade.106 was ready in their forward staging area near Audun-le-Roman around 20:00 hours, but the supporting infantry of Grenadier-Regiment.59 were nowhere to be found. On contacting 19.Grenadier-Division, it quickly became apparent that the higher commands had not informed them of the plans. As a result, the troops from Grenadier-Regiment.59 did not arrive until the early morning hours around 01:50 on 7 September. The spearhead of the Kampfgruppe reached Briey around 03:05 but found no evidence of U.S. troops. Scouting patrols were sent west and southwest of Briey, all without enemy contact. A planned linkup with the 15.Panzergrenadier-Division near Landres failed to occur, and there was no sign of the division in the area. About all that was accomplished that night was the destruction of a bridge near Auboue, southeast of Briey. Around daybreak, Bäke ordered the Kampfgruppe to return to its staging area around Audun-le-Roman.

The countryside around the village of Mairy is gently rolling, occasionally interrupted by small wooded areas. This is a view south of the staging area for Panzer-Brigade.106 near Audun-le-Roman on Route D156 heading towards Mairy. This photo was taken by the author fifty-five years after the battle, in September 1999.

Panzer-Brigade.106 was based in the small village of Audun-le-Roman. This is the view from southwest of the town on the route taken by the brigade on the night of 7 September 1944 for its attack on the 90th Division. Colonel Bäke's headquarters was in the Saint Donat village church seen in the center of this photo.

Panzer-Brigade.106 had a single platoon of these Flakpanzer IV antiaircraft vehicles armed with a 37mm automatic cannon. They do not appear to have been used in the fighting around Mairy but were probably left in Audun-le-Roman to defend the headquarters.

The failure of Bäke's battle groups to engage American forces was due to the lingering effects of the fuel shortage still affecting XX Corps. The advance towards the Moselle by the 90th Division was delayed until the morning of 7 September 1944 when Bäke's troops were returning to their staging areas.

The principal German unit in this sector was the 559.Volksgrenadier Division, which held positions from northwest of Thionville to the northern outskirts of Metz around St. Privat.[80] The 19.Grenadier-Division held positions immediately to the north of the 559.Volksgrenadier-Division. The attacks by the 90th Division on 7 September pushed back both the 19.Grenadier-Division and the 559.Volksgrenadier-Division. Chevallerie's 1.Armee headquarters became concerned enough about the extent of the American advance that Bäke received instructions at 19:15 hours on the evening of 7 September 1944 to prepare his brigade for another attack towards Briey with the intention of helping the 19.Grenadier-Division to regain its old defense line.

PANZER-BRIGADE.106 FHH ORDER OF BATTLE, 7–8 SEPTEMBER 1944 (in order of march)	
1.Stoßgruppe (Shock Group)	**Sr. Lt. Strauch**
2./Panzer-Abteilung.2106	Sr. Lt. Strauch
1./Panzergenadier-Batallion.2106	Sr. Lt. Hobel
1.Zug, Panzer-Pioner-Kompanie.2106	Lt. Sturm
2.Stoßgruppe (Shock Group)	**Col. Franz Bäke**
3./Panzer-Abteilung.2106	Sr. Lt. Struck
2./Panzergenadier-Batallion.2106	Sr. Lt. Papke
Stab./Panzer-Abteilung.2106	Capt. Erich Oberwöhrmann
1./Panzer-Abteilung.2106	Capt. Wiede
Stab Kp., Panzer-Brigade.106	Capt. Ewald Bartel
Stab Kp., Panzergenadier-Batallion.2106	Capt. Münzer
5./Panzergenadier-Batallion.2106	Sr. Lt. Hollfelder
3./Panzergenadier-Batallion.2106	Sr. Lt. Anding
2.Zug; 3.Zug., Panzer-Pioner-Kompanie.2106	Capt. Scheske
Reserve (in Aumetz)	
4./Panzergenadier-Batallion.2106	Sr. Lt. Büchting
Panzerjager-Kompanie.2106	
Security Group (in Audun-le-Roman)	
4./Panzer-Abteilung.2106	Sr. Lt. Auer
Drilling Flak Zug	

The attack was scheduled to start in the predawn hours of 8 September 1944 as soon as the brigade could be made ready. The brigade's tank strength was around twenty-two Panther tanks because eight to ten tanks had broken down over the course of the past few days and were under repair.[81] The brigade was divided into two Stoßgruppen with the majority of the force assigned to the 2.Shock Group. The 1.Shock Group was commanded by Sr. Lt. Strauch, who led his own 2.Kompanie, Pz.Abt.2106, reinforced with 1.Kompanie, Pz.Gren.Btl.2106 and a platoon from the brigade's Pioner (engineer) company. This group was the eastern arm of the attack and was assigned to move southward along Route D906, relieve the trapped battalion from the 559.Volksgrenadier-Division in Briey, and then secure the town.

The 2.Shock Group was led by Colonel Bäke himself and included most of the remainder of the brigade's strength, including the headquarters company and two Panther tank companies of Pz.Abt.2106, the headquarters company, and three grenadier companies of Pz.Gren.Btl.2106. The 4./Pz.Abt.2106 was to be left in Audun-le-Roman as a security screen, and the 4./Pz.Gren.Btl.2106 along with the brigade's antitank company were deployed near Benvillers and Aumetz as a reserve. Bäke's 2.Shock Group formed the western arm of the attack and was instructed to move down Route D156 to Murville, then turn south towards Mont, Mainville, and finally meet up with the 1.Shock Group at Briey.[82]

By nightfall on the evening of 7 September, the 90th Infantry Division had taken up defensive positions after a hard day of fighting. The three component regiments were deployed along a line slightly to the east of Route N43 with the 359th Infantry around Xivry-Circourt, the 358th Infantry around Mairy, and the 357th Infantry around Avril. The 357th Infantry had trapped a battalion of the 559.Volksgrenadier-Division in Briey, and 2/357th Infantry was left behind to reduce this position the next day. In view of the rapid pace of the advance in the last week of August, General McLain decided to position his tactical command post very far forward to avoid the need for daily moves. The division headquarters forward echelon command post (CP) was established in the Bois le Rappe woods south of Landres, with the divisional artillery headquarters across the road in a neighboring farm field. "During this period, it was decided to move the Divisional Command Post well forward to avoid the continual changing of location brought about by the fast advancing situation."[83] In view of its exposed forward location, three M4 Sherman tanks of Company A, 712th Tank Battalion were positioned around the divisional CP.

Both sides were equally ignorant about each other's locations. The weather that night was cloudy with occasional moonlight to illuminate the landscape.

This is a view from the west of the Bois le Rappe woods outside of Landres from along Route D156. The forward tactical command post of the 90th Division was located in these woods during the night of 7 September 1944, and this photo was taken by the author in 1999.

THE BATTLE OF THE CPS

The spearhead of Bäke's 2.Shock Group consisted of four to five Panther tanks from Sr. Lt. Struck's 3./Pz.Abt.2106 followed by a similar number of SdKfz 251 armored half-tracks of Sr. Lt. Papke's 2./Pz.Gren.Btl.2106. After reaching Mont, they headed down the D952 country road to reach the main D643 road to the objective of Briey. As a result, they passed between the main divisional CP in the Bois la Rappe and the divisional artillery CP on the other side of the road. The spearhead passed through the American positions, unaware of their presence. Then Bäke, along with Captain Oberwöhrmann, followed with the headquarters company of Pz.Abt.2106. They reached the road between the American command posts a few moments later around 02:30 hours. The German command group halted at this point. American officers later speculated that the German column had spotted the large sign for the divisional artillery CP along the road and decided to investigate.

Scattered on either side of the road, the tank crews of the Company A, 712th Tank Battalion quickly decided it must be a German column. George Bussell later recalled: "I could tell by the tracks it wasn't ours. The noise was altogether different. They had steel tracks and we had rubber."[84] 2nd Lt. Harry Bell, commanding three M4 Shermans stationed at the divisional CP, radioed to 1st Lt. Lester O'Reilly, commander of Company A, to report German actions. O'Reilly asked if he was sure that they were German and not American. Bell responded that he was positive they were German. O'Reilly radioed to "Give 'm hell." The crewman on an M4 medium tank guarding the divisional artillery CP fired at the trailing vehicle. A German Sd Kfz 251 half-track exploded in flames, but the fire illuminated the American tank, which was then brought under fire from the lead Panther tanks. The U.S. tank exploded and collateral casualties among the artillery staff were heavy. Another M4 Sherman started its engine, alerting a nearby Panther tank that hit it in the suspension with its first shot. Sgt. George Colton, a gunner on one of the M4 tanks, scored the first hit on a German tank moments before his own tank was hit and disabled. Colton leapt out of his own tank, ran to a neighboring

tank, and disabled a second German tank. In a matter of a few moments, there were two burning Sherman tanks and two burning Panther tanks near the edge of the Divisional CP. In the wild firing that ensued, two more M4 Sherman tanks were hit and knocked out.

Grenadiers of Pz.Gren.Btl.2106 began dismounting from their half-tracks along the road and began assaulting both divisional CPs on foot. Machine-gun teams began raking the American positions, and a few of the SdKfz 251/21 half-tracks armed with triple 20mm autocannons circled around the artillery CP and opened fire. A 90th Division account recalled that "The first wave of German foot troops was thrown back by the small arms fire of the defenders. At 03:45, the second German infantry attack began. A volunteer was called for to man the machine gun on the abandoned tank. Pvt. George Briggs jumped on to the tank and started firing. The tanks and armored cars of the enemy cut loose with a barrage. The German machine guns to the north and west chattered forth their torrents of lead. The German infantry, throwing egg grenades, and firing machine pistols, came forward, again to meet a hail of small arms fire. The men of the army message center threw grenades to augment their small arms fire and the enemy beat a hasty retreat, gathering up their wounded as they went."[85] The divisional artillery CP was particularly hard hit.

The assistant divisional commander, Maj. Gen. William Weaver, recalled "No CP could function with Panzer guns shoved down its throat, so it was decided to evacuate the principal personnel and paraphernalia north to Bob Bacon's 359th Regimental set-up temporarily . . . [divisional commander] Ray McLain loved to fight, and he was going to stay and slug it out personally. But he was persuaded, after much argument, with the fact that he had to direct the affairs of the whole division and just the HQ defense platoon. He departed grudgingly."[86] In the meantime, McLain had instructed the neighboring regiments to dispatch troops towards the command posts to join in the fray. The 2nd and 3rd Battalions of the 359th Infantry started moving southward, along with Company C, 712th Tank Battalion.

The German columns broke up into smaller groups and began bumping into other elements of the American force. Company D, 712th Tank Battalion had their M5A1 light tanks in a bivouac area south of the 80th Division command post. The confusion that evening is evident from their subsequent report:

At about 0300, an enemy column, consisting of about 5 Panther tanks and 6 half-tracks, moved down a road between the [tank] companies, circled the [712th Tank] Battalion area and was believed totally destroyed. The presence of this company was known, but to fire on it in the darkness would endanger our own troops.[87]

Instead of retreating in the face of a surprise night attack as the Germans had expected, the American infantry began to methodically attack the intruder. By dawn, Bäke's 2.Shock Group realized it had stumbled into a hornet's nest. Around 08:35, Bäke radioed 2.Shock Group to shift its attack back east to escape, giving up on the main objective at Briey. Bäke also ordered the 1.Shock Group, which had not yet encountered U.S. defense, to turn westward and support their beleaguered comrades.

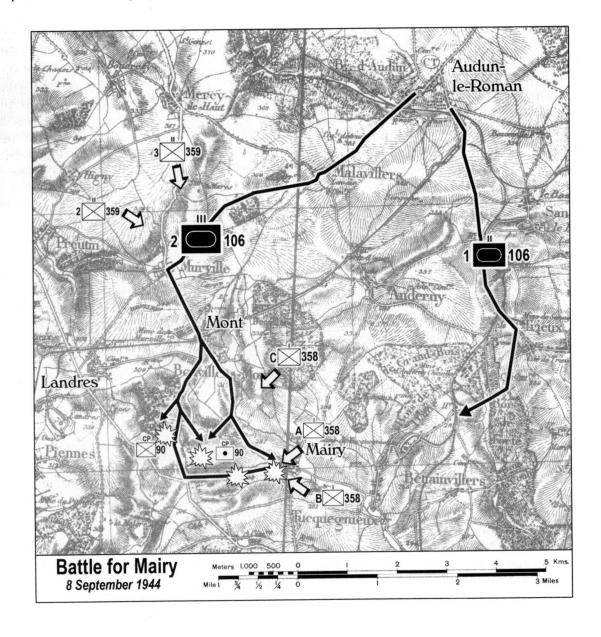

Battle for Mairy
8 September 1944

BATTLE FOR MAIRY

The main body of Bäke's 2.Shock Group changed direction towards the northeast, moving through a shallow valley between two hills that lead to the village of Mairy from the west. This area was defended by the 1st Battalion, 358th Infantry, supported by a platoon of four towed 3-inch antitank guns from the 607th Tank Destroyer Battalion. Mairy is in a shallow depression surrounded by hills. The 2.Shock Group tried to form a regulation arrowhead formation to muscle its way through the American defenses. "It made a formation like a T; the cross of the T was at the front of the column headed straight for the 1st Battalion's motor pool. . . . The tanks and the many armored transporters were camouflaged with brush, and it really looked for awhile like that report of 100 tanks was no exaggeration."[88] The column included several Sd Kfz 251/9 armored half-tracks armed with short 75mm guns that were used in panzergrenadier units for close fire support. They added to the firepower of the Panther tanks.

Major Lytle, the commander of the 1st Battalion, 358th Infantry, instructed the artillery liaison officer from the 344th Field Artillery Battalion "to paste the enemy column with all the artillery he could get, irregardless of how close he had to shoot to our own troops." The task was made somewhat easier when 1st Lt. Cud Baird, commanding Company A, 1/358th Infantry, went tank hunting with a bazooka. He managed to knock out the lead German vehicle in the sunken road, halting the German column at least temporarily. Within a few moments, the column was hit with over 300 rounds of 105mm and 155mm howitzer fire from two field artillery battalions, as well as direct fire from the infantry cannon company, several 3-inch antitank guns, and an assortment of bazookas, mortars, and rifle grenades. The fighting in the gully led to the loss of thirty-one SdKfz 251 armored half-tracks and three tanks. The SdKfz 251 half-tracks were especially vulnerable to artillery fire due to their thin armor and open roofs.

A view inside the town of Mairy taken in 1999. This street is now called "Rue de 8 Septembre 1944" in commemoration of the heavy fighting that took place here between the 1st Battalion, 358th Infantry and the 1.Shock Group, Panzer-Brigade.106.

The panzergrenadiers dispersed away from the stricken column and attempted to fight their way into Mairy. This led to a series of scattered skirmishes in the town between the German and American infantry. Elements of 2.Shock Group farther back in the column tried to escape the death trap at the front of the column. A small group of Panther tanks began firing at the village from the high ground near Mont. They were engaged by the 3-inch antitank guns, and two tanks were hit. Around 10:00 hours, a panzergrenadier company broke free of the trapped column and charged into the town from the south along the Mainville road in seventeen Sd.Kfz. 251 armored half-tracks with a single Panther tank sandwiched in the middle of the column. Two half-tracks were blown apart at close range by M3 105mm howitzers of the battalion's cannon company. Two more were knocked out by bazooka fire from the tank destroyer platoon, and four more were lost to 3-inch antitank guns as they tried to retreat out of the town to the north. The column became trapped in the middle of the town with the leading and trailing half-tracks burning fiercely and preventing the escape of the rest. The column was subjected to further small-arms and mortar fire. An officer, presumed to be the column commander, was hit by rifle fire while peering out of the cupola of the Panther tank. With the fate of the column painfully clear, a German soldier at the rear of the column began waving a white flag. A total of 209 troops surrendered of whom 65 were wounded; a tally of the dead was never recorded.

Besides the morning fighting in Mairy, there was scattered fighting all though the area between elements of the 90th Division and the rest of the 2.Shock Group. The wooded divisional CP area was reinforced by troops of the 359th Infantry, who rebuffed small-scale attacks by German armored vehicles and dismounted infantry. The area around the battalion CP of the 712th Tank Battalion was also the scene of several engagements. Company D reported that "At about 1000 hours, two enemy Panther tanks broke through our defenses and moved full speed toward the Company and Battalion Headquarters Company area. Guns from several directions opened up on them and destroyed both tanks before they had done any harm. Five P.W.

[prisoners of war] were taken, one of whom stated they were trying to get out instead of in."

One of the most peculiar engagements of the day took place late in the morning when a lone Panther tank was seen escaping northward by an L-4 Piper Cub spotter plane of the 915th Field Artillery Battalion piloted by Lt. George Kilmer. Along with his observer, Lt. George Pezat, the light plane continued to try to direct artillery fire against the tank to no avail. In frustration, the pair buzzed the tank repeatedly, firing their .45 caliber pistols at it. After an hour's chase, the plane headed back to base low on fuel; the Panther tank escaped to Audun-le-Roman. Patton visited the 90th Division a few days later and recalled that "One of the few tanks to escape was a Panther. I saw the tracks where it had gone straight into our line, oblivious of what we could do to stop it, and then turned sharply left on a road leading to Germany. It disappeared in a cloud of dust and sparks where our tracers were hitting it."[89]

Strauck's 1.Shock Group had only modest contact with the 90th Division during the day and lost all contact with 2.Shock Group around 13:30 hours in the afternoon. It eventually withdrew towards Aumetz that evening around 19:00 hours along with supporting infantry.

The attack by Panzer-Brigade.106 had been a complete shambles. The conduct of the attack was so poorly executed that the senior officers of the 90th Infantry Division believed that the brigade was simply conducting an administrative movement between Audun-le-Roman and Briey and had inadvertently stumbled into the U.S. positions. Bäke's 2.Shock Group lost the majority of its troops and vehicles. At the end of the day, the 90th Division claimed to have knocked out thirty tanks, fifty-four SdKfz 251 half-tracks, about one hundred trucks and other vehicles, and two platoons of towed antitank guns. At least one account suggests that only seven Panther tanks from the original twenty-two Panther tanks returned, suggesting that fifteen had been lost. The war dairy of Army Group G reported only nine operational tanks and tank destroyers on 9 September, and the OB West war diary on the same day lists the brigade strength as only a quarter of normal strength.[90] A 16 September

An illustration of a Panther Ausf. G of 3.Kompanie, Pz.Abt.2106 that took part in the fighting at Mairy.

1944 report put the brigade's AFV strength as seventeen Panthers and nine Pz IV/70(V) of which nineteen were operational, suggesting that at least nineteen Panthers and two Pz IV/70(V) had been lost in the fighting to that point.[91]

A total of 764 prisoners were taken by the 90th Division of whom 125 were wounded; no count of the dead was recorded. Total casualties were probably about half of the brigade's starting strength. The prisoners and casualties included the commander of Panzer-Abt.2106, Captain Oberwöhrmann, the commander of Panzergrenadier-Btl.2106, Captain Münzer, two tank company commanders, Captain Wiede of 1./Pz.Abt.2106 and Sr. Lt. Struck of 3./Pz.Abt.2106, and one panzergrenadier company commander, Sr. Lt. Hobel of 1./Pz.Gren.Btl.2016. The German garrison in Briey from the 559.Volksgrenadier-Division, the ostensible objective of the Panzer-Brigade.106 attack, surrendered that afternoon, adding 442 prisoners of war to the day's tally.

Casualties in the 90th Division were eleven killed and sixty wounded; nearly half of the casualties were suffered by the divisional artillery CP.[92] The 712th Tank Battalion lost four M4 Sherman tanks; data on their personnel casualties is lacking.[93] The 712th Tank Battalion claimed to have knocked out nineteen German tanks, but the number is probably high due to double counting and confusion. The

90th Division resumed its advance later in the day and reached the Moselle River by 13 September.

One of the more bizarre outcomes of the fighting was the claim that Panzer-Brigade.106 knocked out 110 American tanks and 33 light armored vehicles during the 6–11 September fighting and fought a "fierce meeting engagement" with the 7th Armored Division.[94] This fiction was contained in the war diary of the intelligence section of OB West, most likely as a face-saving measure for the brigade's debacle on 8 September. In the days after the Mairy defeat, the remnants of the brigade were ordered to withdraw back north into Luxembourg. The brigade's war diary does not mention these kill claims, suggesting it might have been inserted by a higher command as a shield against Hitler's wrath for the brigade's embarrassing losses. The brigade's war diary for the period mentions a fight with American tank units west of Dippach in neighboring Luxembourg on the afternoon of 9 September, claiming to have knocked out twenty-six tanks and eight armored cars.[95] This was not the 7th Armored Division as claimed, which at the time was farther south, but the 5th Armored Division, part of the V Corps of the First U.S. Army. American losses during this skirmish were only a small fraction of the Panzer-Brigade.106 claims, amounting to two M4 tanks from the 34th Tank Battalion.[96]

The panzergrenadier units in the panzer brigades were provided with additional fire support in the form of the Sd.Kfz. 251/9 assault gun based on the standard armored half-track with a short 75mm howitzer. These were variously nicknamed "Stummel" or "Kanonewagen."

The 712th Tank Battalion supported the 90th Infantry Division during most of the July–September 1944 fighting. An M4 tank from the 712th Tank Battalion moves through the contested town of Periers on 27 July with an M10 3-inch GMC tank destroyer behind it.

The 607th Tank Destroyer Battalion was attached to the 90th Division during the Lorraine fighting. These towed 3-inch guns were cumbersome to deploy but, in the right circumstances such as at Mairy, proved very effective in the antitank role. This is a view from later in the Lorraine campaign during the fighting around Metz in November 1944.

After the 8 September 1944 attack, the 90th Division continued to move towards the Moselle around Thionville. These troops from the 358th Infantry Regiment are taking shelter in a trench leading into an old German bunker with the inscription "Viel feind, viel Her" (Many enemies, much Honor). This area of Lorraine was ceded to Germany by France in the wake of the 1870 Franco-Prussian War and returned to France at the end of World War I. As a result, it is heavily fortified with both French and German bunkers.

A rifleman of the 90th "Tough 'Ombres" Infantry Division.

Cannon companies in the U.S. infantry regiments used the lightweight M3 105mm howitzer instead of its larger field artillery counterpart. These were not intended for use against enemy tanks, but they proved very effective against lightly armored German half-tracks in the fighting around Mairy.

This Panther Ausf. G tank from Sr. Lt. Anding's 3.Kompanie, Pz.Abt.2106 was left abandoned west of Metz after the Mairy fighting. It was left by the roadside with a small sign to serve for vehicle recognition for passing American troops.

An M1 57mm antitank gun covers an intersection in Algrange during the fighting between the 358th Infantry, 90th Division and the 559.Volksgrenadier Division on 10–12 September. The 57mm gun was a license copy of the British 6-pdr. antitank gun and was the standard antitank weapon of infantry divisions in 1944. There were eighteen in each regiment, three per battalion. The 90th Division also had an attached towed 3-inch tank destroyer battalion to supplement their firepower.

The town of Mairy is surrounded by hills on all sides. This is a view from looking north into the town from Route D145 from Mainville as would have been seen by the panzergrenadiers who entered the town from this direction during the 8 September attack.

A GI from the 90th Infantry Division inspects some of the German equipment captured by the division during the fighting with Pz.Gren.Batallion.2106 near Mairy. These are both armed versions of the standard Sd.Kfz. 251 Ausf. D armored infantry half-track. On the left is a Sd.Kfz.251/21 with a triple MG151 20mm autocannon mounting. On the right is a Sd.Kfz. 251/9 "Stummel" assault gun armed with a close-support 75mm howitzer.

The Panzer-Brigade.106 had a number of these Sd.Kfz.251/21 "Flakwagens" armed with a triple 20mm MG151 automatic cannon on a pintle mount. Although primarily intended for defense against Allied fighter-bombers, they were also used for close fire support of the panzergrenadiers. This vehicle, with the Panzer-Brigade.106 insignia to the left of the rear door, was knocked out during the Operation Nordwind offensive in January 1945. It may have been with the brigade during the September 1944 fighting as Bäke ordered a platoon of six of these vehicles to remain behind in the relative safety of the Audun-le-Roman area to protect key bridges.

AFTER-ACTION ASSESSMENT

Hitler's original scheme had been to mass the new panzer brigades for a violent blow against Patton's spearheads. One of the four new panzer brigades was lost as a result of the defeat of Panzer-Brigade.106 at Mairy on 8 September 1944. The ill-considered release of one of the new brigades to conduct a local counterattack was a mistake, particularly when Bäke's brigade was thrown away in such a slapdash fashion. There was little or no tactical justification for its sacrifice. Its mission changed from day to day, and there was a serious mismatch between an untested panzer force and an experienced infantry division. This was a repeat of the wishful thinking of past German panzer counteroffensives such as Le Dezert and Mortain. German command and control in the Moselle sector was still in turmoil after the retreat by the 1.Armee, and planning for the attack was abysmal.

Patton's role in the German defeat was indirect, and he had no immediate contact with the units during the fighting. It was his previous actions that helped shape the course of the battle. As the fuel crisis deprived his units of mobility in late August and early September, he might have allowed his corps to adopt defensive positions. Instead, he encouraged his units to keep probing forward to the extent possible. His mechanized cavalry probes captured stocks of German fuel, permitting further aggressive reconnaissance. His relentless pressure on his subordinate commanders to keep the Moselle offensive rolling was his principal contribution in shaping this battle. The cavalry probe of Thionville particularly alarmed local German commanders and was the most immediate catalyst for the plan to use Panzer-Brigade.106. As a result of Patton's aggressive direction, the 1.Armee was kept off balance. German commanders hoped that a sharp rebuke against one of the spearheads of Patton's XX Corps might temporarily derail the Moselle offensive. However, they grossly overestimated the combat potential of the inexperienced panzer brigade and assigned it a desperate mission far beyond its modest capabilities.

A fresh panzer force, led by hardened Russian front veterans, and amply equipped with the best new tanks and armored infantry vehicles, might seem formidable on paper. But the brigade's recent formation, its lack of experience, and its slapdash training created a paper tiger. The brigade's attack on a dispersed infantry division exaggerated its organizational shortcomings. The main killer of infantry in World War II was field artillery, and Panzer-Brigade.106 had none. Nor was the technological superiority of its Panther tank at all influential on the battle. The Panther tank may have been a superb tank killer, but its long 75mm gun had a very modest high-explosive projectile when the main target was dispersed enemy infantry.

CHAPTER 6

The Épinal Debacle

DURING THE SECOND WEEK of September, Patton's Third U.S. Army was reinforced by a third corps, Maj. Gen. Wade Haislip's XV Corps. This corps had served under Patton earlier in the summer, and it was returned to the Third U.S. Army in Lorraine to cover Patton's exposed right flank. Patton had been able to ignore this sector in late August due to the disarray in German forces. By early September, Lt. Gen. Jacob Devers' 6th Army Group was advancing towards Patton. German troops retreating from southern and central France were being squeezed between Patton's and Devers' advancing armies. Haislip's XV Corps shielded Patton's main operation along the Moselle River. On 10 September, a mechanized patrol from the French 2e Division Blindée (2nd Armored Division), the southernmost unit in XV Corps, linked up with a patrol from the 6th Army Group to the west of Dijon, joining the Allied forces in the European Theater of Operations from the North Sea to the Mediterranean. The arrival of XV Corps around Épinal threatened the last substantial foothold of Army Group G on the west bank of the Moselle River, and thereby threatened the staging area for Hitler's Vosges Panzer Offensive. This would provoke yet another panzer skirmish prior to the main offensive.

Patton's Third U.S. Army and Patch's Seventh U.S. Army met at Dijon on 10–12 September, marking the linkup of the Allied forces from the North Sea to the Mediterranean. To commemorate the event, this photo was staged for the *Stars and Stripes* newspaper in front of the Autun town hall on September 13 with the crew of a French M20 armored utility car of the 2e Dragons shaking hands with the crew of an M8 light armored car of CCB, 6th Armored Division.

OPPOSING FORCES: THE FRENCH 2ND ARMORED DIVISION

The French 2e Division Blindée, usually known by its abbreviation as the 2e DB, was the only Free French division under Patton's command.[97] The vast majority of Free French units were part of the First French Army serving under Devers' 6th Army Group to the south. The reason for this division's isolation from the rest of the Free French forces was due to its talented and irascible commander, the legendary Gen. Jacques Leclerc.[98] Leclerc's difficulties with other senior French commanders are described in detail in the appendix later in this book on the commanders.

In 1943, the U.S. Army agreed to organize the Free French 2e Division as a U.S.-pattern armored division. The division kept traditional French regimental names, though in fact these units were organized in the same fashion as U.S. tank battalions. The 501e Régiment de Chars de Combat was based around the 342e Compagnie de Chars, a separate company of Hotchkiss light tanks that had served in the Norwegian campaign in 1940, moved to England after that campaign, and then took part in Leclerc's legendary campaign in

equatorial Africa. The 12e Régiment de Chasseurs d'Afrique had earlier taken part on the Allied side during the fighting around Kasserine Pass, equipped with Somua S-35 cavalry tanks. A cadre from this regiment was also used to reconstitute the new 12e Régiment de Cuirassiers in August 1943. The three mechanized infantry battalions originally derived from the Régiment de tirailleurs sénégalais du Tchad (Senegalese Rifle Regiment of Chad), which was renamed as the Régiment de marche de Tchad (RMT) when De Gaulle decided against using black African troops in the division in favor of French and Spanish volunteers. The most exotic formation in the division was the Régiment Blindée de Fusiliers Marins (RBFM), formed from French naval infantry units based in Bizerte and Toulon who volunteered for the Free French forces after the Vichy French fleet was scuttled in November 1942. They served as the personnel for the division's tank destroyer battalion and retained bits of their distinctive naval garb through the 1944 fighting. Further details of the origins of the 2e DB will be found in the section on Jacques Leclerc in appendix 1.

The RBFM tank destroyer regiment was foisted on Leclerc by De Gaulle for political reasons. Leclerc warmed to the regiment after its sterling performance at Dompaire. Here, French Minister of the Navy Jacquinot visits with the crews who had distinguished themselves during the fighting at Dompaire.

One of the officers of the RBFM was Ensign Philippe De Gaulle, son of Charles De Gaulle, an adjutant in the 1/3rd Squadron. As can be seen, officers of the unit retained their naval cap.

Another difference between the U.S. and French pattern was the naming of the division's three combat commands. Instead of the American practices of letters (CCA, CCB, CCR), the 2e DB's Groupements Tactiques were lettered after their commanders (GTD, GTL, GTV); French Task Forces were called Sous-Groupements (Sub-Groups).

De Gaulle wanted at least one French division to take part in any campaign to liberate Paris. Leclerc's 2e DB was the obvious choice. Leclerc and his senior officers had demonstrated their loyalty to De Gaulle's vision of a Free France, and they had demonstrated their military talents time

and time again in the fighting in equatorial Africa and North Africa in 1941–1943. Leclerc had also made clear that he did not want to serve under the First French Army due to the mutual antipathy between the senior commanders. The 2e DB was transferred from Morocco to England in April 1944 and landed in Normandy in July 1944. It was attached to Haislip's XV Corps and entered combat on August 10, 1944. Its combat debut was against the 9th Panzer Division in the Écouves forest on the approaches to Argentan during the attempts to seal the Falaise pocket.[99] Its most famous action of the war was its central role in the liberation of Paris in mid-August 1944.

Leclerc in his command jeep during the liberation of Paris on 23 August 1944. The young officer near the windshield is Aspirant Bergamin, giving Leclerc a report from the operations near Rambouillet. The officer in the kepi immediately behind Leclerc is Lieutenant Colonel Repiton-Préneuf, head of the division's headquarters staff. To the right are Lieutenant Colonel Crépin, head of the divisional artillery staff, and Commandant Jacques Weil, liaison officer to the U.S. Army.

M4A2 No. 28 "Tarentaise" comes ashore at Utah Beach on 1 August 1944. This tank served in the 2nd Platoon, 2nd Squadron of the 12e RCA and was knocked out during the fighting on 12 September 1944 on the approaches to Dompaire.

An M4A2 tank No. 26 "Iseran" of the 2nd Squadron, 12e RCA commanded by Sergeant Martin. This unit originally served in the 1943 Tunisian campaign on Somua S35 tanks, and many of the Sherman tanks had the "Somua" manufacturer's plate attached to memorialize the unit's past actions. This particular tank was knocked out during the fighting in March 1945.

The crews of a platoon of M10 3-inch GMC tank destroyers of the RBFM prepare their well-camouflaged vehicles for a road march. The crews' distinctive naval headgear is evident here.

On 10–11 September, Haislip's XV Corps returned to Patton's control and began operations against the weak German 64.Korps. The 79th Infantry Division pinned down the 16.Infanterie-Division by frontal attack, while Leclerc sent one of his three combat commands, the GTL (*Groupement Tactique Langlade*: Combat Command Langlade) through the gap between the Kampfgruppe Ottenbacher and the 16.Infanterie-Division. The 16.Infanterie-Division had only recently completed a nearly monthlong retreat from the Bay of Biscay on the French Atlantic coast all the way to the Moselle, a distance of more than 600 miles. At this stage, it was a division in name only. This unit was fairly new, having been converted

from the Luftwaffe's 16.Feld-Division in August 1944. By the time it reached Lorraine, it consisted of a motley selection of exhausted infantry troops, interspersed with Organization Todt construction workers, customs police, Luftwaffe ground crews, and assorted hangers-on. The division had barely arrived when the French attacked. The French armor columns raced deep behind German lines, approaching the Moselle River near Épinal by 12 September.

Even though Hitler had explicitly warned the local commanders to keep the new panzer brigades in reserve for the forthcoming Vosges Panzer Offensive, Panzer-Brigade.112 was chosen to prevent the onrushing disaster west of Épinal.

OPPOSING FORCES: PANZER-BRIGADE.112

Panzer-Brigade.112 was part of the second wave of the new formations created in the summer of 1944. The brigades of the second wave were larger and more powerful than first-wave brigades such as Panzer-Brigade.106 FHH that had fought at Mairy against the 90th Infantry Division. Instead of having only a single battalion of tanks, it had two battalions, giving it an overall strength of about ninety tanks and ten assault guns. This was comparable to the tank strength of most panzer divisions at this time. The brigade numbered 4,622 troops, about 150 troops short of the official tables of organization. Unfortunately, the personnel shortages were mostly in the area of officers and noncommissioned officers.[100]

Panzer-Brigade.112 was formed at Grafenwöhr in Military District V in southwestern Germany on 4 September 1944. Its commander was Col. Horst von Usedom, a heavily decorated veteran of the Russian front. To speed up the formation of the brigades, its Panther battalion came from Panzer-Regiment.29, formerly a part of the 12.Panzer Division on the Russian front. Although it was formed around a cadre of Panzer-Regiment.29 veterans, most of its troops were new. At the time of the September fighting, it had forty-six Panther tanks, delivered only on 3–7 September and so giving its new crews little time for training. Allied troops inspecting captured tanks a week later found that most were brand-new and had been built in mid-August 1944. Its Pzkpfw IV battalion, Pz.Abt.2112, was formed from scratch and did not receive its 46 tanks until 3–7 September. They were brand-new and one of them captured by the French had barely one hundred miles on its odometer.

A Panther Ausf. G of I./Pz.Regt. 29 knocked out during the fighting at Dompaire on 13 September 1944.

A Panther Ausf. G of I./Pz.Regt. 29 that suffered a catastrophic ammunition fire and explosion that knocked the turret off the hull.

In contrast to Panzer-Brigade.106, which was fully outfitted with SdKfz 251 armored half-tracks, Panzer-Brigade.112 had only thirteen half-tracks, mainly used in the brigade's reconnaissance company. It depended on ordinary trucks to transport its two panzergrenadier battalions. Panzergrenadier-Regiment.2112, commanded by Major Haecke, was hastily formed from Infantry Replacement and Training Battalion.119 and Panzergrenadier Replacement Battalion.215.[101] These troops had originally been intended for rebuilding the 23. Panzer-Division on the Russian front but were diverted to Panzer-Brigade.112 instead.

Although very well equipped on paper, the brigade was so hastily formed that most units had little or no time for proper training except for the Panther battalion. Brigade officers in many cases had not even met each other until the brigade disembarked in Lorraine. An OB West combat value assessment rated the brigade as "2" on a scale of 1 to 4, meaning limited suitability for offense; good but not great.[102] The brigade was transported to Lorraine by rail, via St. Dié, and it began reaching Épinal starting on 7 September 1944. An Allied air attack en route led to the loss of five Panther and two PzKpfw IV tanks and seven StuG III assault guns. A French villager who watched the column of Panthers move through Lamerey towards Dompaire the evening before the battle recalled that the crews "had the air of children about them."

A Panther Ausf. G of 3.Zug, 3.Kompanie, I./Pz.Regt.29 abandoned inside Dompaire after the 13 September 1944 fighting. At least four Panthers were found more or less intact in and around Dompaire.

This was one of the two intact Panthers that were cleaned up and sent to Paris to commemorate the victory at Dompaire.

OPPOSING PLANS: THE WEHRMACHT

Hitler continued to press for an activation of the Vosges Panzer Offensive, and on 10 September 1944, he sent another set of instructions to the 5.Panzer-Armee to launch the attack on 11 September from the Langres Plateau area against the northern spearhead of Devers' 6th Army Group. This was impossible since the forces for this mission were still in transit to the area. Indeed, Manteuffel and the 5.Panzer-Armee headquarters were not effectively in place until 14 September.

The attack by Leclerc's 2e DB on 12 September created yet another crisis, threatening to encircle 66.Armee-Korps and effectively seizing the Langres Plateau area that was supposed to be the pivot point for the Vosges Panzer Offensive. Gen. Walther Lucht, commander of the 66.Armee-Korps, suggested withdrawing the threatened 16.Infanterie-Division back towards Épinal, essentially conceding the northern shoulder of the Langres Plateau to the Allies. Hitler was infuriated by this suggestion and insisted that Army Group G give up no further ground west of the Moselle.[103] Col. Gen. Johannes Blaskowitz, the commander of Army Group G, had few resources at his disposal. Aware that some elements of 5.Panzer-Armee had begun to arrive in the Langres Plateau area, he decided to use these in an attempt to halt the French attack towards Épinal. Panzer-Brigade.112 was already in the area, and parts of 21.Panzer-Division were also arriving.

A battle group from the 21.Panzer-Division was put under Col. Hans von Luck. At the time, the division had no tanks and Kampfgruppe von Luck was simply a weak infantry force with barely 500 combat effectives. Luck was called to divisional headquarters to receive instructions from the divisional commander, General Feuchtinger. "Hitler is sticking to his intention of attack from the area west of Épinal, northward deep into Patton's flank. Madness, if one considers the physical state of both sides."[104]

The plan was to use Panzer-Brigade.112 in two battle groups, one based on the PzKpfw IV battalion, Pz.Abt.2112, and the other on the Panther battalion, I./Panzer-Regiment.29, to halt the French attack. A battle group from 21.Panzer-Division, Kampfgruppe Luck, was instructed to support the Panther battle group of I./Panzer-Regiment.29. The intention was to advance through Dompaire and Darney, and then swing north to cut off the 2e DB spearhead. In the event, Kampfgruppe von Luck would not arrive in time. More critically, the German planning underestimated their French opponent.[105] The prevailing view was that the French attack was simply a reconnaissance-in-force that could be easily brushed aside. The German assessment was no doubt colored by the contemptuous view that many Germans had for the French army after the 1940 campaign in France.

PLANS: U.S. XV CORPS

Patton had been warned by Bradley that the forthcoming Operation Market-Garden airborne attack in the Netherlands would lead to another round of fuel cutbacks in mid-September. Bradley gave Patton until 14 September to get over the Moselle, and as Patton later recalled, "Had I not secured a good bridgehead by that time, I was to stop arguing and assume the mournful role of a defender."[106] Patton tried to visit Haislip at his headquarters on 12 September to further urge

him forward, but by mistake, he only reached the rear echelon of XV Corps. However, Haislip and his tactical commanders were well aware of Patton's intentions, and the disintegration of the 16.Infanterie-Division defenses on 11–12 September encouraged their bold advance. The southernmost element of XV Corps, GTL of the 2e DB, was assigned to reach Thaon-les-Vosges, a town astride the Moselle River, immediately to the north of Épinal.

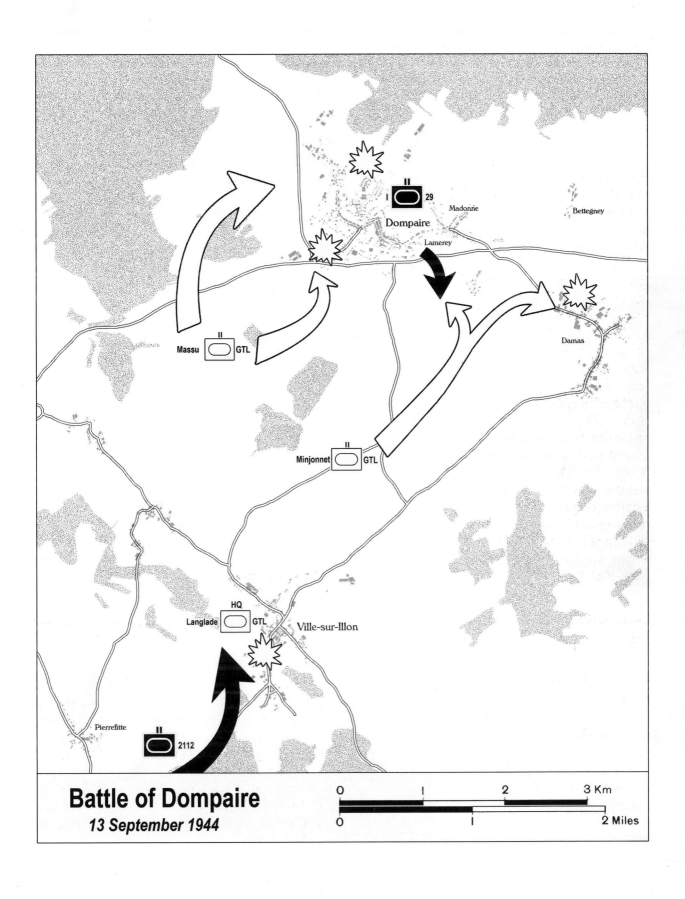

Battle of Dompaire
13 September 1944

Langlade GTL HQ

Massu GTL

Minjonnet GTL

Dompaire I 29

Madonne

Bettegney

Lamerey

Damas

Ville-sur-Illon

Pierrefitte

2112

| 0 | 1 | 2 | 3 Km |
| 0 | 1 | | 2 Miles |

ADVANCE ON DOMPAIRE

In the early afternoon on 12 September, Panzer-Brigade.112 moved out of Épinal in two battle groups. The plan had been to start around 06:00 hours, but there were problems with fuel supply. The Panthers of I/Panzer-Regiment.29 along with a battalion of panzergrenadiers reached the town of Dompaire in the early evening, and the Pz.Kpfw.IV tanks of Pz.Rgt.2112 and a panzergrenadier battalion moved separately towards Darney. This would prove to be a fatal mistake since the two battle groups were widely spaced apart in an area with few good roads, and they could not provide mutual support.

The formation in the lead of the opposing 2e DB was Groupe Tactique Langlade (GTL) led by Col. Paul de Langlade. He was another of Leclerc's desert veterans, having originally commanded the 12e Regiment de Chasseurs d'Afrique (RCA) in Tunisia and remaining in command when it converted from obsolete Somua S35 tanks to new M4A2 Sherman tanks in 1943. He was assigned to lead one of the 2e DB's three combat commands prior to the Normandy landings.

GTL was a combined-arms force consisting of mechanized infantry from the Regiment de

A view towards Dompaire from the southwest on the approach route of Group Minjonnet on 12–13 September 1944. Dompaire is in the shallow valley in the distance, obscured by the numerous stands of trees.

A view of the town of Dompaire from the hills to the southwest of the town with the Saint Nicolas church evident in the center. The plaza in front of the church is now called Place de Général Leclerc. Groupe Minjonnet approached the town from this direction during the 13 September 1944 fighting.

Marche du Tchade (RMT), mounted on American armored half-tracks, and companies from two tank battalions, the 12e Regiment de Chasseurs d'Afrique (RCA) and the 501e Regiment de Chars de Combat (RCC). Langlade's force was divided into three task forces, Group Putz near Darney and Groups Massu and Minjonnet heading towards Dompaire.[107] Each of these groups had ten to fifteen M4A2 medium tanks with 75mm guns, one of the new M4A3 with a 76mm gun, three to four M10 3-inch tank destroyers, and one or two companies of mechanized infantry. The total strength of GTL was close to the Panzer-Brigade.112 battle group in Dompaire, with about forty M4 Shermans and seven M10 tank destroyers facing forty-five Panthers. Langlade had the advantage of better positions and better intelligence, as well as artillery and air support that the Germans completely lacked. In addition, the French group was well trained and combat experienced. The balance was more in the German favor if the other Panzer-Brigade.112 battle group in Darney was counted in the balance.

The French division had a very active intelligence service under Capt. André Gribius. He was linked into the U.S. Army's G-2 operations from XV Corps. But the division conducted its own intelligence operations. One of the simplest and most obvious methods was the use of the local telephone network. Lorraine had not been as badly damaged by Allied air strikes as had been the case in Normandy, and much of the telephone network was still functional. Gribius and his men used the simple expedient of calling up the local postmaster and other town officials in the path of their advance and asking them about the presence of German units in their area. The local French officials were happy to oblige. The one hole in Langlade's intelligence picture on the evening of 11 September was the lack of knowledge of the PzKpfw IV battalion and panzergrenadier group, which was behind them and to the southwest in Darney.

A view from the outskirts of Dompaire as would have been seen by the German defenders looking to the west. The ridgeline over the town in this direction is forested.

First contact by Group Massu on the morning of 12 September was made southwest of the town of Vittel. The M4A2 tank "Ancinnes" and the M10 tank destroyer "Cyclone" were hit while advancing near Route D429, probably by a concealed German antitank gun. The spearhead reported a Panther in the town, but it was more likely a StuG III or other armored vehicle supporting a battle group of 16.Infanterie-Division. The town was taken after a brisk fight, and GTL continued moving eastward towards Dompaire against "light, scattered resistance." By the late afternoon, 2e DB was aware that a panzer brigade had deployed in this area, with concentrations at Dompaire and Bains-les-Bains. Dompaire is the last major town to the west of Épinal and sits astride the main east-west route D166 leading over the Moselle River in this area.

A platoon of M10 3-inch tank destroyers of the RBFM led by Midshipman Durville was brought forward to lead Massu's task force. This group included the tank destroyers named Siroco and Simoun, already famous for their skirmishes with Panther tanks around the Place de la Concorde in the center of Paris three weeks before. Capt. Jacques Massu, commander of the task forces, recalled the first skirmish on the outskirts of town at dusk:

We continually hear the faint sound of tanks in the distance. Approximately 600 meters to the right of the road, a curious shape of foliage attracts our attention. Opinions are divided: Is it a tank or bush? . . . The mass moves, and suddenly out pops a long tube aiming at us: It's a Panther! Guns, tank destroyers, Shermans all open fire. Our guys push forward. The Panther abandons the fight and disappears. A second is immediately spotted, and as it moves, it exposes its flank. Gunfire sets it ablaze and it is abandoned by its crew. Cries of victory. The next moment a third Panther, probably understanding the danger, flees. In so doing, it exposes to us the most vulnerable part of its hull. The hill is steep, and it moves very slowly. Bracketed by dozens of projectiles, hit by several, it seems impossible it could go any further. Painfully,

One of the best-known M10 3-inch GMC tank destroyers of the RBFM was Siroco, named after a prewar French destroyer. Commanded by Second Mate Krokenberger, it was the highest scoring M10 during the Dompaire fighting. It survived the war and is currently preserved at the tank museum at Saumur near France's cavalry school.

it reaches the crest and disappears behind it. Certainly it is out of action. First tally: one destroyed Panther, two seriously damaged.[108]

The second Panther was numbered IN2, the command tank of the Panther battalion's executive officer. The third Panther was hit by the M10 named Mistral.[109] Group Massu attempted to take up its position for the night on a hill close to the town. Massu later recalled the German reaction:

Our infantry dismount their half-tracks. Our first tanks are hardly in position when we are violently attacked on our left flank by at least three Panther in perfect defilade, from a range of about 800 meters. Others fire on us from about 2,000 meters away. Red dots of tracers searching for targets, the hum and slap of enemy shots, shots from our own tanks. It is a stunning din, a real fireworks display. Impossible to give an order, I had to run from one unit to the other. One of our half-tracks, hit early on in the fight, burns like a torch. . . . The Panthers in front of us have nothing to fear. They are repeatedly hit, but our projectiles ricochet off their armor. At the height of the brawl, three other Panther tanks leave Dompaire by the southern route and are preparing to attack us from the front. The lead one is hit with two shots and burns. The other two hold their ground and hit one of our tanks. . . . To the left, the battle is still violent: two of our half-tracks are hit without being set on fire. Our situation is difficult. I order a withdrawal to our departure point.

A view of the memorial to Leclerc and the 2e DB located on the eastern side of Dompaire in the hamlet of Madonne-et-Lamerey.

The M4A3 (76mm) of Officer Cadet J. P. Nouveau named "Champagne" was knocked out during the fighting at Ville-sur-Illon. It was recovered after the war and placed in the town square as a memorial to the fighting there in 1944. (Pierre-Olivier Buan)

Group Massu withdrew to a point beyond the view of the German tanks. It became quiet after nightfall as darkness descended, and it began raining. Massu radioed back to Langlade's headquarters that he didn't think the Germans would try to attack that night and they seemed to be moving their tanks around in the town, trying to set up a defensive strongpoint. Obviously facing a well-equipped opponent, both French groups took up bivouac positions for the night, anticipating a major fight the next day. As Massu had surmised, I./Panzer-Regiment.29 spent most of the night moving their Panther tanks around in Dompaire arranging their defenses. Town residents, fearing a battle the next day, fled the town towards the French lines or towards neighboring Épinal.

Haislip's XV Corps had assigned Colonel Tower, a TALO (tactical air liaison officer) from the XIX Tactical Air Command, to Langlade's command. One of Patton's preferred tactics was to use airpower to shield his flanks. Since GTL was the southernmost element of the Third U.S. Army, it received added attention. Tower moved his radio-equipped M4 tank to the group command post on the high ground southwest of Dompaire overlooking the Guitte valley, which had a clear view of the German positions below. Air support would prove to be instrumental in the forthcoming battle.

Patton's Third U.S. Army was supported by the XIX Tactical Air Command. One of the most active fighter-bomber units in the Metz fighting was the 405th Fighter Group, equipped with P-47 Thunderbolts as seen in the illustration here. A typical armament load was a pair of 250-pound bombs and two triple-tube 4.5-inch rocket launches.

A critical ingredient in the air-ground team was the tactical air liaison officer (TALO), an air force officer assigned an M4 Sherman tank with special radios capable of linking between the ground units and overhead aircraft.

Group Massu took up defensive positions to the southwest of Dompaire, while Group Minjonnet took up positions on the high ground immediately south, short of the village of Damas. Langlade's headquarters were behind Minjonnet, in the village of Ville-sur-Illon. The French expected the Germans to conduct vigorous night patrols to reconnoiter their positions. Instead, there were no probes of French lines, allowing the French to prepare for the next day's battle in peace. The French crews spent the night in muddy farm fields under a continual rain. The tank and tank destroyer crews laboriously carried fuel and ammunition from trucks on the roads well behind their camouflaged vehicles, making certain that they had a full fuel tank and a full load of ammo for the battle expected the next morning. The soldiers got very little sleep.

Most of the panzer brigade's infantry was with the other battle group in Darney, and the inexperienced Panther crews were unaccustomed to conducting night patrols on foot. They spent much of the night camouflaging their vehicles, often removing doors from garages for this purpose. The French began preparatory artillery bombardment of the town during the night.

The morning of 13 September began with the noisy demolition of one of the main water towers in Dompaire by German engineers, along with the demolition of a large building to create some maneuver space inside the town. The rain of the previous evening stopped and the skies began to clear. On the French side, a Piper Cub artillery observation aircraft was sent aloft to reconnoiter for planned artillery strikes.

Group Minjonnet continued their advance into the hamlet of Damas, running into a German outpost of about fifty troops but encountering no serious resistance. The French infantry company continued to advance northward towards the main road leading between Dompaire and Épinal. They adopted standard defensive positions with a platoon of RBFM M10 tank destroyers taking up camouflaged ambush positions near the road to Dompaire.

The main German force in Dompaire eventually sent a small group of tanks eastward towards Damas. Two M10 tank destroyers of the RBFM, Orage and Tempête, were covering the road and were well camouflaged. The crews knew quite well that it was futile to fire on the Panther's thick frontal armor. When the more visible sides of the Panthers became visible, they let go with a volley, hitting three. During the morning skirmishes, Group Minjonnet knocked out seven Panther tanks and lost two of their own M4 tanks, hit by the Panthers from the eastern side of the town.

Panther 332 ended up at the plaza around Les Invalides in central Paris in the early winter of 1945. The tactical symbol for Groupe Tactique Langlade has been painted on the turret side, and the insignia for the 2e DB on the glacis plate. The two Dompaire Panthers there were removed in 1962 prior to the signing of the Élysée Treaty with Germany when they were retired to the cavalry school at Saumur.

Group Massu launched an infantry attack against the southwest corner of Dompaire, hoping to distract the defenders while two small groups of tanks and tank destroyers under Captain Rogier and Captain Eggenspiller moved to the nothern side of Dompaire. A clump of woods shielded their approach route from the view of the German troops in Dompaire. They maneuvered behind the town and around noon set up a position in the town cemetery overlooking the exits from the town towards the northeast.

While the two French groups were maneuvering against Dompaire, Colonel Tower called in an air strike by a squadron of eight Thunderbolts. Captain Massu recalled the first air attack:

The first Thunderbolt . . . appeared at 08:30 hours. The time has come to display our cherry or orange identification panels, to avoid becoming targets. The planes turned upon reaching Dompaire. Never has that scene faded from my memory! Colonel Tower had his headphones on, a microphone to his lips while standing outside of his turret. Lifting myself next to him, I handed him my map, every moment adding new assignments communicated to me from Captain Rogier's radio. The positions of newly discovered tanks were communicated to the pilots with

a brief order in a language both conventional and barbaric to my ears. Obediently, the aircraft began their dives, despite the desperate reactions of the German 20mm guns. No movie since then could recreate in my mind that pinnacle of excitement, violence, wild beauty, and horror! Bombs, machine-gun fire, and rockets are the musical melody of this show, leaving us breathless. Columns of smoke from the burning Panthers rise into the sky, greeted by screams of joy from my over-excited men. We count 8 tanks burning.[110]

The first strike was credited with destroying eight Panther tanks. If so, the strike was unusually accurate. These sorts of claims were almost always exaggerated, but no doubt the sight of the screaming Thunderbolts demoralized the exposed German troops. A second strike by P-47 Thunderbolts followed around 11:00 hours. Six P-47s of the 406th Fighter-Bomber Group concentrated against the Panther tanks strung out in the hamlets of Lamerey and Madonne next to Dompaire. They were raked with rocket fire, bombs, and machines guns, and the Germans responded with 20mm fire. At least one P-47 went down. The French claim the pilot belly-landed after not pulling up fast enough, while the Germans claim he was shot down. In the

Patton dubbed the XIX TAC commander, Brig. Gen. Otto Weyland, as "the best damned general in the Air Force" due to the excellent close support provided by his command to the Third U.S. Army.

event, the French troops saved the pilot. A French tanker recalled that this second attack was "the most impressive and terrifying spectacle imaginable." French villagers later reported that the strike terrified the inexperienced German tank crews and that a number of crews deserted and tried to steal civilian clothes in order to escape.

Leclerc visited Langlade's headquarters to check on progress. While there, Langlade received a phone call from the postmistress of the neighboring hamlet of Pierrefitte. She reported that another German tank column was heading for Dompaire from Darney. This was a rescue group of PzKpfw IV tanks of Pz.Abt. 2112 requested earlier in the morning by I./Panzer-Regiment.29 in Dompaire. The phone call estimated their strength as forty tanks and about a thousand infantry, but Langlade later estimated the group as closer to two companies and twenty tanks. This attack posed a serious risk to Langlade's battle group, since it not only threatened to overrun the command post, but could sandwich Group Minjonnet against the German tanks in Dompaire. The headquarters in Ville-sur-Illon was defended by a squadron of M4 medium tanks, a few M5A1 light tanks, and a few M10 tank destroyers of the RBFM. Langlade sent a few of the M10 tank destroyers to reinforce an existing antitank gun screen in the direction of the advancing PzKpfw IV tanks. Though not known to Langlade at the time, the German infantry was delayed when some troops found a large cache of kirsch liquor in a garage along the route and took an extended break to enjoy their spoils.

The skirmish south of Langlade's command post began when the M4A3 (76mm) No. 55 "Champagne" of Officer Cadet J. P. Nouveau spotted the lead PzKpfw IV in a knoll in the valley below. He fired two rounds against it, with one round grazing the turret and the other hitting the side and damaging the suspension and transmission. The crew was machine-gunned when they tried to abandon the tank. While this was occurring, two more PzKpfw IVs emerged from the nearby woods. Nouveau's tank was hit twice, once on the lower hull passing under the driver's legs and another against the rear side, setting the gasoline tank on fire. The tank was temporarily functional and Nouveau had the crew back it to the cover of apple trees before abandoning

it. Another M4 moved up and began engaging the PzKpfw IV with 75mm fire, eventually hitting one tank. By mid-afternoon around 15:30 hours, a total of three PzKpfw IV tanks had been knocked out.

Two P-47 Thunderbolts, returning from a bombing mission at Dompaire, were directed to strafe the remaining German tanks. "They had no bombs, but strafed so continuously that two maddened German tanks were still trying to make their way north and paid no attention of the tank destroyer shells that were landing among them." Both PzKpfw IV were knocked out by the M10 tanks destroyers. Nouveau later inspected these two tanks. The skirts around the turret were penetrated numerous times by .50 cal machine-gun fire from the Thunderbolts. It also appeared that protective glass in the driver's view slit was completely battered by machine-gun fire, blinding the driver. This may be the reason that one tank was driven into a stream bank, losing a track when it became stuck in the mud. As this tank was trying to escape, it was knocked out with a hit through the thin rear-hull armor.

Scattered tank fighting continued until late afternoon when the accompanying panzergrenadiers launched an attack around 17:00 hours from the woods to the west of Ville-sur-Illon. This area was defended by only two jeeps armed with .30 cal machine guns. They opened fire, and then boldly raced out into the forest clearing, raking the panzergrenadiers with machine guns. This surprise attack put a temporary halt to this threat as the German troops retreated into the nearby woods. A pair of half-tracks from an engineer platoon were rushed in to assist and managed to capture a few prisoners. At least one Sherman tank was brought forward to engage the German infantry with high-explosive rounds and machine-gun fire. With so many German tanks and troops still operating in the area, Langlade moved his command post out of the town to a less conspicuous location on a neighboring hill overlooking the battle site.

As the fighting was taking place around Langlade's command post, a third air strike began at 15:30 hours when a flight of six P-47s conducted a bombing run against Lamerey. This attack was partly wasted on burnt-out tanks due to difficulties in establishing a radio link with the TALO. The I/Panzer-Regiment.29 in Dompaire staged a series of weak, intermittent attacks through the afternoon, usually consisting of two or three Panthers trying to find weak points in the French positions. It was a futile exercise as the French had carefully established camouflaged hull-down positions around the village and were able to destroy the more heavily armored Panthers with flank shots from close range. One probe in the early afternoon nearly found a gap, protected only by an exposed 57mm towed antitank gun. A field artillery barrage from a battery of 105mm howitzers put an end to that attempt. Captured German prisoners made it quite clear that they feared the artillery even more than the air strikes. Due to the excellent observation positions afforded by the plateau, the French were able to bring down precision artillery strikes all day long regardless of the changing weather. A fourth air strike left many of the Panthers in the hamlets east of Dompaire burned or abandoned.

After a day of weak and futile probes against the plateau to the south and east, I/Panzer-Regiment.29 began to try to escape the death trap in Dompaire by exiting to the northeast. This exit route was clearly visible to Group Massu's blocking positions up on the hill near the town cemetery. An initial foray of three Panthers around 14:30 hours proved halfhearted after the lead vehicle was struck ineffectively at 1,600 meters by M10 fire. Two more platoons of Panthers, accompanied by panzergrenadiers, appeared next. Several were put out of action from the M10 tank destroyers. This temporarily broke up the attack, which resumed about 18:30 for the loss of two more Panthers. The attacks petered out by evening. The I/Panzer-Regiment.29 and its supporting panzergrenadiers abandoned Dompaire after dark, leaving behind a small rearguard.

The following morning, Group Massu occupied the western side of Dompaire, finding four abandoned Panther tanks in the streets of the town along with numerous charred wrecks. Langlade's CP was reinforced on the morning of 14 September by his third team, Group Putz.

The Kampfgruppe of the 21.Panzer-Division under Colonel von Luck finally arrived in the area on the morning of 14 September and tried to help extricate the remainder of I/Panzer-Regiment.29 that was still holding positions on the eastern side of Dompaire against Groupe Minjonnet. Luck's battle group, consisting of a handful of armored

Following the defeat of Panzer-Brigade.112 at Dompaire, Patton ordered XV Corps to push across the Mortagne River. Here, the 314th Infantry, 79th Division advanced through Gerbeviller after Manteuffel had ordered 21.Panzer-Division to withdraw from this sector.

vehicles and 240 infantry, made an attack on Group Minjonnet from the east near Hennecourt, supported by 17 PzKpfw IV tanks of Pz.Abt.2112.[111] This force was brought under fire by divisional artillery and halted after an hour of fighting. The 47.Panzer-Korps headquarters concluded that any further attacks would be futile. Luck and the surviving elements of Panzer-Brigade.112 were ordered to withdraw towards positions west of Épinal, hoping that these remnants might be used later in the planned Vosges counteroffensive. The hapless survivors of Panzer-Brigade.112 were put under 21.Panzer-Division command.

In less than two days of fighting, the brigade had been reduced to only twenty-one operational tanks of its original ninety tanks. This engagement is usually known as the Épinal Debacle in German accounts. Casualties were estimated to be 350 dead and about 1,000 wounded, or about a third of its original manpower strength. Accounts of German tank losses vary. Langlade indicates that forty-two tanks were counted in the Dompaire-Damas area and that a further nine were found from the fighting around the Ville-sur-Illon command post and in the Damas-Chatel area, for a grand total of fifty-one tanks.[112] This number is also cited in Massu's memoirs. A German report claimed that there were only thirty-four total losses.[113] The I/Panzer-Regiment.29 was "practically annihilated" according to an OB West report. The battalion had lost most of its Panther tanks except for four that were still operational and four more in repair. Of the thirty-three German tanks counted in Group Massu's sector, thirteen had been knocked out by tank or tank destroyer fire, sixteen by aircraft attack, and four were abandoned undamaged. Pz.Rgt.2112, which had seen far less fighting, lost two PzKpfw IV totally destroyed in the fighting, twenty-six battle damaged or broken down, and only seventeen of its original 45 PzKpfw IV tanks operational. In its StuG III assault gun company, two vehicles were operational and two battle damaged or broken down. French losses in the fighting around Dompaire were five M4 medium tanks, two M5A1 light tanks, two half-tracks, and two jeeps; as well as 44 killed and 70 wounded.

The failure of the Panzer-Brigade.112 counter-attack also had dire consequences for the 16.Infanterie-Division, which lost more than 7,000 men killed or captured in the ensuing encirclement; only 500 troops escaped the XV Corps trap. In addition, the failure forced the Wehrmacht to abandon their only large foothold on the west bank of the Moselle.

AFTER-ACTION ASSESSMENT

The German attack was poorly planned, in large measure due to overconfidence and poor intelligence. The separation of the two battle groups allowed the French to destroy the brigade bit by bit. This battle was another clear reminder of the shortcomings of the panzer brigade's organization, particularly its lack of artillery.

The victory of the 2e DB's Groupement Tactique Langlade at Dompaire impressed Patton. He invited Leclerc to Haislip's XV Corps headquarters on 18 September 1944 to express his congratulations. They enjoyed a fine meal with chilled champagne. Afterwards, Patton took out a jeweler's box containing a Silver Star, which he pinned to Leclerc's tunic. Patton remarked, "It is a decoration for courage on the battlefield. You have done a lot for the honor of the US Army." Patton also brought along six more Silver Stars and twenty-five Bronze stars as awards for members of Langlade's battlegroup.

Patton's role in the Dompaire fighting was peripheral. Unlike Gerow's V Corps, Patton had been happy to have the 2e DB under his command. Patton's most direct impact in the fighting was his enthusiastic support for airpower and its lavish use in support of the Third U.S. Army.

CHAPTER 7

Breaching the Moselle Line

THE ATTACKS BY PATTON'S THIRD U.S. ARMY in Lorraine in the first two weeks of September brought American forces to the Moselle River, the last major river barrier in front of the central German frontier.[114] Patton was anxious to advance over the Moselle, as the terrain on the east bank up to the German frontier was mostly rolling hills and farmland, well suited to mechanized operations. With enough fuel and supplies, Patton was convinced he could reach the Rhine by the end of the month. The three corps of the Third U.S. Army had varying degrees of success in achieving this goal. The advance of the XII Corps near Nancy and the setbacks of XX Corps near Metz reoriented the direction of the delayed Vosges Panzer Offensive.

Of Patton's three corps, Walker's XX Corps near Metz had the most difficulty in executing a river crossing.[115] This was in no small measure due to the heavy concentration of old German and French forts that had been built in the nineteenth century specifically to prevent river crossings.[116] Although the artillery in the forts was antiquated, it was still more than capable of retarding the advance over the river in this sector.

The German defenses in this sector had been reinforced by one of the least known, but most effective German combat formations in Lorraine, a battle group of the Metz Officer Candidates School (Fahnenjunkersschule VI Metz).[117] This school consisted of combat-hardened noncommissioned officers who had received field promotions on the eastern front. They were sent to Metz to complete formal officer training. On 27 August 1944, the local military district commander ordered the school to convert its students into an improvised battle group to defend the Moselle sector near Metz. It was called Kampfgruppe Stössel after the school commander. The unit was organized into three Lehrgange (training battalions), each with four Inspektione (training companies) composed of three infantry and one heavy weapons company. The regiment numbered about 1,500 troops. In early September, the unit organized straggler collection points around Metz to cull retreating columns for troops and equipment; some 4,000 troops and 400 vehicles were collected in the process, which were amalgamated into its battalions. Kampfgruppe Stössel was deployed along a twenty-kilometer frontage from Armanvillers through Gravelotte to Ars-sur-Moselle to defend against the approaching American XX Corps. These battalions constructed fieldworks along the Moselle River until first contact with U.S. troops in early September.

One of the most effective of these battalions was Lehrgang.3, assigned to the Ars-sur-Moselle sector. It was commanded by one of the school instructors, thirty-year-old Capt. August Weiler, a decorated combat veteran with two Iron Crosses. Its main defense line was established behind Fort Driant since the senior German commanders felt that the old forts had no defensive value. A single platoon was placed near Fort Driant as an outpost in front of the main line. The commander of the battalion's heavy weapons company, Captain Hinkmann, found that there was ample ammunition in the fort even if most of the guns were not immediately functional. Hinkmann began steps to rejuvenate the two 100mm Krupp howitzers in the Moselle battery. These guns overlooked the Moselle River and were sited to block key river-crossing sites.

Walker's XX Corps attempted to secure several Moselle River crossings from the run starting on September 7.[118] The 2nd Battalion, 11th Infantry, 5th Infantry Division secured a shallow bridgehead at Dornot on 8 September, but its expansion was stopped. The 17.SS-Panzergrenadier-Division re-peatedly counterattacked the bridgehead.[119] On September 10, Hinkmann's crews began firing on the Dornot bridgehead. The bridgehead was battered by constant artillery fire from Fort Driant and the neighboring Fort Jeanne d'Arc, making the site untenable. To cover its withdrawal, XX Corps

artillery targeted the Moselle battery, hitting one of the armored cupolas and killing three crewmen. However, the gun was functional again within half an hour, ample testament to the battery's thick armor. In the meantime, the 2/11th Infantry troops on the east bank of the Moselle were withdrawn back to the west bank. The 2nd Battalion had suffered nearly 50 percent casualties in its attempt to hold the Dornot crossing site.

The withdrawal of the 2/11th Infantry back across the Moselle was also due to the 5th Division's success in securing a broader and more useful bridgehead near Arnaville. This was less than three miles away from Fort Driant, and the site quickly came under fire from Hinkmann's gunners in Fort Driant. Engineers attempting to erect a bridge across the Moselle at the Arnaville site were continually harassed by fire from the fort. On 13 September, the Fort Driant artillery sank a ferrying raft, partially demolished the treadway at the river ford, and broke up a pontoon bridge that was nearly completed.

In view of the problems facing the 5th Infantry Division in front of the forts, Patton hoped that the 7th Armored Division could still push across the river to the south of Metz and envelop it by a drive to the northeast. However, the 7th Armored Division attack stalled due to stiff German resistance, the timely destruction of key bridges, and the effective use of the old fortifications. Fort Driant would remain a thorn in Patton's side until the Third U.S. Army staged Operation Thunderbolt later in the month to overwhelm the fort.[120]

On Wednesday, 12 September, Patton was called to Bradley's headquarters at Dreux. The supply situation had again reached a critical point, and Bradley warned his subordinate commanders that it would inevitably mean a slowdown in operations. Eisenhower had agreed to give priority to Montgomery's 21st Army Group for their Operation Market-Garden airborne campaign in the Netherlands. General Patton estimated he had four days of ammunition, but enough fuel to "roll on to the Rhine." The Third U.S. Army had captured several large German fuel dumps during the initial fighting in Lorraine. Bradley warned Patton that he would have only two more days to cross the Moselle in force in the Nancy-Metz region, and if he was unable to do so, the Third U.S. Army would have to go over the defensive from Nancy to the Luxembourg border. Fuel deliveries to the Third U.S. Army had averaged 400,000 gallons through the second week of September, but by late September, they would fall to 270,000 gallons.

With Walker's XX Corps tied down on the approaches to Metz, Patton placed his hopes on Eddy's XII Corps. Eddy's divisions were opposite the old provincial capital of Lorraine, the city of Nancy. The geography in the immediate vicinity of Nancy was not favorable for a river-crossing operation. The sector west of Nancy forms a triangle where the Meuse, Moselle, and Meurthe Rivers meet. The area immediately west of Nancy consists of Grand Couronne ridgeline and the wooded Forêt de Haye (Haye forest). The city was not fortified like Metz, but the terrain on its western approaches was forbidding. Instead, Eddy's XII Corps decided to stage landings north and south of Nancy and conduct a concentric envelopment.

On 5 September, a regimental combat team from the 80th Infantry Division secured a crossing near Pont-à-Mousson. There was a sharp counterattack by the 3.Panzergrenadier-Division that quickly overwhelmed the small force. The Germans created a defense zone on the western side of the Moselle using the 92.Luftwaffe Feld-Division and Fallschirmjäger-Regiment.3. These units resisted the 80th Infantry Division attack until 10 September, when they withdrew to the eastern bank of the Moselle. The 80th Infantry Division shifted its attention from Pont-à-Mousson to a crossing site near Dieulouard. The vestiges of Celtic earthworks, a Roman fort, and a medieval church-fortress testified to the military significance of the crossing site. Before dawn on 11 September, two battalions from the 80th Infantry Division crossed the river and took the high ground overlooking the river. The Germans counterattacked at 01:00 on 13 September with a battalion from the Panzergrenadier-Regiment.29, 3.Panzergrenadier-Division backed by ten StuG III assault guns. In a vicious nighttime battle, the attack pushed the GIs back within a hundred yards of the bridges by 05:00 hours. But in the meantime, a company of M4 medium tanks from the 702nd Tank Battalion had moved forward, engaging the German armor at ranges of only 200 meters. The American bridgehead came very close to being overrun, but the area near the crossing site was stoutly defended by the engineers who had erected the bridges. In the face of growing American resistance, the German attack lost its momentum. A morning counterattack by the 80th Division supported by the 702nd Tank Battalion recovered the lost ground and halted the German counterattack.

Due to the difficulties in the 80th Infantry Division sector, Eddy directed the 35th Infantry Division to seize a crossing south of Nancy. This area had its own complexities due to the series of interconnected waterways and industrial canals that could frustrate an attack. On 10 September, a battalion of the 134th Infantry, 35th Infantry Division gained a foothold using an undamaged bridge. The Germans responded by air attacks and managed to down the bridge using artillery in the early morning hours of 11 September. This was followed by a counterattack by the 15.Panzergrenadier-Division that overwhelmed the 134th Infantry bridgehead. In the meantime, the 137th Infantry, 35th Infantry Division gained several small bridgeheads during the course of the day.

Eddy ordered the 4th Armored Division towards Nancy with the intention to use it to exploit any firm bridgehead that was obtained. Combat Command B (CCB) of the 4th Armored Division decided to try its own luck at crossing and found a shallow stretch of the Bayon canal. The streams of the Moselle in this area were shallow enough to push over tanks, and soon CCB was moving out of the bridgehead. On the evening of 11–12 September, the 137th Infantry linked up with CCB near Lorey. A battalion of the 15.Panzergrenadier-Division tried to counterattack this sector, but it became trapped and was destroyed.

To complete the encirclement of Nancy, the commander of the 4th Armored Division, Maj. Gen. John P. Wood, ordered the division's CCA to cross the river at Dieulouard early on the morning of 13 September to link up with the CCB bridgehead near Bayon. At the lead were the M8 armored cars of D Troop, 25th Cavalry Recon Squadron, which reached the western end of the bridges around 04:00 hours while the fighting on the east bank was going

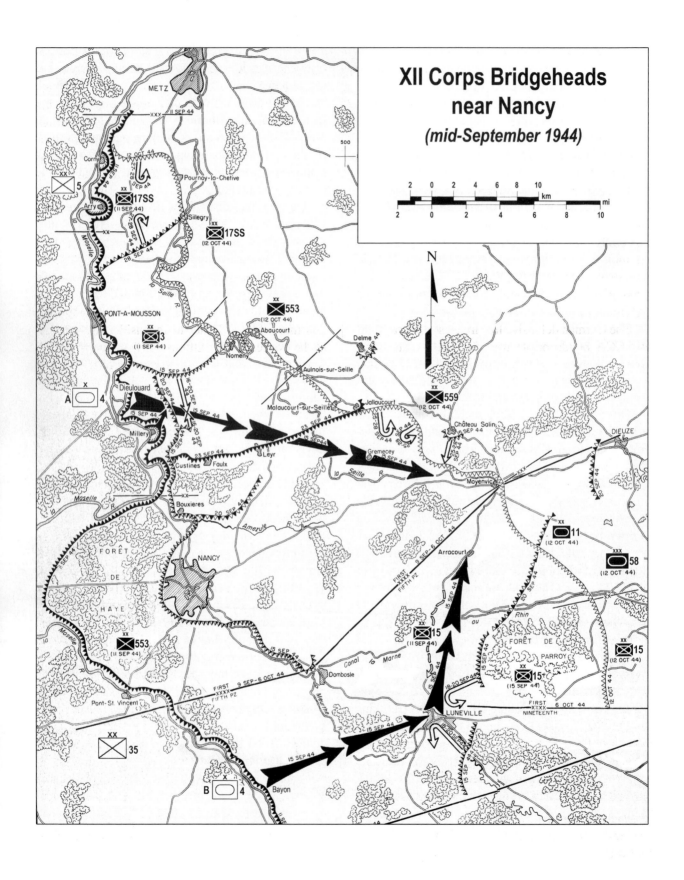

XII Corps Bridgeheads
near Nancy
(mid-September 1944)

on. The regulating officer wouldn't let the cavalry across until 06:15 hours due to concerns about artillery coordination. After crossing the bridge, the armored cars fought their way through the German infantry before finally being forced to stop by some entrenched StuG III assault guns.

A council of war had formed on the west bank, including the corps commander, General Eddy, and the CCA commander, Col. Bruce Clarke. Eddy had some doubt whether it was sensible to deploy a large mechanized force in such a small bridgehead, especially in light of the unexpectedly fierce German attack. Clarke turned to the pugnacious commander of the 37th Tank Battalion, Lt. Col. Creighton Abrams, who replied, "That's the shortest way home!"

The German defensive line in the sector was thin, and CCA bulldozed its way through the attacking German infantry near Dieulouard with few losses.

Once past the German main line of resistance, the tanks raced deep into the enemy rear towards Château-Salins, destroying twelve German armored vehicles, eighty-five other vehicles, and some artillery in the process. By the end of the day, the armored force was deep behind German lines and threatening to complete the envelopment of Nancy. The division log noted, "The rapid drive of CCA through the enemy lines has so disrupted the enemy forces that small groups have been apprehended wandering, almost aimlessly, through their bivouac areas."

The successful crossings of the Moselle and Meurthe Rivers around Nancy put Patton's Third U.S. Army in position to rapidly advance towards the Rhine. In combination with the loss of the Langres Plateau to the XV Corps in mid-September, this threat forced Hitler to reconsider the mission of the Vosges Panzer Offensive. The advancing 4th Armored Division became its new target.

A motorized column from the 7th Armored Division descends into the Moselle valley on 8 September on the approaches to Metz. This division took part in the early stages of the Lorraine campaign with XX Corps, but it was transferred to the Netherlands later in the month.

The 11th Infantry, 5th Infantry Division made a crossing of the Moselle in the XX Corps sector near Dornot on 8 September, but counterattacks drove it back over the river on 11 September.

The initial crossing of the Moselle in September 1944 was conducted using engineer assault boats.

The vulnerability of the Dornot bridgehead to artillery fire from the forts is evident in this aerial view. The Dornot crossing of the Moselle took place in the center of the lower foreground, while the two forts are evident in the background, with Fort St. Blaise to the left and Fort Sommy to the right.

The scene at Fort St. Blaise more than a month later when the troops of the 11th Infantry, 5th Division raised the American flag following the fort's surrender on 26 November. This view clearly shows how the fort overlooked the Moselle valley below, including the Dornot crossing site.

The commander of Fort Driant was Capt. August Weiler, commander of Lehrgang.3 of Kampfgruppe Stössel during the Moselle fighting in September 1944.

Fort Driant was heavily damaged by U.S. artillery and air strikes in late September. After the battle, two U.S. infantrymen examine the extensive but superficial damage to one of the casernes.

Ammunition shortages became so acute in some units of Patton's Third U.S. Army that special batteries of captured German artillery were organized to exploit stockpiles of captured German ammunition. This unit operating near Metz in September 1944 is armed with a German 88mm PaK 43 antitank gun.

The Arnaville bridgehead proved to be more successful after the engineers were able to erect a pontoon treadway bridge over the Moselle. In addition, the site was shielded from observation of nearby Fort Driant and the Verdun-fortified group by smoke generators as seen here on 23 September.

The 134th Infantry, 35th Division ford across the Madon River at Pierreville, five miles from the Moselle. Curiously enough, the regiment's 57mm antitank guns are being carried in their ¾-ton trucks rather than being towed.

The first successful crossing of the Moselle was conducted by the 137th Infantry, 35th Division, which overcame the defensive positions of the Panzergrenadier-Regt.104. at Neuviller-sur-Moselle south of Bayon late on the afternoon of 11 September. The engineers later erected a pontoon treadway bridge at the site, and it is seen here the following day with an M10 tank destroyer crossing.

Tankers of the 8th Tank Battalion, CCB, 4th Armored Division found some suitable fords across the Bayon Canal and so were able to cross without bridges.

An M4A1 medium tank of the 8th Tank Battalion crosses the Bayon Canal through a shallow but muddy ford on 12 September 1944. The crossing was made possible when a tank platoon used their 75mm guns to reduce the steep banks of the canal on the opposite shore. The 8th Tank Battalion used foliage camouflage much more extensively than other tank battalions of the 4th Armored Division, as is evident on this M4 medium tank.

The 8th Tank Battalion crossing of the Bayon Canal was made possible by the low water level in several sections. This is evident here as several of the barges are left high and dry in the mud. The M4 exiting the canal is one of the newer M4A3 medium tanks armed with the long 76mm gun. These were not in widespread service in the 4th Armored Division at the time.

The Wehrmacht responded to the Bayon crossing with a series of counterattacks, including a brief tank attack by PzKpfw IVs of the 15.Panzergrenadier-Division near Mehoncourt in which one M4 medium tank of the 8th Tank Battalion was knocked out. It can be seen in the background while a medic tends to a wounded tanker in the foreground.

The northern crossing of the Moselle took place near the town of Dieulouard. The area is laced with several small tributaries of the Moselle, which complicated the crossing. Here an M4 bulldozer tank is used to create a roadway across a narrow tributary of the river on 12 September.

The XII Corps made numerous crossings of the Moselle in the Nancy area in September. An M4A3 tank and Jagdpanzer IV are seen here at a crossroad on the eastern bank of the Moselle near Dieulouard where the 80th Division supported by elements of the 4th Armored Division fought off a major counterattack by the 3.Panzergrenadier-Division in mid-September 1944.

Troops of the 80th Infantry Division cross the Moselle near Dieulouard on 12 September across an improvised bridge. The next day, the engineers had erected a pontoon treadway bridge elsewhere on the river to permit heavy traffic to cross.

The Dieulouard bridgehead was the scene of intense fighting in the early morning hours of 13 September as the 3.Panzergrenadier-Division attempted to crush it. The bridgehead was held and served as the springboard for the CCA, 4th Armored Division's drive on Arracourt. Here, German prisoners pass through the town later in the day after the attack had been beaten back.

The destruction of bridges can slow but not stop a river crossing if the opponent is prepared. Here, an M4 crosses the Moselle on a treadway bridge, while in the background, the destroyed local bridge can be seen. The commander of the CCA, 4th Armored Division, Col. Bruce Clarke, had been instrumental in the development and fielding of engineer bridging for U.S. armored units before the war.

The bridgeheads south of Metz in the XX Corps sector proved even more difficult than around Nancy, with the crossing sites under fire from the artillery of Fort Driant. On 12 September, a heavy bridge was finally completed near Arrnaville, allowing the 7th Armored Division's CCB to send reinforcement to the beleaguered infantry on the west bank. This is an M32 armored recovery vehicle crossing the bridge on 13 September.

The Germans destroyed most of the bridges over the Moselle. However, in the days following the first crossings, engineers began to use the pilings of the bridges to create improvised crossings, like the one at Arnaville in use by medical teams on 21 September.

With the CCB, 4th Armored Division and 35th Infantry over the Moselle, the tanks began moving on to encircle the regional capital of Nancy. Here, an M4 medium tank of the 737th Tank Battalion fires on buildings near Dombasle, along the left flank of the advance on 15 September 1944 in support of the 320th Infantry, which was crossing a nearby canal at the time.

CHAPTER 8

The Battle of Lunéville: Monday, 18 September

THE SUCCESS OF EDDY'S XII CORPS in crossing the Moselle posed a serious threat to Army Group G's fading control of Lorraine. Unless the XII Corps bridgehead was smashed, Patton's Third U.S. Army was likely to advance all the way to the German frontier. Having lost the pivot point of the planned Vosges Panzer Offensive, the mission now shifted to an attack on the east side of the Moselle to trap and destroy Patton's spearhead, the 4th Armored Division. The Vosges Panzer Offensive belatedly started on 18 September 1944.

5.PANZER-ARMEE ARRIVES IN LORRAINE

The centerpiece of the Vosges Panzer Offensive, Manteuffel's 5.Panzer-Armee, did not begin to coalesce until the second week of September 1944. The staff began to arrive at Hochwald on 8–9 September, but Manteuffel was called back to the Wolf's Lair on 10 September for briefings with Hitler. Due the unrelenting pressure of Patton's Third U.S. Army against Army Group G, the original plan of 5 September had to be abandoned. The revised plan envisioned an attack from the Langres Plateau and Épinal towards Reims, with an aim towards cutting off Patton's Third U.S. Army as it was entangled in the battles along the Moselle River. The American advances threatened to create a breach between the 1.Armee and 19.Armee that would allow the American tank columns to race ahead into the Saar basin across the German frontier. The date for the offensive was now postponed to 15 September, but Hitler was adamant that it start no later, even if only part of the allotted forces were ready. Manteuffel came to realize that the Vosges Panzer Offensive plan "was beyond all hope."

Manteuffel left the Wolf's Lair and finally arrived at Army Group G headquarters on 11 September. He was briefed by the Army Group G commander, Col. Gen. Johannes Blaskowitz, and his operations staff about the local situation. That day, patrols of the First U.S. Army were the first Anglo-American troops to cross the German frontier. They began to approach Aachen, the first major German city to be threatened on the western front. This new threat distracted Hitler's attention. At Hitler's insistence, Rundstedt's OB West headquarters began stripping forces from all over the theater to reinforce the Aachen sector.

The staff at Blaskowitz's headquarters was deeply skeptical about the Vosges Panzer Offensive plan in view of the constant drain of resources to other sectors and the slow arrival of the new panzer brigades. Their main operational concern was to prevent a breach between the 1.Armee and 19.Armee and to create the "Vosges Outpost Line" to serve as the next line of defense once the Americans breached the Moselle River line.

On 11 September, Blaskowitz was able to convince Berlin to allow him to use the newly arrived Panzer-Brigade.112 in the hopes of retaining the west bank of the Moselle near Épinal, as related in chapter 6. As described before, the Panzer-Brigade.112 attack ran into the French 2e DB and was crushed.

The crippling losses suffered by Panzer-Brigade.106 at Mairy on 8 September and Panzer-Brigade.112 at Dompaire on 12 September reduced the size of the panzer force for the Vosges Panzer Offensive from six to four brigades. To make matters worse, Hitler's new focus on the threat to Aachen led to the transfer of both Panzer-Brigade.107 and Panzer-Brigade.108 from their temporary allotment to Army Group G back to the Führer reserve. This left Manteuffel with only two of the new panzer brigades for the offensive, along with several battered panzer and panzergrenadier divisions.

Manteuffel, to the left, discusses the planned offensive with Col. Heinrich von Bronsart-Schellendorf, the commander of Panzer-Brigade.111, near Blanche-Église in the days before the start of the offensive.

Manteuffel gives instructions to Maj. Gerhard Tebbe, the commander of I./Panzer- Abteilung.16, the Panther battalion of Panzer-Brigade.111.

Manteuffel continued his discussions of the plans with two of the staff officers of I./Panzer-Abteilung.16, Sr. Lt. Horst Gitterman, with the map, and Sr. Lt. Walter Schubert to the right, the battalion's executive officer.

The 5.Panzer-Armee headquarters finally became operational on 14 September. Due to its intended mission, Manteuffel was allotted two subordinate corps headquarters, the 47.Panzer-Korps and 58.Panzer-Korps. The 47.Panzer-Korps, located in Remiremont, was an experienced headquarters, led by General der Panzertruppe Heinrich Freiherr von Lüttwitz. His counterpart in the 58.Panzer-Korps was General der Panzertrupp Walter Krüger, like Lüttwitz a highly decorated commander. The 47.Panzer-Korps was headquartered in Languimberg, but it did not become operational until 18 September, the day the offensive started.

The divisions assigned to the 5.Panzer-Armee included the 15.Panzergrenadier-Division and 21.Panzer-Division. The 15.Panzergrenadier-Division had been broken up into numerous battle groups and was playing a vital role in defending the 1.Armee sector around Metz. Although nominally under the command of Lt. Gen. Eberhard Rodt, he was ill at the time of the Lorraine battles, and the division was led by the divisional artillery commander, Colonel Decker. It would take days to consolidate its scattered battle groups and extract it from the front before transferring it to the 5.Panzer-Armee sector. This division had fought against Patton on Sicily in 1943, served again in the Italian theater in 1943–1944, and was sent to southern France in August 1944 shortly before the Operation Dragoon landings. At the time, it was one of the best-equipped and most-experienced mechanized units in Army Group G. On 1 September 1944, it had thirty-three PzKpfw IV tanks, three PzKpfw III tanks, twenty-nine Jagdpanzer IV tank destroyers, twelve armored half-tracks, and nineteen armored cars. It depended mainly on trucks for mobility due to a shortage of armored half-tracks. It was in reasonably good shape as far as personnel was concerned, with 13,410 men, about 83 percent of authorized strength.[121]

The 21.Panzer-Division had retreated from Normandy after having suffered heavy losses. At the beginning of September 1944, it had no tanks at all. Its armored strength was quite paltry and amounted to only four tank destroyers, nine self-propelled field guns, twenty-seven armored half-tracks, and nine armored cars.[122] Its personnel strength was about 11,700, about 70 percent of its authorized strength. It was refitting in the Monsheim area, though some battle groups of the division were sent forward in mid-September due to the desperate situation facing Army Group G.

The next of the panzer brigades to see combat was Panzer-Brigade.113, organized in Military District XII in western Germany starting on 4 September 1944. It was commanded by Col. Erich Freiherr von Seckendorf. The brigade's Panther battalion was I./Panzer-Abteilung.130. This

battalion had been raised in early August 1944 in the neighboring Military District XIII as part of the Panzer-Lehr Division. It did not receive its Panther tanks until 15 August–5 September, so it was not sent to Normandy with the rest of the division, ending up instead in Panzer-Brigade.113. As a result of its earlier formation and a better selection of personnel, it was the best-trained element within the brigade. The brigade's other tank battalion, Panzer-Abteilung.2113, received its PzKpfw IV tanks only on 3–8 September and so had very little unit training prior to being deployed to Lorraine. The brigade was at full strength when committed, with 4,895 troops, 46 Panther tanks, 45 PzKpfw IV tanks, 10 assault guns, and 8 Flakpanzers. Like most of the second-wave panzer brigades, Panzergrenadier-Regiment.2113 depending on ordinary civilian trucks for transport. It lost about half of its trucks during its rail transport to Saarebourg when two of its six rail shipments were struck by Allied fighter-bombers.[123] German reports about the unit showed concern over the numbers of Alsatians drafted into the unit since they were not considered as reliable as regular German troops. One report from before the fighting noted that of the eighty Alsatians in Panzergrenadier-Regiment.2113, four had already deserted.[124]

A close-up of a German officer of Panzer-Abteilung.2111 in the cupola of a PzKpfw IV command tank taken prior to the start of the offensive. His decorations include the Iron Cross Second Class and the Crimea medal. Although never positively identified, this is probably Captain Junghans, the commander of the battalion.

The crew of a Befehlspanzer IV Ausf H command tank of Panzer-Abteilung.2111. The command tank version had an additional FuG 8 radio, evident from the crow's-foot antenna, which was used to communicate with higher commands. The captain in the middle of the group is believed to be the battalion commander, Captain Junghans, but it might also have been the 1st Company commander, Captain Muckert.

The next of the new panzer brigades to arrive was Panzer-Brigade.111. This unit had only been organized on 4 September, and it was created at the Sennelager camp in Military District VI in the Westfalen region of northwestern Germany. It was commanded by Col. Heinrich-Walter Bronsart von Schellendorf, a highly decorated officer. To speed its formation, the brigade's Panther battalion was based on the 1st Battalion of Panzer-Abteilung.16 from the 116.Panzer-Division. This unit was re-equipped with forty-five new Panther tanks from 24 August to 6 September. Its companion unit was the newly created Panzer-Abteilung.2111 that was organized in Bielfeld on the basis of the Panzer-Ersatz-Abteilung.11, a tank replacement battalion originally stationed in the Netherlands.[125] It was equipped with forty-five brand-new PzKpfw IV tanks on 3–5 September along with ten StuG III assault guns and eight Flakpanzer IV antiaircraft tanks. The brigade's infantry element, Panzergrenadier-Regiment.2111, was raised in Bocholt on the basis of Panzergrenadier-Ersatz-und-Ausbildungs-Regiment.57 (replacement and training regiment) and had not received unit training before being sent to Lorraine.[126] The infantry officers came from replacement units and most had been previously wounded in combat. The enlisted men consisted of a mixture of previously wounded veterans or very young recruits. There were insufficient armored half-tracks so mobility for the unit depended on trucks. Fuel shortages led to the use of trucks powered by wood and coal gas converters.[127] The brigade was slightly overstrength in personnel. It was dispatched by train towards Lorraine but was hit by an Allied bombing attack near Schirmeck, where it lost a Panther tank, a Bergepanther recovery vehicle, ten trucks, and two vehicles. It was initially deployed near Rambervillers, south of Nancy, in the early morning hours of 15 September.[128] The Panther battalion lost about ten additional tanks to mechanical breakdown along the route before being committed to combat.[129]

A fairly typical scene in Lorraine as a column of Panthers of Panzer-Brigade.111 advance down a tree-lined road.

CHANGING HITLER'S MIND

The eventual direction of the Vosges Panzer Offensive was shaped more by Patton's actions than by Hitler's original intentions. By 14–16 September when the 5.Panzer-Armee was finally ready for battle, two developments on the Army Group G front required immediate attention. The attacks by Haislip's XV Corps pushed German forces off the Langres Plateau, the intended pivot point for the Vosges Panzer Offensive. The penetration of the Moselle Line by Eddy's XII Corps, and especially the thrust by the 4th Armored Division past Nancy, created a significant crisis in Army Group G. This attack threatened to separate the 1.Armee from 19.Armee, and unless this advance was checked, Patton's Third U.S. Army would soon be on the German border. These developments made Hitler's plans for an offensive on the western side of the Moselle impossible to carry out.

Blaskowitz, the Army Group G commander, was fully aware of the precariousness of his defenses along the Moselle and the weakness of his forces. The best he thought he could accomplish was to staunch the penetration near Nancy. He knew that Hitler did not entertain defeatism, so he was careful to couch the proposal in suitably offensive phraseology. Blaskowitz suggested a more feasible, though more limited, offensive that would emanate out of the Épinal area to the northeast and cut off elements of Patton's Third U.S. Army from the rear. The intent of Blaskowitz's plan was to use the 5.Panzer-Armee attack to accomplish the more limited tactical objective of closing the gap between the 1.Armee and 19.Armee. The plan was couched in more ambitious terms to mollify Hitler's predilection for the grandiose. An initial version of the plan was transmitted on 14 September, and Blaskowitz knew he would need permission from higher authorities including both Rundstedt's OB West headquarters and the OKW in Berlin, acting under Hitler's direction. The initial version of the plan intended to launch the attack along the western bank of the Meurthe-Moselle River. The OKW approved the plan early in the morning of 15 September. Hitler directed that 11.Panzer-Division and Panzer-Brigade.113 be added to the attack group, and he rescinded the OKW decision to deploy Panzer-Brigade.107 and Panzer-Brigade.108 to Army Group B, reserving this decision to himself should the need arise to reinforce the Vosges Panzer Offensive.[130]

By the time the plan was received by the 5.Panzer-Armee on the evening of 15 September, it was already obsolete.[131] The encirclement of the 16.Infanterie-Division west of Épinal made the new plan impossible since the area west of the Moselle was no longer safe as a launch point. Furthermore, the capture of Nancy by Patton's forces on 15 September changed the dynamics of the Lorraine fighting.

Since Patton's breakthrough near Nancy presented the most immediate threat, Blaskowitz altered the plan accordingly. The first wave of the attack would consist of the 5.Panzer-Armee seizing a base of operations at Lunéville and then attacking Patton's armored spearhead, the 4th Armored Division, from its southern flank. In the meantime, the 1.Armee was supposed to join with its own attacks from the north side of the penetration around Château-Salins to prevent any enlargement of the bridgehead.

Rundstedt knew better than to approve the change in Hitler's plan on his own authority, and he deferred to the OKW in Berlin for the final decision. With Hitler's acquiescence, the OKW approved the revision. Rundstedt did win a concession from the inspector of the panzer forces on the western front, Lt. Gen. Horst Stumpf, that priority in new tanks would be given to units slated for the attack, especially the tankless 21.Panzer-Division. This never materialized. None of the tanks allotted by OB West in September went to this division.[132] There are some hints in the postwar memoirs, especially those of General Balck, that there was unease over the divisional commander and a feeling that the division was not pulling its own weight. Balck cited one panzer division that was holding only two kilometers of front line with 300 men while holding 9,000 troops over the German border; this describes 21.Panzer-Division.[133] These shenanigans may explain the marginal role played by the division in the September fighting, and the reluctance of Rundstedt's headquarters to waste precious resources on it. In the event, the remnants of the shattered Panzer-Brigade.112 eventually were absorbed into 21.Panzer-Division.

Hitler insisted that the Vosges Panzer Offensive begin no later than 18 September even though it was unlikely that all of the forces would be assembled. On 16 September, detailed orders were issued for the attack. The 58.Panzer-Korps, consisting primarily of Panzer-Brigade.113 and the 15.Panzergrenadier-Division, would attack southwestward along the north bank of the Marne-Rhine canal towards Lunéville. The 47.Panzer-Korps would strike northwestwards towards Lunéville using Panzer-Brigade.111 and a battle group made from elements of 21.Panzer-Division and Panzer-Brigade.112 from the Épinal area. The objectives were to eliminate the XII Corps from the east banks of the Moselle by seizing Lunéville as a base of operation, then crushing the bridgeheads at Pont-a-Mousson and Nancy. Manteuffel protested that the 5.Panzer-Armee was not strong enough to conduct such an ambitious attack, but he was told in no uncertain terms that he would attack on 18 September regardless of his opinion.

ROUND ONE: THE BATTLE FOR LUNÉVILLE

The plans for the Vosges Panzer Offensive were based on the use of the town of Lunéville to serve as the launch point for the attack along the Moselle. Neither side had a firm control of the town at the outset of the fighting on 18 September.

Two squadrons from "Patton's Ghosts," the 2nd Cavalry Group, had been ordered to scout the town on the morning of 15 September. C Troop of the 42nd Cavalry Squadron was instructed to send two platoons into the city, one mounted and the other dismounted. The mounted platoon came under intense fire as soon as it approached the town as recalled by one of the armored car crewman:

> Something gave the M8 [armored car] a helluva jolt and driver looked at me and said he couldn't steer any more. We climbed out and saw than an 88 had blown off our right front wheel, and we immediately dived into the ditch alongside the road. We were no more

than on the ground when a second 88 drilled the car right through the middle. After that, we did just what the rest of the dismounted men were doing—we ran![134]

At the time, Lunéville was being loosely held by a battle group of the 15.Panzergrenadier-Division. While C Troop was engaged with the German forces in the town, other troops from the 42nd Cavalry Squadron infiltrated around Lunéville, with A Troop passing to the east of town through the Forêt de Mondon and to the village of Benaménil, where they located and destroyed an ammunition dump. Other elements of the squadron reached within five miles of the town of Baccart, where a local French civilian reported six "Tiger" tanks to be present. A German officer who was captured indicated that 160 Panther tanks were unloading nearby in the town of Saint Die.

Due to the apparent presence of German armor in the vicinity, the 42nd Cavalry Squadron requested heavier assistance. They received some tanks from the 35th Tank Battalion of the CCR, 4th Armored Division. In the meantime, the 15.Panzergrenadier-Division had reinforced the town with five or six tanks and a few more antitank guns. On 16 September, the 42nd Cavalry Squadron staged a deliberate attack on the town from the south around 13:30 hours, leading to a withdrawal of the 15.Panzergrenadier-Division battle group to the neighboring Forêt de Parroy and Forêt de Mondon. The rest of Col. Wendell Blanchard's CCR, including Companies A and D of the 35th Tank Battalion, a company from the 10th Armored Infantry Battalion, and Company B, 704th Tank Destroyer Battalion, arrived in the Lunéville area around 20:00 hours and set up defensive positions on the northwest side of the town.[135] The infantry forces available to CCR were not sufficient to hold a town of this size, so the American forces inside Lunéville consisted of small outposts.

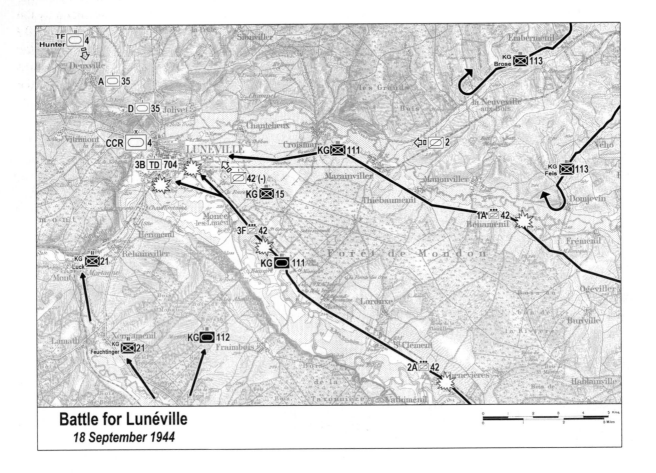

Battle for Lunéville
18 September 1944

INITIAL SKIRMISHES AT LUNÉVILLE: 17 SEPTEMBER 1944

On Sunday, 17 September, a battle group of the 15.Panzergrenadier-Division counterattacked Lunéville, leading to a sharp fight. Details of this attack from the German perspective provide little detail.[136] During the fighting on 17 September, Company A, 35th Tank Battalion claimed the destruction of two German armored half-tracks and estimated that the Germans lost about seventy-five men killed in the attack as well as more than eighty taken prisoner. U.S. losses were one medium tank, two men killed, and fifteen men wounded. The 42nd Cavalry Squadron set up a line of outposts to the southeast of Lunéville facing Baccarat. During the evening of 17 September, German infantry from the 15.Panzergrenadier-Division infiltrated back into Lunéville and reported it was in their hands. Most of CCR, 4th Armored Division remained northwest of the town, and the northern side of the town was still in American hands that night through the morning of 18 September. Neither side had enough infantry to firmly control the town, and much of Lunéville was a no-man's-land.

In spite of Manteuffel's objections that 5.Panzer-Armee was not yet ready to attack, Blaskowitz knew that Hitler would tolerate no further delays and ordered him to begin the offensive on Monday, 18 September. Panzer-Brigade.113 was located north of the wooded Forêt de Parroy with its forward command post in Coincourt, north of the woods and the Rhine-Marne canal. Manteuffel instructed Colonel Schellendorf to divide the Panzergrenadier-Regiment.2113 into two battle groups. Kampfgruppe Brose, led by the regimental commander, Colonel Brose, consisted of the regiment's 1st Battalion, supported by the brigade's Panther battalion, I./Panzer-Abteilung.130. The brigade's mission was to push down the southeast side of Forêt de Parroy, secure control of the villages of Emberménil and Laneuveville-aux-Bois, and link up with the 15.Panzergreadier-Division in this vicinity to conduct a joint attack towards Lunéville from the north. The second battle group, Kampfgruppe Feis, was commanded by the 2nd Battalion commander. It consisted of Feis' II./Panzergrenadier-Regiment.2111, supported by the brigade's StuG III assault gun company. It was to proceed farther to the southeast and secure the village of Domjevin, linking up with elements of

Panzer-Brigade.111 captured several M8 light armored cars from the 42nd Cavalry Squadron, 2nd Cavalry Group, on the approaches to Lunéville on 18 September. This particular example was from C Troop, captured near Moncel.

the 15.Panzergrenadier-Division before proceeding to attack Lunéville.[137] The brigade was suffering from serious fuel shortages and was still awaiting the delivery of a fresh fuel supply. This probably accounts for the decision not to employ the brigade's PzKpfw IV battalion during the first day of fighting.

The southern portion of the attack was assigned to Colonel Bronsart-Schellendorf's Panzer-Brigade.111. This unit was instructed to attack in two columns from Baccart and Ogéviller, on either side of the Forêt-de-Mondon, linking up with troops of the 15.Panzergrenadier-Division before attacking Lunéville. The 47.Panzer-Korps commander, General Lüttwitz, had been informed that Lunéville was in the hands of the 15.Panzergrenadier-Division, but instructions from Manteuffel's staff warned him to expect an American cavalry screen on the approaches to the town. Panzer-Brigade.111 was supported by Kampfgruppe Feuchtinger from the 21.Panzer-Division, which followed behind on a more southerly route in an attempt to control the Mortange River crossings south of Lunéville. This battle group was spearheaded by Kampfgruppe Luck, which included some of the tanks. Panzer-Brigade.112 had been attached to the division after the debacle at Dompaire, but at the time, its operational tank strength was a paltry two Panthers and seventeen PzKpfw IV tanks.[138]

On the approaches to Lunéville, a tank commander from Panzer-Brigade.111, on the left, asks directions from a senior lieutenant of the 15.Panzergrenadier-Division on the right in the town of Croismare. The lieutenant is still wearing a tropical field cap as the division had served on Sicily and in Italy prior to being transferred to France in August 1944.

THE START OF THE PANZER OFFENSIVE: 18 SEPTEMBER 1944

The two battle groups of Panzer-Brigade.111 headed out at 06:00 hours and quickly ran into the cavalry screen southeast of Lunéville. The lead Panther tanks ran into an outpost of the 42nd Cavalry Squadron consisting of M8 light armored cars armed with 37mm guns. The guns on these vehicles were useless against the Panther tank. The squadron's M8 75mm howitzer motor carriages (HMC) rushed forward to provide fire support. The M8 was an assault-gun version of the M5A1 Stuart light tank, with a short 75mm howitzer in an open-topped turret. This weapon was useless against the thick frontal armor of the Panther tank. In moments, three of the six M8 HMCs were quickly destroyed. Four M5A1 light tanks bogged down in the mud and were abandoned. The forward cavalry outposts were ordered to withdraw back towards Lunéville. The German tanks pressed ahead, but a tenacious defense by dismounted cavalry troops delayed the Panzergrenadiers until 11:00 hours. The commander of the 42nd Squadron was killed and the commander of the 2nd Cavalry Group was severely wounded in the fighting.

In addition to three battalions of tanks and armored infantry, the 4th Armored Division also had three armored field artillery battalions, equipped with the M7 105mm howitzer motor carriage. This is Battery B, 22nd Armored Field Artillery Battalion in England in June 1944 before the division deployed to France.

Fire support in the American mechanized cavalry groups came from the M8 75mm howitzer motor carriage (HMC), which consisted of an M5A1 light tank chassis with a new open turret fitted with a short 75mm howitzer.

The 2nd Cavalry Group radioed back to the CCR, 4th Armored Division in the Lunéville area warning them about the onrushing German units. The 35th Tank Battalion set up a defensive perimeter around Deuxville to the northwest of Lunéville. The 3rd Platoon of Company B, 704th Tank Destroyer Battalion along with a platoon of M4 Sherman tanks from Company A, 35th Tank Battalion moved through town and set up a defensive position on the southeastern side of town near the railroad tracks and the village of Moncel. The spearhead of the German attack consisted of four Panther tanks of I./Panzer-Abteilung.16. Two of the Panther tanks were hit at close range by the M18 tank destroyers and the other two began to reverse down the road.[139] Lt. Richard Buss spotted another Panther 300 yards away near the edge of the woods opposite the railroad tracks with its vulnerable side visible. He maneuvered the M18 tank destroyer of Sergeant Romek to the embankment.

Romek briefed the gunner, Corporal Mazolla, and the tube traversed onto the target. I gave the signal to fire. The concussion was deafening. Mazolla rose up from the telescopic sight and signaled a hit, except that nothing happened. I was terribly dissappointed. I called for another round and Mazolla indicated another hit, but still there was no indication we had put the target out of action. Suddenly, I saw billowing flames. It was not the dramatic kind of explosion that one would have expected. The flames were transparent orange, rising with a startling swiftness. They rose through the branches of the trees to a height of nearly sixty feet.[140]

A forward artillery observer in the upper floor of a neighboring building reported that he could see about thirty German tanks advancing up the road. By this time, German infantry from Panzergrenadier-Regiment.2111 were swarming over the railroad tracks heading into the town. The M18 tank destroyers had an open roof and lacked a coaxial machine gun or hull machine gun to defend against infantry. The platoon commander, Lt. Jerome Sacks, radioed the M18 tank destroyers to pull back into town. By the end of the day, the platoon was credited with knocking out nine German tanks. Although no M18 tank destroyers were lost that day, the battalion commander, Lt. Col. Bill Bailey, was killed when struck by mortar fire while directing his troops.

The 2nd Cavalry Group and elements of the CCR, 4th Armored Division were embroiled in close combat against German troops in Lunéville

A GI inspects a StuG III Ausf. G, probably from the Sturmgeschütz Company of Panzer-Brigade.111, knocked out during the fighting around Lunéville on 18 September.

Another StuG III knocked out during the fighting around Lunéville. Besides their use by Panzer-Brigade.111, these assault guns were also used in the area with the 15.Panzergrenadier-Division.

throughout the day. The CCR was able to bring the firepower of several field artillery battalions against Panzer-Brigade.111 and the accompanying troops of the 15.Panzergrenadier-Division, especially at the road junctions leading into the town. Tank losses on 18 September are not known in detail though a later U.S. intelligence report put them as twelve Panther and about ten PzKpfw IV tanks.[141]

Around noon, CCR requested reinforcements, and Task Force Hunter from CCA, 4th Armored Division set off around 13:00 hours. This was a typical combined-arms task force, and it was led by the battalion executive officer, Maj. William L. Hunter. The task force arrived around 16:00 hours. Battery C, 94th Armored Field Artillery Battalion tied into the existing field artillery net. Since it was in direct sight of German targets, it was able to extend the work of the existing forward artillery observers. Many of the participants credited the firepower of the 273rd and 738th Field Artillery Battalions and the 183rd Field Artillery Group with finally forcing Panzer-Brigade.111 out of the town around dusk.

Task Force Hunter, 18 September 1944
Company B, 53rd Armored Infantry Battalion
Company A, 37th Tank Battalion
Company C, 704th Tank Destroyer Battalion
Battery C, 94th Armored Field Artillery Battalion

The halfhearted advance south of Lunéville by the battle groups of 21.Panzer-Division contributed little to the struggle for Lunéville. Kampfgruppe Feuchtinger made a token advance from Domptail to Gerbévillier, having some minor encounters with scattered U.S. cavalry outposts.[142] Kampfgruppe Luck pushed ahead in an attempt to gain control of the river crossings along the Mortagne River. However, this battle group was quite weak. It had two battalions of panzergrenadiers but numbered only 240 men in total, of whom only 100 were given the task of attacking Lunéville from the south.[143] This battalion was supported by some tanks of the battered Panzer-Brigade.112, but they only advanced as far as the Bois de Bareth, the woods west of Xermamenil, before taking

An M18 76mm GMC tank destroyer guards the intersection on Rue Carnot in Lunéville in the direction of Frambois. Although sometimes identified as a vehicle from the 704th Tank Destroyer Battalion, this is in fact from the 603rd Tank Destroyer Battalion from CCB, 7th Armored Division that took over defense of this sector from the task forces of the 4th Armored Division.

up defensive positions near the woods. Luck's dilemma was that elements of his command were being threatened by the continued advance of the French 2e DB to the southeast, and he was reluctant to entangle his depleted command in the Lunéville battle.

Manteuffel and Blaskowitz were under the impression that the Americans had been pushed out of Lunéville and that the town had been occupied by troops of 15.Panzergrenadier-Division by 14:00 hours.[144] In fact, the battle group had reported only that it had repulsed all of the American counterattacks. This misunderstanding was due in part to the confused chain of command. Instead of a unified command controlling the two panzer brigades, a field army headquarters and two corps headquarters were involved. The right hand did not know what the left hand was doing.

While the fighting was taking place around Lunéville on 18 September, the rest of the 4th Armored Division had continued its advance to the northeast past the Forêt de Parroy. Thinking that Lunéville was already in German hands, Manteuffel ordered Panzer-Brigade.113 to disengage from its advance towards Lunéville and proceed to Parroy for the next day's attack. As a result, it took no part in the fighting for Lunéville. By late in the day, this confusion had been cleared up, but it was too late to redirect Panzer-Brigade.113 back to Lunéville. As a result, the attack on Lunéville was conducted by only about half the force that Manteuffel had intended to employ. As a result, the operation fell far short of its ambitious goals.

CHANGE OF PLANS

After dark, CCB, 4th Armored Division had pushed into the outskirts of Château-Salins with the intention of continuing on to Saabrücken. This put the spearhead of the 4th Armored Division only fifty miles (eighty kilometers) from their first major objective in Germany and deepened the wedge between the 1.Armee and 19.Armee. Under these circumstances, Manteuffel decided to shift the focal point of the panzer offensive from Lunéville farther north around Parroy and the Metz-Strasbourg Road.

The senior tactical commanders of the 4th Armored Division were divisional commander Maj. Gen. John Wood (center), CCB commander Brig. Gen. Holmes Dager (left), and CCA commander Col. Bruce Clarke (right). This group photo was taken in Britain in June 1944 before the division deployed to France.

Manteuffel instructed Luttwitz's 47.Panzer-Korps to continue the struggle for Lunéville the next day, but he took away Panzer-Brigade.111 and transferred it to Krüger's 58.Panzer-Korps to form the southern flank of the next day's attack. Luttwitz was left with the badly weakened 15.Panzergrenadier-Division and the weak battle groups from the 21.Panzer-Division.

The fighting around Lunéville continued into 19 September, and the 15.Panzergrenadier-Division took over fighting. In the four days of combat around Lunéville from 16 to 19 September, U.S. forces estimated they killed or captured 1,070 German troops and knocked out 13 tanks. Patton planned to use the 4th Armored Division as his main spearhead towards the German frontier and so withdrew Task Force Hunter and CCR from the Lunéville sector. The newly arrived 6th Armored Division was instructed to send a combat command to Lunéville to take over from CCR, 4th Armored Division. They arrived there in the early morning hours of 20 September 1944, freeing up CCR to move north.

Panzer-Brigade.111 was not instructed to break off its activities in the Lunéville area until the early evening of 18 September and to move to the Parroy sector for the next day's attack. It was still entangled in the Lunéville fighting after dark. After it began moving north, Panzer-Brigade.111 became lost during the night road march, allegedly after receiving bad instructions from a French farmer. Other accounts blamed a German military police traffic control officer who told the lead column that the bridge over the Vezouze River at Croisemare had been destroyed, forcing a more prolonged route of march. The brigade spent all night driving past the Forêt de Parroy and did not arrive at the staging area until early the next day. Krüger complained to Manteuffel that it was not ready for action on the morning of 19 September. Feeling pressure from Blaskowitz to get the offensive moving, Manteuffel telephoned Krüger and told him that his corps would start the offensive towards Arracourt on the morning of 19 September or he would suffer the direst consequences.

The disorganized condition of the German panzer forces and persistent demands for action from Berlin forced Manteuffel into hasty commitment of his forces. Furthermore, the 2nd Cavalry Group had prevented German reconnaissance units from determining much about the dispositions of the 4th Armored Division around Arracourt, and the Luftwaffe had proven to be useless in this regard as well. Manteuffel was operating in an intelligence void, exacerbated by the tendency of the eastern-front veterans to launch tank attacks without adequate scouting.

A portrait of Capt. J. F. Brady, who led Company A, 35th Tank Battalion of the 4th Armored Division during the fighting around Lunéville.

On 20 September 1944, a patrol of the 106th Cavalry drives past a demolished PzKpfw IV Ausf. H of Panzer-Abteilung.2111 near Moncel on the outskirts of Lunéville that had been knocked out during the fighting on 18 September.

Following the 18 September fighting around Lunéville by elements of the 4th Armored Division, the 6th Armored Division was brought in to replace them in this sector. This is an M4 medium tank and M2A1 half-track of the 6th Armored Division knocked out in the fighting in the area in late September 1944.

During clean-up operations around Lunéville, a GI from the 6th Armored Division escorts a German prisoner of war towing a small cart used for laying field telephone wire.

PATTON'S ASSESSMENT

The weakness of the initial German attack at Lunéville on 18 September was evident from the American reaction. Eddy's XII Corps, which bore the brunt of the fighting around Lunéville, regarded it simply as a local counterattack. Third U.S. Army intelligence had already been aware that Panzer-Brigade.111 was in the area, so its role in the battle was no surprise.[145] Panzer-Brigade.113 had not yet been noticed by U.S. intelligence. Likewise, it was not immediately apparent to Patton that a major panzer offensive had begun. There was no signals intelligence on German intentions, and the attack on Lunéville was so weak and disjointed that it was presumed to be a minor local action.[146] Not anticipating a major attack by 5.Panzer-Armee, Patton's plan for 19 September was to continue the 4th Armored Division attack towards the German border. CCB was instructed to push from Delme and Château-Salins towards Saabrücken, while CCA would attack from Arracourt towards Saareguemines.

CHAPTER 9

The Fields of Arracourt: Tuesday, 19 September

ON THE NIGHT OF 18–19 SEPTEMBER, there were numerous reports along the American front lines of the sounds of German tanks. The 25th Cavalry Squadron picked up several German prisoners who told them of a forthcoming panzer attack. Shortly before midnight, an outpost of Company C, 37th Tank Battalion east of Lezey heard German tanks moving on the road near Ommeray. This was a column from Panzer-Brigade.113 moving to their assigned staging area in preparation for the next day's attack. The tankers informed the 94th Armored Field Artillery Battalion, which fired on the German bivouac area around 01:30 hours, forcing the German column to shift its positions.

The 5.Panzer-Armee attack was supposed to start at dawn with Panzer-Brigade.113 attacking in the northern sector along the Metz-Strasbourg Road in the direction of Bourdonnay-Lezey-Moyenvic while Panzer-Brigade.111 attacked in the center sector from Parroy towards Arracourt. The ultimate objective of the day's attack was to link up with the 553.Volksgrenadier-Division of 1.Armee north of Nancy in the Château Salins area.

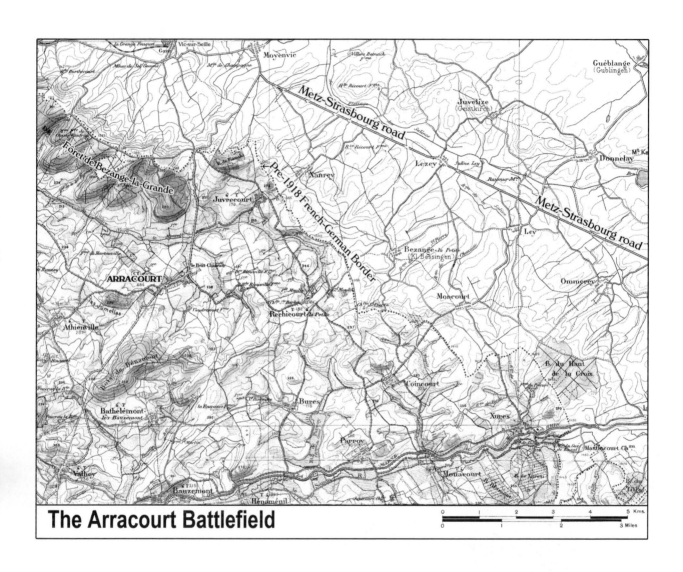

The Arracourt Battlefield

The countryside around Arracourt consists of rolling hills with occasional wooded areas. This is a view taken from the outskirts of Arracourt looking southeast towards Parroy in 1999.

This aerial view of the Arracourt area was taken in August 1947 and shows the relative flatness of the terrain. Arracourt is in the upper center of the photo, and the wooded area behind it is the Fôret de Bézange la Grande. The village of Rechicourt-la-Petite is barely visible in the upper right. The foreground includes Hill 318 to the left, the site of considerable fighting towards the end of September.

This view from Arracourt to the southeast shows how even, shallow hills dominated the surrounding rural terrain.

Small roadside shrines dotted the rural landscape in the Arracourt area, with this one still standing in 1999.

Standing in their way was Col. Bruce Clarke's Combat Command A, 4th Armored Division. During the advance past Nancy, CCA had covered the northern sector and CCB the southern sector, but in the intervening days, their responsibilities had been reversed with CCB in the northern sector around Château-Salins and CCA in the southern sector around Arracourt.

On 18–19 September, CCA, 4th Armored Division was based around the 37th Tank Battalion and 53rd Armored Infantry Battalion. The 25th Cavalry Squadron was screening CCA to the north and east. CCA was somewhat understrength at the start of the day, having sent Task Force Hunter to Lunéville the previous day, 18 September. Task Force Hunter had about a third of the combat command's strength: a company each of tanks, armored infantry, armored field artillery, and tank destroyers. Clarke's command post was in a cluster of farms sometimes called the Riouville farms, about a half mile east of Arracourt. The CCA command post had a single platoon of M18 tank destroyers for defense. Its units were oriented northward

since instructions from divisional headquarters indicated that the attack would continue on 18 September. CCA had a substantial artillery element in the vicinity of the command post, including two battalions of M7 105mm HMC and a tractor-drawn 155mm field artillery battalion.

CCA's left flank consisted of a small task force based on B/37th Tank Battalion and C/10th Armored Infantry Battalion, serving as a link to CCB farther west. The center consisted of the remainder of the 53rd Armored Infantry Battalion on the southeast ridge of the Forêt de Bezange overlooking the crossroads to Moyenvic. The right flank consisted of the headquarters company and Company C of the 37th Tank Battalion in the village of Lezey. A single platoon of M5A1 light tanks of D/37th Tank Battalion was on the extreme right flank in the village of Moncourt. The 25th Cavalry Squadron had a number of outposts screening CCA's front lines. The 166th Engineer Combat Battalion, minus one company, had been attached to CCA from the XII Corps and was located near the center of the command's positions.

Col. Bruce Clarke, CCA commander, speaks with the 4th Armored Division commander, Gen. "P" Wood, in his jeep.

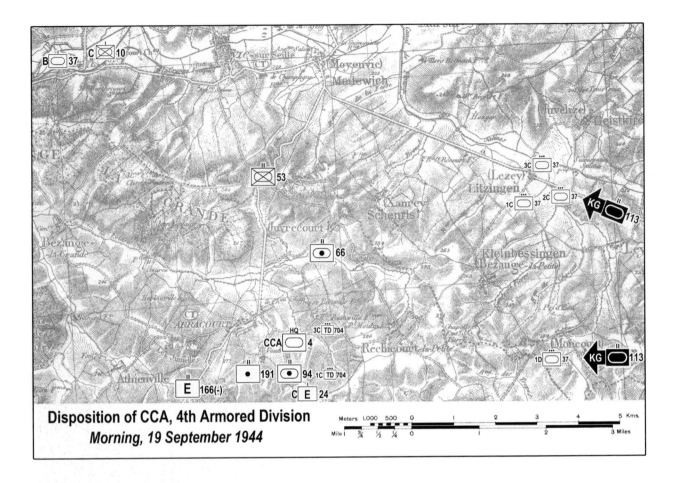

Disposition of CCA, 4th Armored Division
Morning, 19 September 1944

The morning of 19 September dawned as it had for the past several days with a thick fog in the low-lying areas. There was intermittent rain throughout the morning. The area around Arracourt was agricultural and consisted of gently rolling hills. The geography played an important role in the subsequent fighting. Even though the hills were not especially high, some of them offered a vantage point over large areas of the farmland.

The early morning advance by Panzer-Brigade .113 was along the Metz-Strasbourg Road, the contemporary Route D955. The German panzer columns began moving northwest in the predawn hours from the village of Bourdonnay towards Lezey and Moyenvic with other columns paralleling the road to the south by heading cross-country from the Ommercy area.

In the fog, several advance parties of German troops stumbled into U.S. outposts along the Metz-Strasbourg Road and were captured. Col. Creighton Abrams' 37th Tank Battalion was stationed in and around Lezey on the Metz-Strasbourg Road and so was directly in the path of the northern German columns. Shortly before dawn, an outpost of Company C, 37th Tank Battalion captured a German motorcyclist who revealed that there was a column of twenty-one Panther and PzKpfw IV tanks on the way up the highway from Ley towards Lezey.

A view of the town of Arracourt from its southern side looking northward.

Col. Erich Freiherr von Seckendorf talks to two of his men from Panzer-Brigade.113 prior to the start of the offensive.

Panzer-Brigade.111 used one or more of the M8 light armored cars captured from the 2nd Cavalry Group on the approaches to Lunéville on 18 September. It is seen here with German insignia hastily applied in the vicinity of Parroy.

THE FIGHTING BEGINS

The first fighting near Arracourt involved the M5A1 light tanks of 1st Platoon, Company D, 37th Tank Battalion under Staff Sergeant Mallon in a screening position near the village of Moncourt. This outpost was the easternmost position of CCA. Mallon's light tank engaged a German armored half-track, knocking it out along with an accompanying truck. Moments later, five Panther tanks appeared out of the fog, from behind the burning vehicles. After radioing to Colonel Abrams at the 37th Tank Battalion command post to warn him, Mallon ordered his platoon to withdraw. They were a screening force, and not expected to fight. They withdrew towards Bézange-la-Petite in order to join up with the rest

of the 37th Tank Battalion. Another German column moving along the Metz-Strasbourg Road was spotted by an outpost of Lieutenant Smith's platoon of Company C, 37th Tank Battalion, slightly north of the Metz-Strasbourg Road, which also notified Abrams' command post.

Around 07:30 hours, Capt. William Dwight, a 37th Tank Battalion liaison officer, was returning to the battalion command post in Lezey in a jeep with routine reports from the forward units. Between Bézange-la-Petite and the CCA headquarters, he encountered the rear of the German tank column near Moncourt. Dwight heard the firing by Smith's tanks and radioed ahead, asking if he could join the

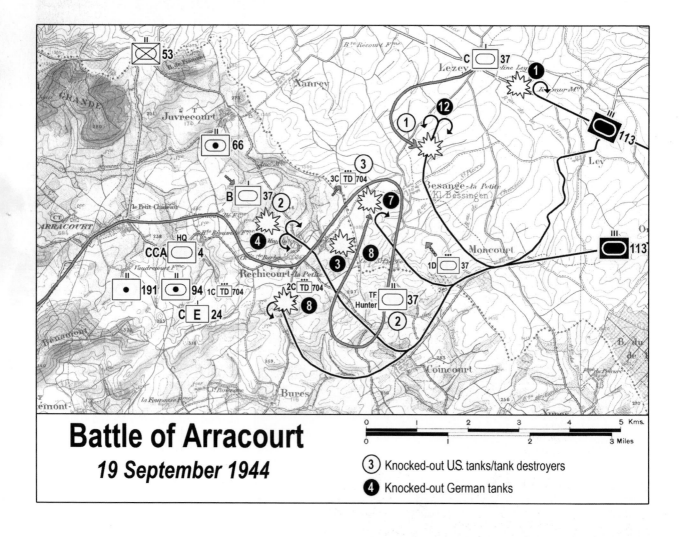

Battle of Arracourt
19 September 1944

(3) Knocked-out U.S. tanks/tank destroyers

(4) Knocked-out German tanks

outpost. Due to the chaos in the area, Smith radioed back and told him it was not safe and not to attempt to join the outpost. In the thick fog, Dwight went unnoticed by the Germans and radioed his warning to the 37th Tank Battalion commander, Lt. Col. Creighton Abrams.

Dwight headed instead to the CCA command post near Arracourt, arriving at 07:45 hours. The CCA commander, Col. Bruce Clarke, told Dwight to take the command post's guard detachment, Lieutenant Leiper's 3rd Platoon, Company C, 704th Tank Destroyer Battalion, and head through Réchicourt-la-Petite to establish a blocking position on Hill 246 about 800 yards north of the village.

Dwight and Leiper took the lead of the column in their jeeps with the M18 tank destroyers following behind. While the column was passing through the village of Réchicourt-la-Petite, it came under fire. However, it was so foggy that the source of the fire was unidentified. After Lieutenant Dwight and Lieutenant Leiper reached the hill, they deployed the four M18 76mm GMC tank destroyers. Leiper almost immediately spotted a German tank emerging out of the woods at the base of the hill.

"The lead tank destroyer, commanded by Sgt. Stacey, had evidently seen the German tank at the same time as Lt. Leiper, and opened fire immediately. Its first round scored a direct hit, exploding the

The M18 76mm GMC tank destroyer was lightly armored and had an open roof. It was the fastest U.S. tracked armored vehicle of World War II, capable of speeds of fifty-five mph on the road.

Creighton Abrams' M4 command tank was named "Thunderbolt V." One of the few modifications on it was the addition of a large reel for field telephone wire on the rear of the turret.

"Bazooka Charlie," Maj. Charles Carpenter, headed the 4th Armored Division's spotter planes. He modified his L-4H aircraft, named "Rosie the Rocketeer," to carry six 2.36-inch bazooka rocket launchers as seen in this illustration. He made several attacks on German tanks around Arracourt during the course of the battle.

German tank. The flames of the burning tank revealed others behind it in a V-formation and Sgt. Stacey's next round hit the second German tank. But immediately afterwards, he had his own tank destroyer knocked out by fire from a third German tank. This enemy Mark IV was taken under fire by the number two tank destroyer and was destroyed. The maneuver and fire of the third tank destroyer got another German tank as it tried to back out of this unhealthy situation, and a fifth enemy tank was destroyed almost immediately thereafter."[147]

Stacey's M18 had been hit in the right front hull, instantly killing the assistant driver and injuring the remainder of the crew. The tank destroyer was sent back to headquarters under its own power. Leiper's three remaining M18 tank destroyers withdrew to the crest of a neighboring hill. At the base of the hills was a stream variously called the Loutre Noire (Black Otter) or the Moncel River that wandered through low-lying areas. The fog clung to the marshy areas around the stream, but the hilltops above were relatively clear of fog. Leiper's platoon noticed a tank column on a road running along the hills between Réchicourt and Bézange-la-Petite. After determining that they weren't American, the platoon began to fire on the enemy column. They estimated that they had hit four or five of the

PzKpfw IV tanks. They called in the location over the radio, leading to an artillery strike on the hill by the supporting M7 105mm HMC of the 66th Armored Field Artillery Battalion.

Flying in the area was "Bazooka Charlie," Maj. Charles Carpenter, the commander of the 4th Armored Division's spotter aircraft. He had modified his L-4H aircraft, named "Rosie the Rocketeer," to carry three 2.36-inch bazookas under the wing braces on both sides of the fuselage for impromptu ground attacks. An article about Carpenter in *Liberty Magazine* in 1945 described him as "a legend in an outfit where reckless bravery is commonplace." Carpenter had spotted several German tanks trying to work their way around Leiper's position and dove through the fog, firing bazooka rockets. This alerted the tank destroyers to the threat to their rear.

"Lt. Leiper pulled a tank destroyer around and brought its fire on the tanks, destroying two of them before the third one's fire hit the right sprocket, knocking it out of action. Lt. Leiper signaled for another tank destroyer to come up with a tow and pull the damaged tank destroyer back. Before the plan could be put into action, the second tank destroyer was also hit, this time through the gun shield."

The area around Réchicourt-la-Petite was a tank graveyard after the September 1944 fighting. In early 1945, some crews of the 704th Tank Destroyer Battalion revisited the battlefield and took photos of the tank wrecks dotting the landscape.

Leiper subsequently withdrew his sole surviving tank destroyer. Colonel Abrams sent a section of three M4 tanks to reinforce Leiper, but one was hit by a German Panzerfaust while mopping up a platoon of dismounted German infantry of Panzergrenadier-Regiment.2113 in the area. Leiper's surviving M18 tank destroyer was directed to join the 2nd Platoon, Company C, 704th Tank Destroyer Battalion, which had set up a defense on a hill between Athienville and Arracourt.

When Lieutenant Smith's outpost from Company C, 37th Tank Battalion first spotted the German tanks earlier in the morning, he radioed to the rest of his platoon as well as the commander of Company C, 37th Tank Battalion, Capt. Kenneth R. Lamison, warning about the German approach. Smith's M4 tank platoon was the first element of the 37th Tank Battalion to engage the German tanks along the Metz-Strasbourg Road, knocking out two or three Panthers as they emerged from the fog. The German tank column pulled back away from the fire, south of the road. Captain Lamison raced a platoon of M4 medium tanks to a commanding ridge near Bézange-le-Petite to trap the withdrawing panzer column. As the eight surviving Panthers appeared, four were quickly knocked out at close range from the flanks. Before the Germans could respond, the M4 tanks moved behind the cover of the reverse slopes. In the dense fog, the Panther crews had no idea where the American tanks were located, and seconds later, the M4 tanks reappeared from behind the ridge and destroyed the remaining four Panthers.

"Bazooka Charlie" had in the meantime engaged the German tanks again. A squad of engineers maintaining the CCA water point were startled when two Panther tanks appeared out of the fog. "The plane attacked the tanks, but on the first pass missed. The second try he came in from 1,500 feet at an angle of 80 degrees, fired, and hit both tanks."[148]

Another German tank column began approaching the CCA command post around 09:30 hours. Company B, 37th Tank Battalion had been ordered to move to the command post earlier in the morning around 08:00 hours when the fighting had first started, and they arrived around 09:45, shortly after the German tank column was spotted. Clarke ordered them to move forward from the CCA command post to deal with the threat. They took up positions on a ridge about 500 yards from the command post and engaged the German column, knocking out several tanks.

While this fighting was taking place, Colonel Clarke ordered the 2nd Platoon, Company C, 704th Tank Destroyer Battalion to move from their position south of Arracourt and replace Leiper's

Most of the tanks of the 37th Tank Battalion were decorated with cartoons that had been applied back in Britain. Blockbuster was the M4 tank of Capt. Jimmie Leach, leader of Company B during the Arracourt fighting.

platoon guarding the CCA command post. This proved to be a prudent decision, as around noon, a German tank company numbering fourteen tanks appeared near the CCA headquarters. This was the southernmost attack of the day and may have been a company from Panzer-Brigade.111. In a quick set of engagements, the M18 tank destroyers knocked out eight tanks, most probably Panthers. The remainder of the German column pulled back.

Company A, 37th Tank Battalion had been attached to Task Force Hunter in Lunéville the day before, and this detachment arrived back in the Arracourt area around 14:30 hours. Having beaten back repeated German tank attacks, Abrams and Clarke decided to take a more active posture. Abrams radioed to Hunter: "Dust off the sights, wipe off the shot, and breeze right on through."

Hunter was instructed to take Companies A and B, 37th Tank Battalion and sweep across the area east of Arracourt to deal with any remaining German tanks. One platoon from Company A was left at the CCA command post for security. Task Force Hunter had about five tank platoons numbering about two dozen M4 tanks, and it formed up southwest of Réchicourt with Dwight's M18 tank destroyers.

"Company A hit head on, opening up at 400 yards. Lt. Turner's platoon swung full left, wheeled and smashed the enemy on the flank, opening at a range of 250 yards. B Company to the right came up on the other flank and finished off the enemy, Total score was 8 tanks and an estimated 100 infantry. Lt. Turner claimed 5 tanks for his own gun. Our losses, three tanks."[149] This was the last major engagement before nightfall.

A pair of knocked-out Panther Ausf. G tanks in the Réchicourt-la-Petite area after the September fighting. The German tank force did not usually use two-digit tactical numbers on the turret as seen here, and the reason for this anomaly is not clear.

At the end of 19 September, Patton visited John "P" Wood, 4th Armored Division, and they both agreed to continue the advance towards the German frontier the following day.

AFTER-ACTION ASSESSMENT

Patton visited the front later in the day, starting with a visit to Eddy's XII Corps command post. Eddy was concerned that Lunéville remained contested, and he was wary of pushing on to Germany with a lingering threat to his rear right flank. Patton tried cheering him up with an adage that he attributed to Gen. Robert E. Lee at the battle of Chancellorsville: "I was too weak to defend, so I attacked." Patton then drove off to see the progress of the 4th Armored Division. By this time, Gen. John Wood had reached the CCA headquarters outside Arracourt and the meeting took place there. Wood indicated that CCA had destroyed forty-three enemy tanks during the fighting, mostly factory-fresh Panthers, at a cost of six killed, three wounded, plus three M18 tank destroyers and five M4 tanks knocked out. Patton later recalled that "Wood's division was spread pretty thin, but I still believed we should continue the attack. This I felt was particularly true against Germans, because as long as you attack them, they cannot find the time to plan how to attack you."[150] Patton believed that the German strength in the area had been spent due to their heavy losses at Lunéville and Arracourt over the previous two days, and so he ordered Wood to continue the advance on Saareguemines the next day.

Panzer-Brigade.113 returned to its staging area late that afternoon near its new command post in Moncourt. Details of its losses are lacking, though the 53.Panzer-Korps daily report indicated "heavy losses around 50%."[151] The poor results of the day's attack were in large measure due to the failure to coordinate both brigades. As mentioned earlier, Panzer-Brigade.111 became lost during its night move from Lunéville. Manteuffel had been receiving such intense pressure from Army Group G headquarters that he pushed Panzer-Brigade.113 into the attack alone. Besides the disruptive delay, Panzer-Brigade.111 did not arrive at full strength, having been badly beaten up in the previous day's fighting and having left behind one battalion and an assault gun company to continue the fight in the Lunéville area.[152] Panzer-Brigade.111 did not reach the battlefield until around 17:30 hours, by which time the Panzer-Brigade.113 attack had already been smashed. There is little detail of the Panzer-Brigade.111 actions that day, though it is possible that it was responsible for the late-afternoon attack southeast of Arracourt. Blaskowitz was furious at the failure of the 58.Panzer-Korps and ordered Manteuffel to continue the attack the next day regardless of the casualties.

CHAPTER 10

Arracourt Day 2: Wednesday, 20 September

CCA, 4TH ARMORED DIVISION was substantially reinforced for its planned mission towards the German frontier on 20 September and contained almost two-thirds of the division's strength. This included both the 35th and 37th Tank Battalions, the 10th and 53rd Armored Infantry Battalions, and the 66th Armored, 94th Armored, and 191st Field Artillery Battalions.

While Kruger's 58.Panzer-Korps had enjoyed numerical superiority over CCA on 19 September, the battlefield ratio on 20 September was now in the American favor. Krüger reported to Manteuffel that an attack against the 4th Armored Division was no longer possible due to the losses in his own units and the reinforcement of the 4th Armored Division. A German assessment put the ratio at 200 versus 45, though the actual ratio was closer to 130 to 45 if CCA's M5A1 light tanks are discounted. Panzer-Brigade.113 reported that it expected the 4th Armored Division to counterattack on 20 September.

Manteuffel continued to receive pressure from Army Group G to press the attack. As a result, Krüger decided to lead the 20 September actions with an attack by Panzer-Brigade.111 through Arracourt towards Moyenvic. If repulsed, the plan was to draw the Americans back towards the Marne-Rhine canal, where a line of flak guns would be established. The battered Panzer-Brigade.113 was instructed to link up with Flak-Regiment.45.[153]

A hasty conference on 20 September 1944 in Parroy. To the left is Col. Heinrich von Bronsart-Schellendorf, the commander of Panzer-Brigade.111, discussing plans with Gen. Walter Krüger, commander of the 58.Panzer-Korps. The figure between them is Major Beck, the executive officer of 58.Panzer-Korps, and to the extreme right is Captain Junghans, commander of Panzer-Abteilung.2111, the brigade's PzKpfw IV battalion.

CCA ON THE OFFENSIVE

During the early morning of 20 September, CCA, 4th Armored Division moved out from the area near Lezey on their planned offensive towards the German frontier. Once again, the weather was foggy with intermittent rain. Visibility was only about 300 yards. The advance was in two columns: Task Force Abrams to the east was based around Abrams' 37th Tank Battalion, and Task Force Odem to the west was based on Colonel Odem's 35th Tank Battalion. The lead tank columns began moving about 08:00 hours with the other battalions following. Clarke's CCA command post had moved from the Arracourt area farther north to Juvrecourt. Around 11:00 hours, Clarke was startled when tank fire began to impact in the command post area. They came from the Réchicourt-la-Petite area to the southeast.

The source of the tank fire was the attack by Panzer-Brigade.111 against the trailing end of the CCA columns, the 191st Field Artillery Battalion. This was a tractor-towed 155mm howitzer battalion attached to the 4th Armored Division from XII Corps reserve. The battalion was "limbering up" and attaching their howitzers to the M5 high-speed tractors when a forward observer noticed the German tanks approaching. The observer called for the howitzer crews to deploy and load "Charge

1," the lowest powder charge due to the very short range to the German tanks. At a frantic pace, the gunners swung their guns into action, unloaded a few rounds off the tractors, and prepared to fire. The howitzers were ready when the tanks were only about 200 yards away, point-blank range. The 155mm high-explosive round could not penetrate the frontal armor of the German tanks, but the impact of the 95-pound projectile containing a 15-pound high-explosive charge was more than enough to cripple any tank and immobilize the crew. Two tanks were quickly hit, and the remainder withdrew.

On hearing the radio warnings, the 35th Tank Battalion sent Company A to intervene. They arrived after the German tanks had departed. The 602nd Tank Destroyer Battalion, attached to the 2nd Cavalry Group, arrived in the area around 11:00 hours after having returned to the area following some early morning fighting around Lunéville. The CCA after-action report credits the counterattack and artillery fire with six tank kills in the area. An afternoon spot report of 58.Panzer-Korps indicated the loss of five Panther tanks on a scouting mission by Panzer-Brigade.111 near Bathelémont, presumably the same action.[154]

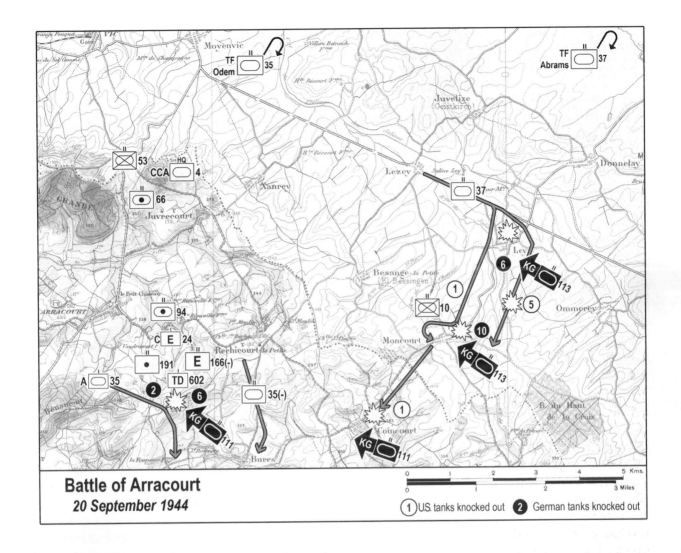

Battle of Arracourt
20 September 1944

TF Odem | 35

TF Abrams | 37

53 | CCA | HQ 4

66 | Juvrecourt

37 | Lezey

94 | 10

C | E 24

E 166(-)

191

TD 602

A | 35

2

6 | KG | 111

35(-) | Bures

KG | 113

6

5

10 | KG | 113

1

1 | Coincourt

KG | 111

Moncourt

0 1 2 3 4 5 Kms.

0 1 2 3 Miles

① U.S. tanks knocked out ② German tanks knocked out

A close-up of a PzKpfw IV Ausf. H of Panzer-Abteilung.2111 of Panzer-Brigade.111.

By 11:00 hours, Abrams' task force had reached the town of Dieuze, about six miles from the start line, and Oden's task force was to the west around Hampont. The German tank attack suggested that there might be additional German forces in the Forêt de Parroy area, and General Wood decided to settle the issue once and for all. He ordered both task forces to halt, return to their start positions, and clear the Arracourt area of German tanks.

Abrams dispatched a team from the 37th Tank Battalion and half-track infantry from the 10th Armored Infantry Battalion to sweep down towards the Rhine-Marne canal on the northern side of Forêt de Parroy. After passing through Donneley, they headed for Ley. The Germans had set up an ambush position with a mixture of tanks and some 75mm PaK 40 antitank guns. When Company C, 37th Tank Battalion crested the rise, they were hit with a volley from the tanks and antitank guns below, losing a half-dozen M4 tanks in a few seconds. "On this occasion, a platoon leader went berserk and despite orders from other officers, handled his platoon so that 5 tanks were lost."[155] The details of this particular incident were controversial. The commander of Company C, Captain Lamison described it differently than the official battalion account. He indicated that the first of the five tanks that were lost were hit during an exchange between Sgt. Roy Grubbs' 3rd Platoon and seven stationary German tanks in the Mannecourt hill area. When Sgt. Howard Smith's 1st Platoon arrived on the scene, two tanks were knocked out by emplaced antitank guns before the tanks were able to adopt hull-down positions. Subsequently, two tanks from Lt. Wilbur Berard's 2nd Platoon were knocked out in a similar fashion slightly to the west by German antitank guns as they came over the brow of a hill.[156] All seven German tanks were knocked out in the subsequent gun duel, as were three of the antitank guns.

While the 37th Tank Battalion assaulted Ley, Oden's 35th Tank Battalion approached Bures to the south, where there were reports of German tanks. There was a short exchange of fire before the onset of darkness without either side scoring any damaging hits.

Late in the day, Company A, 10th Armored Infantry Battalion with support from Company A, 37th Tank Battalion staged an assault on Moncourt, where Panzer-Brigade.113 had established a forward headquarters the day before. "By this time it was nightfall but the same tactics were used, perhaps even more effectively because all of the weapons of the line firing at once, and at night, presented a rather weird and frightening spectacle."[157]

The battalion diary of the 37th Tank Battalion described the night action:

> Night was falling, and from the battalion CP area, the glow of burning Ley began to light up the sky. Despite gathering darkness, the order was still "attack." The attack against Moncourt, executed at night, was a new departure from the "book" which said that tanks could not be successfully employed in the dark. Preceding the attack, the artillery laid down a preparatory fire on Moncourt. The attack on Moncourt was delivered from the west of the Ley-Moncourt road which was the general line of advance. In a tight and intermingled formation, three tank companies and two infantry companies approached Moncourt. The whole formation opened fire as one, presenting an awesome sight, and the storm of incendiary bullets and high explosive set Moncourt afire as the forces moved in, grinding under the opposition outside the town. All this was in complete contradiction to the German conception [as reported in intelligence channels] that Americans never attack at night and always stick to roads. Lt. Donnelly's A Company platoon then went into the town with A Company of the 10th Infantry. The infantry used bayonets, grenades and sub-machine gun and rifles, slaughtering the Germans in their fox-holes where they were immobilized by fear and the shock of the assault.[158]

The 37th Tank Battalion claimed enemy casualties on 20 September to have been 16 tanks, 15 to 80 prisoners, and 257 dead. There are no detailed casualty statistics from 58.Panzer-Korps records during the two days of fighting around Arracourt on 19–20 September. However, it is very

OPERATIONAL TANK STRENGTH, 58.PANZER-KORPS, 10–21 SEPTEMBER 1944[160]							
	10 Sep	17 Sep	18 Sep	20 Sep	21 Sep	22 Sep	24 Sep
Pz.Brig.111							
Panther	45	9	n/a	18	10	3	4
PzKpfw IV	45	20	n/a	13	11	4	6
Pz.Brig.113							
Panther	45	42	40	4	6	5	10
PzKpfw IV	45	n/a	37	19	13	14	9
Total	**180**	**71**	**77**	**54**	**40**	**26**	**29**

evident that casualties were heavy. A report at the end of 20 September by 58.Panzer-Korps listed the day's panzer losses as 11, which was probably based on incomplete reports. The two brigades had less than a third of their tank strength at the end of 20 September 1944, 54 tanks of the original 180. The 58.Panzer-Korps claimed to have knocked out 18 Sherman tanks during the fighting on 20 September, 15 Shermans credited to Panzer-Brigade.111 and 3 to Panzer-Brigade.113.[159]

Blaskowitz was becoming increasingly frustrated by the negligible results of the attacks and accused Manteuffel of limiting his units to defensive action.

Panzer-Brigade.113 had remained largely inactive during the fighting on 20 September after its battering on 19 September. Panzer-Brigade.111 managed to put only a couple of companies of tanks into action during the whole day after having bungled their part in the previous day's attack. Manteuffel complained about the poor combat value of the panzer brigades, but he was lectured by Blaskowitz on tactics. When American tanks pushed German troops out of Moncourt that night, Manteuffel used it as a rationale to request a general withdrawal of the 58.Panzer-Korps east of the Parroy woods. Outraged, Blaskowitz ordered him to counterattack again the next day.

COMMAND CHANGE

Hitler was furious to learn that the carefully husbanded panzer brigades had been squandered with so little effect and that his plans for an early and quick victory over Patton had been frustrated. In spite of Blaskowitz's exceptional performance in reconstructing a defense in Alsace-Lorraine days after the demoralizing withdrawal of Army Group G, he had never been favored in Berlin. He was a stiff-necked and traditional Prussian officer of the type despised by Hitler. He further

earned Hitler's distrust when he complained about Waffen-SS atrocities in Poland in 1939. His fate was sealed when he crossed swords with Himmler over control of the Vosges defense line. Himmler began using his new powers after the 20 July bomb plot to take away army control of the home defense sector. Blaskowitz complained to Wehrmacht High Command about interference by local party officials in the construction of defenses in the Vosges Mountains in Alsace. This triggered political intrigue behind the scenes by the Nazi Party regional officials to have him removed.[161] Hitler had already purged most of the senior commanders in France since the 20 July bomb plot, and he apparently decided to relieve Blaskowitz around 18 September. The dismal results of the Vosges Panzer Offensive on 17–20 September was merely the excuse, and Blaskowitz was formally relieved on 20 September 1944.

Blaskowitz's replacement was Gen. Hermann Balck, another distinguished panzer commander from the Russian front. Balck and his chief of staff, Maj. Gen. Friedrich von Mellenthin, were briefed by Hitler at the Wolf's Lair before being sent to Alsace.

In a voice ringing with indignation, Hitler severely criticized the way in which Blaskowitz had commanded his forces, and reproached him for timidity and a lack of offensive spirit. In fact, he seems to have thought that Blaskowitz could have taken Patton's Third Army in the flank and flung it back to Reims. . . . The absurdity of this criticism soon became clear to us. [Blaskowitz] had just extricated his army group from the south of France under extremely difficult conditions. But his offense was that he had quarreled with Himmler, first in Poland and recently in Alsace. Like many others, Blaskowitz was made a scapegoat for the gross blunders of Hitler and his entourage.[162]

The grenadiers of Panzer-Grenadier-Regiment.2111 mount up on the Panther tanks of I./Panzer-Abteilung.16 in the village of Bures on the morning of 20 September 1944 for the attack towards Arracourt.

A close-up of the panzergrenadiers on the engine deck of a Panther tank of Panzer-Brigade.111 in Bures prior to the attack on the morning of 20 September. The two nearest soldiers are armed with panzerfaust antitank rockets.

A Panther Ausf. G of Panzer-Brigade.111 moves out of Bures at the start of the attack on 20 September. There was a single, company-strength Kampfgruppe in Bures that morning, with fourteen Panther tanks. The remainder of the Panther battalion struck out from other starting points farther north.

The attack towards Arracourt begins. This column ran into elements of the 191st Field Artillery Battalion that was beginning to move out of their bivouac.

The 191st Field Artillery Battalion was equipped with M1 155mm howitzers towed by M5 high-speed tractors.

Panzer-Brigade.111 lacked armored half-tracks, and their trucks did not have sufficient cross-country traction for tactical use. As a result, the panzergrenadiers rode the tanks into the battle area, as seen here on 20 September 1944.

A Panther Ausf. G of I./Panzer-Abteilung.16 of Panzer-Brigade.111 moves off a road outside of Bures past a French road marker.

Besides the basic version of the M4 Sherman tank with a 75mm gun, the M4 (105mm) assault gun was also built to provide fire support. This resembled the normal tank version, but it was fitted with a 105mm howitzer. There was one of these assault guns in each tank company and in a platoon in the battalion headquarters company. During the fighting around Juvelize, Abrams deployed the assault-gun platoon alongside Company A in the orchards above the town. This photo was taken while the unit was still training in Britain in June 1944.

When the weather cleared later on 20 September, the P-47 fighter-bombers of the XIX Tactical Air Force intervened again. German accounts attribute these air attacks as being one of the main reasons for the failure of the day's offensive. The illustration here shows a typical armament load for these fighter-bombers, a pair of 250-pound bombs and two triple 4.5-inch rocket launchers.

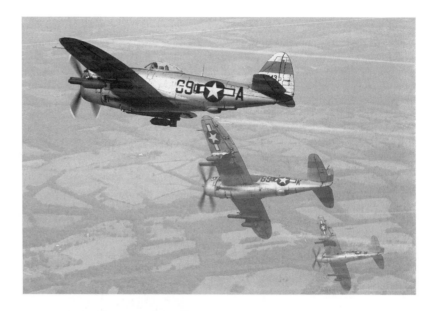

A Panther Ausf. G of the second company of I./Panzer-Abteilung.130 of Panzer-Brigade.113, knocked out in the fighting north of the Parroy forest.

A Panther Ausf. G photographed in the Réchicourt-le-Petite area in early 1945. Most of the Panther tanks of the two panzer brigades fighting around Arracourt were from the August 1944 production batch.

CHAPTER 11

The Battle for Juvelize: 21–23 September

THE ARMY GROUP G COMMAND change led to a temporary halt in the 5.Panzer-Armee offensive. Balck was intent on reinvigorating the offensive, but he decided that it needed to be larger and better coordinated. This meant waiting for the panzer divisions to finally arrive and getting support on the northern side from the 1.Armee. One reason that the attacks against Arracourt continued with such unabated fury was that Hitler had insisted to Balck that Army Group G hold on the old pre-1918 borders. In this sector, the boundary between French Lorraine and Lothringen (German Lorraine) fell roughly south of the Metz-Strasbourg Road running from Moyenvic through Lezey.

On the American side, there were also a series of high-level discussions. Eisenhower called for a conference of the senior commanders at the SHAEF headquarters outside Paris to discuss operational issues. Ike made it clear that until Antwerp was open, there would be no major offensive operations. He reiterated his promise to Montgomery that the British 21st Army Group would continue to receive priority for supplies during the current Operation Market-Garden attack in the Netherlands. Patton took some comfort in the fact that "he was more peevish with Montgomery than I have ever seen him. In fact, he called him a 'clever son of a bitch' which was very encouraging."[163] Patton's main disagreements came with Gen. Jake Devers, commander of the neighboring 6th Army Group. Due to the supply issues, Patton's XV Corps was being supplied through Marseilles via Dijon, the supply route controlled by the 6th Army Group, rather than through the northern routes controlled by Bradley's 12th Army Group. As a result, Devers wanted XV Corps taken over by his command. Patton made his case with Ike over lunch, and even though no decision was made on the matter, Patton felt relieved when it became clear that Eisenhower was not favorable to Devers' position and that in fact "Ike hates him." Patton summed up his day's activities: "One has to fight one's friends more than the enemy."

For the 5.Panzer-Armee, the day passed without any major actions while Manteuffel awaited orders from the new Army Group G commander. For the 4th Armored Division, 21 September was written off as a day of rest and maintenance while higher authorities decided the future conduct of the campaign.

On 20 September, OB West ordered Army Group G to focus its attention on the gap between the 1.Armee and 19.Armee and push Eddy's XII Corps back across the Moselle River.[164] The main focus of the counterattack would again be Manteuffel's 5.Panzer-Armee, but Knobelsdorff's 1.Armee was also ordered to participate on the northern flank.

The principal change in the 5.Panzer-Armee sector was the arrival of the 11.Panzer-Division. This unit was the only panzer division under Army Group G at the time of the withdrawal in late August and early September. It had done an exemplary job serving as the rearguard of the 19.Armee during the retreat to Alsace. However, these actions had proven to be very costly in men and equipment. At the beginning of September, it had been reduced to only nineteen Panther and five PzKpfw IV tanks. When it arrived in the 5.Panzer-Armee sector on 20 September, it had ten Panther and twenty PzKpfw IV tanks, though not all were operational. "The morale of the troops was good and the preceding fighting had not discouraged them. More importantly, they were well trained and had the necessary combat experience from the battles on the western front."[165] Furthermore, the division had received a replacement battalion of about 2,000 young Luftwaffe ground crew, who were being integrated into the division to make up combat losses. Panzer-Brigade.111 was attached to the division. This added about thirty tanks to the overall strength, but only a small fraction of the tanks were operational due to combat damage and mechanical problems. The 11.Panzer-Division was

discouraged by the quality of the panzer brigade troops, who they described as being "for the most part from older military age groups, or partially disabled . . . [and eventually] about eighty percent were returned to Germany to replacement units."[166]

The objective for the 22 September attack was much the same as before. The 11.Panzer-Division was to seal off the 4th Armored Division penetration by gaining control as far west as the Forêt de Bézange-le-Grande, Arracourt, and the Bois de Bénamont. The contribution of the 1.Armee was supposed to include a supporting attack eastward by the 553 .Volksgrenadier-Division supported by a panzer Kampfgruppe from the 17.SS-Panzergrenadier-Division. In any event, the armored support did not arrive for the 22 September attack.

At 04:20 hours on the morning of 22 September, the 5.Panzer-Armee headquarters sent out the orders for the renewal of the offensive. Since the attempts to push through Lezey along the Metz-Strasbourg Road had been continually frustrated by the 37th Tank Battalion, the direction of the attack was changed. The main force would strike from the area north of Lezey from around Blanche-Église and Guéblange, seize the village of Juvelize, and then push through Lezey from the north. A secondary attack would be conducted from the south by the remnants of Panzer-Brigade.113, heading first for Ley. Panzer-Brigade.111 was supposed to begin its attack at 07:00 hours from Guéblange, but this was delayed until 09:00 hours due to delays in meeting up with elements of the brigade that had to travel through Donnelay to join the main force at Guéblange.

The 37th Tank Battalion was bivouacked around Lezey with a cavalry screening force north of Juvelize, and the M5A1 light tanks of Company D, 37th Tank Battalion were covering the southern approaches. The first contacts occurred around 09:15 hours when dismounted panzergrenadiers encountered an outpost of Troop D, 25th Cavalry Squadron on Hill 252. The cavalry units were holding a series of small outposts in the open farm country north of Juvelize. Due to the fog, visibility was only about one hundred yards. As skirmishing began, a reinforced cavalry platoon of M5A1 light tanks of the squadron's F Company headed out to disperse the German infantry. A panzer company of about a dozen tanks appeared out of the fog and

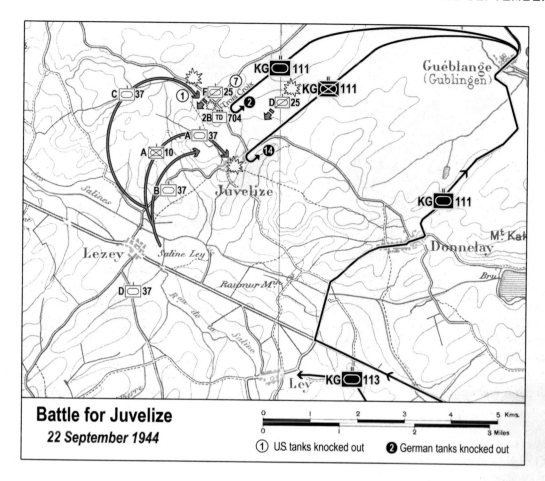

Battle for Juvelize
22 September 1944

0   1   2   3   4   5 Kms.

0   1   2   3 Miles

① U.S. tanks knocked out   ② German tanks knocked out

began to engage the light tanks. The outcome of a confrontation between the puny M5A1 light tanks and Panther tanks was enitrely predictable. The 37mm gun on the M5A1 light tank had no ability to penetrate the frontal armor of either the PzKpw IV or Panther, and within moments, four of the light tanks were burning.

A few M18 tank destroyers of the 2nd Platoon, Company B, 704th Tank Destroyer Battalion were nearby in a reverse slope position near the Trois Croix road intersection. A few surviving crewmen from the destroyed light tanks withdrew past them and warned them of the approaching German tanks. The tank destroyer detachment commander, Lt. Martin Evans, decided to withdraw his platoon since his instruction had been to cover the flank of the cavalry, not engage in tank fighting. He sent a single M18 to the top of the ridge to serve as a rearguard for the withdrawal. Major Wilcox, the executive officer of the 25th Cavalry Squadron,

appeared and ordered the lead M18 tank destroyer to engage the approaching German tanks The closest German tank was about 600 yards away, and the M18 knocked out three Panther tanks in quick succession. The tank destroyer platoon then withdrew to defend the cavalry command post. During the melee, two more M5A1 light tanks were knocked out by German tank fire and one was abandoned due to mechanical problems. Panzer-Brigade.111 incorrectly reported ten M4 Shermans destroyed in this encounter.[167]

The 37th Tank Battalion's service company near Lezey could see the smoke on the horizon from the burning tanks. As reports began to flow back to Abrams' command post in Lezey, he ordered his battalion to begin deploying for action. Company B was sent to cover the road between Juvelize and Lezey, while Company C was sent in a sweeping motion to the northwest of Juvelize to intervene in support of the retreating cavalry outposts.

This is one of the M5A1 light tanks of Company F, 25th Cavalry Squadron that was knocked out by Panther tanks during the initial exchanges north of Juvelize on 22 September 1944.

A knocked-out M4 medium tank of Company C, 37th Tank Battalion. This tank was hit by a Panther tank located near the Trois Croix crossroads north of Juvelize. In the background can be seen the burned wrecks of several of the M5A1 light tanks of Company F, 25th Cavalry Squadron.

This is another view of one of the M5A1 light tanks of Company F, 25th Cavalry Squadron. It was evidently knocked out by two hits in the rear by the 75mm gun of a Panther tank.

Another view of the M4 Sherman tank of Company C, 37th Tank Battalion knocked out to the west of the Trois Croix crossroads.

By the time that Company C arrived, a few German tanks had veered off to the west towards Moyenvic. These were taken under fire from the M4 medium tanks. By 10:40 hours, as the fog was finally lifting, the tank companies of Panzer-Brigade.111 and the truck-mounted infantry of Panzergrenadier-Regiment.111 were advancing towards Juvelize across the open farm fields. For the first time in several days, the P-47 Thunderbolts of the XIX TAC came roaring over the battlefield, strafing and bombing the German columns. Shortly after noon, the lead column of Panzer-Brigade.111 had occupied Juvelize. Panzer-Brigade.113, after a late start, reached Ley around noon.

To get a better picture of the confused situation, Abrams drove his command tank, "Thunderbolt V," to an orchard on top of Hill 257 that overlooked Juvelize from the northwest.[168] Finding it unoccupied, he ordered his remaining tank company, Captain Spencer's Company A, to occupy it to preempt a German advance farther south. He also ordered the battalion headquarters' assault gun platoon with M4 (105mm) tanks to accompany them to provide further fire support. An attached company of half-track infantry from Company A, 10th Armored Infantry Battalion followed the tanks towards Juvelize.

With German troops already in Juvelize, Abrams ordered supporting field artillery and mortars to bombard the town with white phosphorus smoke and high explosives. The white phosphorus was intended to cover the movements of the 37th Tank Battalion and was so effective that none of the columns came under fire during the movement. An observation aircraft in the area reported more German tanks moving towards Juvelize, so Abrams instructed Company C to move forward to cover Company A's left flank.

At this time, Company A was down to two platoons with nine tanks instead of the usual fifteen tanks due to casualties over the previous several days. As the tanks took up position on the hill, three German tanks emerged from the nearby "Trois Croix" roadside shrine. The tank platoon under Sergeant Walters quickly engaged and destroyed all three from the flank. One of the tanks in Lieutenant Donnelly's platoon was hit by tank fire from nearby

woods. When Spencer's company reached the top of the hill, they could see about twenty-five German tanks and vehicles in the fields beyond Juvelize moving into the town. The eight remaining M4 Sherman tanks began to fire on the moving German tanks at ranges of 400 to 2,000 yards. They knocked out many of the German vehicles while suffering only a single crewman wounded in the exchange.

Following the fighting, Spencer's crews found fourteen German tanks and eight trucks knocked out around the town. At least one of the tanks had been abandoned with no signs of any damage. The company also knocked out a German-operated M5A1 light tank during the fighting, presumably the one that had been abandoned by Company F, 25th Cavalry earlier in the morning.

Having halted the German attempts to reinforce Juvelize, Abrams instructed Capt. Jimmie Leach of Company B, 37th Tank Battalion to form a small task force with a platoon of tanks and an infantry platoon from Captain McDonald's Company A, 10th Armored Infantry Battalion and clean out the village. Leach's task force fought their way into Juvelize and killed or captured the remaining infantry of Panzergrenadier-Regiment.2111. The other two platoons of A/10th Armored Infantry Battalion patrolled around the town for stragglers.

After the Luftwaffe refused his pleas for air support, Manteuffel committed his last armored reserve, some surviving tanks from Panzer-Brigade.113, with instructions to attack Juvelize from the south. These instructions had no appreciable effect. The remnants of Panzer-Brigade.111 withdrew from the area north towards Guéblange, harassed by artillery and P-47 fighter-bombers.

During the Juvelize fighting, the Panzer-Brigade .111 commander, Col. Heinrich von Bronsart-Schellendorf, was killed when he dismounted from his command half-track and was hit by machine-gun fire. Some of his officers felt that he had given up hope after another tongue-lashing earlier in the morning from Manteuffel. Exhausted by days of road march and fighting, and disheartened by the destruction of his unit, he had decided to die a soldier's death, carelessly exposing himself to hostile fire.[169] The following day, the Panzer-Brigade.113 commander, Col. Erich von

A PzKpfw IV Ausf H of Panzer.Abteilung.2111 of Panzer-Brigade.111 knocked out in the fighting near Juvelize on 22 September. This tank has suffered hits on the upper surfaces, which suggests it may have been hit by airstrikes, but it also has multiple penetrations of the sides, which suggests it was also hit by tank fire. The level of destruction was probably due to a catastrophic ammunition fire that caused the armor penetrations.

Seckendorf, was killed around 19:15 hours west of La Garde when his half-track command vehicle was strafed by a P-47 from the 405th Group.[170] Both officers were posthumously elevated to the rank of general. Manteuffel later commented that "these leaders attempted to make up for the troop's poor training and lack of organization by an exemplary commitment on the battlefield. This led to their heroic deaths."[171]

The final day report of Krüger's 58.Panzer-Korps reveals the despair of the moment:

By 16:40 the Americans succeeded in halting the attack of Panzer-Brigade.111 toward Juvelize and captured the town as well as the hills to the southeast. Our own units fled under constant enemy air attack back to Blanche Église. Under these circumstances, 58.Korps considers a continuation of the attack fruitless, even if one of the Panzergrenadier regiments of 11.Panzer-Division is brought in.

The 37th Tank Battalion war diary for 22 September noted that "the enemy attempt to breakthrough from that direction was not only repulsed but completely routed." By the end of the day, Panzer-Brigade.111 had been reduced to 7 tanks and 80 men from an original strength of more than 90 tanks and 2,500 troops. The 37th Tank Battalion put the German casualties of the day's fighting in their sector as 16 tanks, 8 vehicles, 250 troops killed, and 85 to 100 prisoners. The 4th Armored Division losses, suffered mainly by Company F, 25th Cavalry Squadron, were 7 M5A1 light tanks, 1 M4 medium tank, 1 half-track, 1 jeep, 7 killed in action, and 13 wounded.

Another outcome of the day's fighting was Manteuffel's decision to consolidate the remnants of the three panzer brigades in his army into neighboring divisions.[172] He was disheartened by the brigade's disappointing performance and felt that the equipment and men could be better utilized within the framework of the more experienced divisions.

A pair of Panther Ausf. A tanks of Panzer-Regiment.15, 11.Panzer-Division in Dieuze, northeast of the Arracourt battlefield on 23 September 1944.

While CCA, 4th Armored Division was engaged in the Arracourt sector, CCB was supporting the 35th Division in the fighting near Château Salins on 22 September. Here, a pair of M4 tanks move through a field of dead cows.

ABSORPTION OF PANZER BRIGADES INTO PANZER DIVISIONS, 22 SEPTEMBER 1944	
Panzer-Brigade.111	11.Panzer-Division
Panzer-Brigade.112	21.Panzer-Division
Panzer-Brigade.113	15.Panzergrenadier-Division

In the three days of fighting from 19 to 22 September, the 4th Armored Division's Combat Command A had lost fourteen M4 medium and seven M5A1 light tanks as well as twenty-five men killed and eighty-eight wounded. In the process, they had effectively shattered two panzer brigades and derailed the Vosges Panzer Offensive.

CHAPTER 12

Stalemate: 24–30 September

ANY THOUGHTS OF FURTHER reinforcing the 5.Panzer-Armee with more armor were rejected by Hitler due to the significant shifts in the strategic situation in late September. The Vosges Panzer Offensive had been planned in early September when Hitler had thought that Patton's thrust would be the first to reach German soil. But by late September, it was becoming obvious that the Allies had other intentions. On 17 September, a day before the Lorraine panzer attacks started in earnest, the Allies had staged Operation Market-Garden, a massive airborne operation in the Netherlands to seize the Arnhem River bridges over the Rhine. More worrisome was an intensified attack by Hodge's First U.S. Army in Belgium. On 15 September, the 3rd Armored Division had punched a hole through the Westwall, threatening the German city of Aachen. Hitler was also aware that the 5.Panzer-Armee was a spent force, and substantial reinforcement would be needed for it to accomplish its original mission. He had other needs for these forces.

By 24 September, after the first series of Lorraine tank battles had ended, Rundstedt pleaded with Hitler to shift the surviving armor northward to prevent an American entry into Aachen. Although Hitler would not provide any more reinforcements to Manteuffel, neither would he completely abandon his plans in Lorraine. The belated arrival of the 11.Panzer-Division marked a new stage in the Lorraine tank fighting.

On the American side, Patton's offensive plans had been deflated by the continuing supply crisis. Bradley contacted Patton on 23 September and informed him that due to a lack of supplies, the Third U.S. Army would have to take up defensive positions. The 6th Armored Division was being taken away from him, so the armored forces needed for a drive on the Rhine would not be available. Furthermore, Haislip's XV Corps would be shifted to Devers' 6th Army Group at the end of the month, removing another armored division. The next day, Patton met with his three corps commanders, Walker, Eddy, and Haislip, and they agreed on a line that could be defended by the remaining forces.

After the disastrous fight for Juvelize on 22 September, 5.Panzer-Armee spent most of 23–24 September licking its wounds and awaiting the arrival of the rest of 11.Panzer-Division. Balck insisted on a new round of attacks to shield the construction of the new Vosges-Stellung, a line of strongpoints and defense works being created in the foothills of the Vosges Mountains. Balck was not aware that Patton's forces had shifted to the defensive. The objectives of the attack on 24 September were the same as two days before. In the 1.Armee sector, two regiments of 559.Volksgrenadier-Division would attack towards Moncel-sur-Seille with the support of surviving elements of Panzer-Brigade.106. In the 5.Panzer-Armee sector, the objective again would be to reach Moyenvic to link up with the 1.Armee, thereby creating a solid defensive barrier in front of the 4th Armored Division.

SUNDAY, 24 SEPTEMBER

Due to the delays in getting the 11.Panzer-Division into position as well as the exceptionally wet and muddy weather, 5.Panzer-Armee took little part in the fighting on 24 September. The day's fighting began in the predawn around 05:35 hours, primarily in the 1.Armee sector around Château-Salins. In contrast to the previous panzer brigade attacks, this attack began with heavy artillery preparation. This was due to the fact that the 559.Volksgrenadier-Division had a normal complement of artillery compared to the panzer brigades, which had none. CCB, 4th Armored Division was holding a screening position in front of the 35th Infantry Division near Château-Salins when the Germans began with a

A medic tends to a wounded tanker from the 37th Tank Battalion in the area north of Arracourt during the fighting on 24 September 1944.

heavy concentration of artillery. The main ground attack followed at 08:30 hours, consisting of about two battalions of infantry supported by about thirty tanks. CCB depended heavily on the divisional artillery to repulse the attack. The weather was considered unflyable due to 80 percent cloud cover, but two squadrons of P-47s were vectored into the area using radar. Around 10:00 hours, the P-47s found a gap in the clouds and made a skip-bombing attack on the German tanks from an altitude of about fifteen feet, then returned to strafe. Within fifteen minutes, the attack had collapsed and the Germans withdrew. CCB captured 194 prisoners and estimated German casualties as 300 killed, 500 wounded, and 21 tanks knocked out. Patton recommended the Medal of Honor for the pilot who led the P-47 attack.

By 25 September, the 11.Panzer-Division was ready to take part in the attacks. Its tank strength was still paltry, even after absorbing the remaining tanks of Panzer-Brigade.111. Manteuffel did not want a repeat of the 22 September fighting and had

troops scout the U.S. lines in advance of the attack. Reconnaissance indicated that the crossroads town of Moyenvic was unoccupied on the evening of 24 September, so this became the initial objective of the attack on 24 September in the 5.Panzer-Armee sector. Balck was not aware of the reasons for this situation, but Moyenvic had been abandoned by the 4th Armored Division as part of Patton's overall plan to withdraw back to shortened defense lines.

The quick, and largely uncontested, advance into Moyenvic in the morning convinced Manteuffel to continue the offensive, and attacks were launched all along the salient held by CCA, 4th Armored Division. The attacks were on a very small scale compared to previous days, usually a battalion or less of infantry with a few supporting tanks. There was steady rain the entire day, which seriously constrained German operations. Attacks were all beaten back, since the Americans held the high ground and had an advantage in both tanks and artillery. CCA estimated German losses that day in their sector as 10 tanks, 2 vehicles, and about 300 troops.

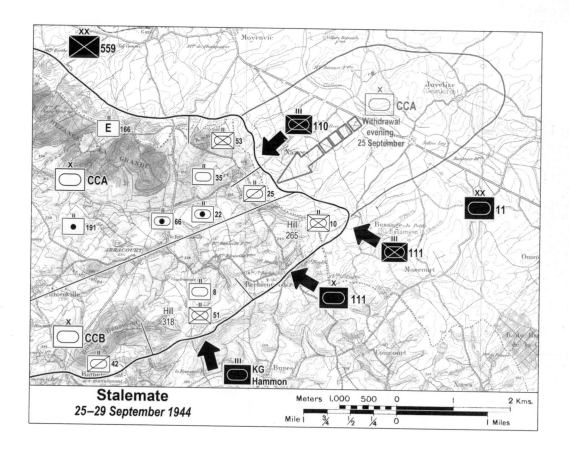

Stalemate
25–29 September 1944

Meters 1,000 500 0 | 2 Kms.
Mile | ¾ ½ ¼ 0 | Miles

CCA WITHDRAWS: MONDAY, 25 SEPTEMBER

The attack resumed on Monday morning, 25 September. The 11.Panzer-Division began to probe beyond Moyenvic, while the remnants of Panzer-Brigade.111 emerged out of Blanche-Église again, heading towards the forward positions of the 37th Tank Battalion and 10th Armored Infantry Battalion. "Steady rain hampered visibility and operations" according to the 4th Armored Division.

The 53rd Armored Infantry Battalion was deployed outside Moyenvic, and it was the first to encounter the 11.Panzer-Division battle groups. The 4th Armored Division after-action report later described the scale of the German actions in this sector as little more than "nuisance attacks." It also concluded that "The objective of the attack is not clear due to the fact that there appears to be no coordination between them." Balck instructed Luttwitz's 47.Panzer-Korps, stationed along the western portion of the Rhine-Marne canal, to engage its artillery against the Bathelémont area in the hopes of drawing away forces from the main assaults. A steady rain throughout the day and the muddy battlefield frustrated many of the German infantry attacks.

The day's largest assault was in the sector around Juvelize and Lezey. The German infantry pushed through the American cavalry screens and also compelled an outpost of the 704th Tank Destroyer Battalion near Ley to pull back, exposing the right flank of the 37th Tank Battalion. By this time, the 4th Armored Division had already decided to compress their forward defenses to less vulnerable positions, pursuant of Patton's instructions to change to a defensive stance.

As a result of the new instructions, Colonel Clarke planned to stage an "Orson Welles Attack." This was a reference to the famous radio broadcast of the *War of the Worlds* on 30 October 1938

cleverly conceived by Orson Welles as a fake news broadcast. Clarke concocted a radio disinformation program, broadcasting a variety of instructions over the CCA radio network "in the clear" to create the impression that CCA was about to stage a major counteroffensive.[173] This was accompanied by "demonstrations" of the forward companies of the 37th Tank Battalion to simulate the start of an attack. There was a great deal of noisy movement near the front lines as well as preparatory artillery bombardments. This deception freed the 10th Armored Infantry Battalion to withdraw first. The CCA withdrawal began at 19:00 hours beginning with the evacuation of the positions west of Lezey. The 10th Armored Infantry Battalion pulled back to new positions east of Réchicourt across the Réchicourt-Bézange Road. Once this was under way, the 37th Tank Battalion withdrew company by company and went into reserve near Arracourt after dark. During the day's fighting, the 37th Tank Battalion estimated it had destroyed 6 German tanks and 20 vehicles and killed about 100 troops. The tally for the 4th Armored Division as a whole was pegged at 300 enemy killed, 10 tanks and 2 other vehicles knocked out. CCA casualties that day were 16 killed, 47 wounded, and 29 exhaustion cases. CCB to the northwest was relieved by elements of the 35th Infantry Division starting around 21:00 hours during the defensive consolidation; CCB casualties that day were 120 men.

The frenetic activity on this front was misunderstood by the 58.Panzer-Korps, which reported to the 5.Panzer-Armee that the Americans had counterattacked with eighty tanks and were preparing for a broader offensive. Krüger's headquarters recommended that the focus the next day should be farther south.

TUESDAY, 26 SEPTEMBER

Balck sent out instructions in the early afternoon of 25 September 1944 for a continuation of the attacks on 26 September. These were fairly predictable,

with instructions for the 5.Panzer-Armee to seize Bézange-la-Grande while the neighboring 1.Armee was to stage an attack towards Moncel-sur-Seille.[174]

In any event, fighting on 26 September was constrained due to the continuing rainy weather and atrocious battlefield conditions. Instead of major ground actions, there were a number of artillery exchanges.

The 4th Armored Division used most of the day to conclude its internal reorganization as it shifted to a defensive posture. The forward defense line was now held by the 4th Armored Division's three armored infantry battalions. CCB took over the southern sector of defenses facing the 47.Panzer-Korps. Clarke's CCA remained concentrated in the Arracourt area and the northern sector. Clarke selected defensive positions on the hills around the town that gave his units a good vantage point, looking down on neighboring German positions in the area. Abrams' 37th Tank Battalion was pulled back to the CCR reserve to rest and refit, and the realignment was completed on 26 September.

The after-action report by the 51st Armored Infantry battalion summarized the situation succinctly: "It was obvious that the Battalion's present position must be held at all costs since the loss of any of the front would give the enemy a vantage point from which observed artillery fire could be placed on any position of Combat Command B's area."[175]

Manteuffel used the withdrawal by Clarke's CCA to claim a local victory. The 11.Panzer-Division passed through the ruins of Juvelize and reached Lezey by 11:45 hours. They eventually reached as far south as Coincourt around 14:00 hours. In the 47.Panzer-Korps sector, the 15.Panzergrenadier-Division moved through Parroy and reached Bures by the afternoon. Manteuffel had hoped to continue the attack into American lines, but the muddy conditions seriously hampered movement. One of the few confrontations of the day occurred during the movement by CCB to new positions. "While on the march, elements of CCB were attacked by an enemy column of half-tracks and other vehicles, but accurate artillery concentrations broke up the attack at its inception, destroying 3 tanks and 5 armored cars."[176]

The fighting along the Moselle became increasingly difficult in late September due to the advent of early autumn rains. Here, a jeep is trapped in the mire in the 35th Infantry Division sector on the left flank of the 4th Armored Division.

One of the few photos of the M4 tank during the Arracourt battles is this shot of a tank from 2nd Platoon, Company C, 37th Tank Battalion commanded by St. Sgt. Timothy J. Dunn. This was the only tank of the five in the platoon that survived the fighting on 19–25 September. The official caption states it was taken in Château-Salins on 26 September 1944, but on that day, Château-Salins was in German hands. It was in fact taken south of Parroy after the 37th Tank Battalion was withdrawn from the front lines for rehabilitation and refit. Curiously enough, the tank had still been fit with a Normandy hedgerow cutter on the bow, and one of the crewmen can be seen after he detached it.

WEDNESDAY, 27 SEPTEMBER

Once the weather cleared and the mud began to dry, the German attacks resumed on 27 September. The panzer forces committed in the sector consisted of twenty-four Panthers, six PzKpfw Ivs, and some assault guns. Manteuffel sought to secure the camelback plateau of Hills 318 and 293 on the southern flank of the 4th Armored Division positions that overlooked the 5.Panzer-Armee positions around the Parroy forest. He ordered the commander of the 11.Panzer-Division, Gen. Wend Wietersheim, to create a battle group to attack from Bures towards Arracourt. Kampfgruppe Hammon consisted of the remnants of Panzer-Brigade.113 and the division's reconnaissance battalion with about twenty-five tanks. From his experience on the western front, Wietersheim was opposed to concentrating all the armor, feeling that it would be too vulnerable to air and artillery attack. Based on his eastern-front experience, Manteuffel was equally adamant that the armor be concentrated and not committed piecemeal.

The day's attacks started with a diversionary advance by the rest of the division on the eastern end of the salient that pushed out from Lezey and Ley, while Panzergrenadier-Regiment.111 supported by a few tanks occupied the village of Bézange-la-Petite below the positions of Company C, 10th Armored Infantry Battalion on Hill 265. The brunt of the attack on 27 September fell on Company A, 10th Armored Infantry Battalion positions near Réchicourt between Hills 265 and 318. The company was very depleted due to previous combat, and its battered 3rd Platoon was down to only fifteen men from a starting strength of more than forty. An after-action account from the neighboring 51st Armored Infantry Battalion described the situation:

The 4th Armored Division set up their defensive perimeter on a line of shallow hills to the southeast of Arracourt. This is a view of Hill 318 from the German perspective looking over Parroy Lake.

This is a view of the reverse slope of Hill 318 from the perspective of the American side. The troops of the 51st Armored Infantry Battalion established defensive positions along the top of this hill line.

Company A's position in Rechicourt became a focal point for enemy artillery. Concentrations consisted of 105's and heavier. The road through town became known as the "Bowling Alley" as it was obviously under enemy observation and more than one vehicle in any one spot immediately brought artillery fire.

Lt. James H. Field of 1st Platoon, Company A, 10th Armored Infantry battalion, received the Medal of Honor for gallantry in the fighting, the first Medal of Honor awarded in Patton's Third U.S. Army. Field's citation read as follows:

For conspicuous gallantry and intrepidity at risk of life above and beyond the call of duty, at Rechicourt, France. On September 27, 1944, during a sharp action with the enemy infantry and tank forces, 1st Lt. Fields personally led his platoon in a counterattack on the enemy position. Although his platoon had been seriously depleted, the zeal and fervor of his leadership was such as to inspire his small force to accomplish their mission in the face of overwhelming enemy opposition. Seeing that one of the men had been wounded, he left his slit trench and with complete disregard for his personal safety attended the wounded man and administered first aid. While returning to his slit trench he was seriously wounded by a shell burst, the fragments of which cut through his face and head, tearing his teeth, gums, and nasal passage. Although rendered speechless by his wounds, 1st Lt. Fields refused to be evacuated and continued to lead his platoon by the use of hand signals. On one occasion, when 2 enemy machineguns had a portion of his unit under deadly crossfire, he left his hole, wounded as he was, ran to a light machinegun, whose crew had been knocked out, picked up the gun, and fired it from his hip with such deadly accuracy that both the enemy gun positions were silenced. His action so impressed his men that they found new courage to take up the fire fight, increasing their firepower, and exposing themselves more than ever to harass the enemy with additional bazooka and machinegun fire. Only when his objective had been taken and the enemy scattered did 1st Lt. Fields consent to be evacuated to the battalion command post. At this point he refused to move further back until he had explained to his battalion commander by drawing on paper the position of his men and the disposition of the enemy forces. The dauntless and gallant heroism displayed by 1st Lt. Fields were largely responsible for the repulse of the enemy forces and contributed in a large measure to the successful capture of his battalion objective during this action. His eagerness and determination to close with the enemy and to destroy him was an inspiration to the entire command, and are in the highest traditions of the U.S. Armed Forces.

Following Field's evacuation, Lieutenant Wilson from the neighboring Company C took over the 1st Platoon. A German tank moved to within 150 yards of the 1st Platoon trenches and began shelling them. Machine-gun and small-arms fire killed the exposed panzer commander and forced the crew to button up. The small-arms fire also killed or wounded the accompanying panzergrenadiers, and so the panzer moved back to a defilade position, where it continued to shell the foxholes. U.S. tank destroyers in the neighboring Company C positions refused to move out of their entrenchments to relieve Company A, and eventually Wilson decided to pull the 1st Platoon back down the hill and closer to the town of Réchicourt. The company commander, Capt. Thomas J. McDonald, concurred since by this stage the company was under direct observation from the Moncourt area, the company had no medical support for the wounded, and it lacked any radio or field telephone links to higher headquarters. Company A had gone into the line with 224 men and was left with 116 men.[177] Patton later told his executive officer that "I did not want Lieutenant Fields sent to the front anymore, because it has been my unfortunate observation that whenever a man gets the Medal of Honor or even the Distinguished Service Cross, he usually attempts to outdo himself and gets killed, whereas, in order to produce a virile race, such men should be kept alive."

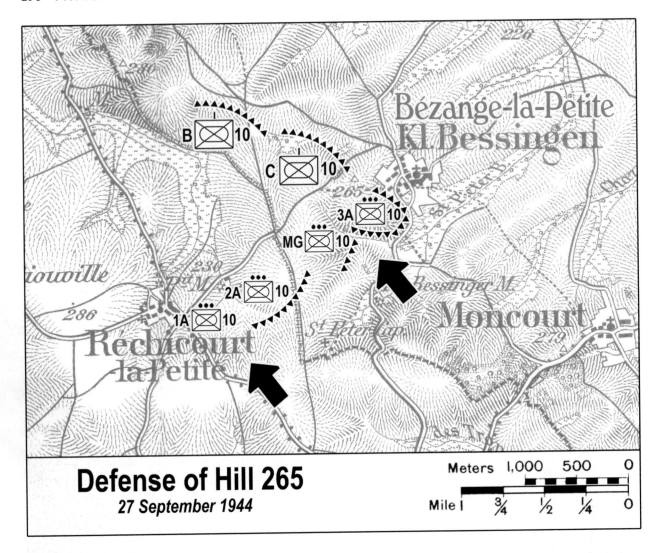

Defense of Hill 265
27 September 1944

The Company C position on Hill 265 was reinforced by a platoon of tank destroyers and a platoon of engineers. A battle group of the Panzergrenadier Regiment.110 conducted repeated attacks against Hill 265, including a night attack on 26–27 September. It was beaten back, but the attacks resumed around 10:00 hours on 27 September from the area around Xanrey. The morning attack advanced only 1,800 yards towards the northern positions of the 53rd Armored Infantry Battalion when it was stunned by a concentrated barrage from the six field artillery battalions supporting Clarke's CCA. The attack faltered and the panzers withdrew. The 35th Tank Battalion formed a small task force with a few tank companies and two platoons of riflemen

to clear out Xanrey. In the subsequent fighting, Lieutenant Colonel Oden estimated about 135 German infantry had been killed before the task force withdrew back to the start positions. Two tanks were lost in the raid after running over mines.

General Wietersheim shifted the II./Panzergrenadier-Regiment.110 to support the southern sector, and the attacks against the 51st Armored Infantry Battalion resumed on 27 September. The panzergrenadiers infiltrated past the farm at the base of Hill 318, and after bitter fighting, Kampfgruppe Hammon reached the top of the hill and the edge of the neighboring woods. The crest of Hill 318 became the focus of the fighting over the next few days between the 51st Armored Infantry Battalion and Kampfgruppe Hammon.

This is a view of the village of Réchicourt-la-Petite facing north with Hill 265 to the upper right. This was the area held by Lt. James H. Field's 1st Platoon, Company A, 10th Armored Infantry Battalion during the fighting on 27 September 1944.

The armored infantry battalions of the 4th Armored Division fought dismounted in the final stages of the Arracourt battles. These are riflemen of the 10th Armored Infantry Battalion later in the Lorraine campaign.

1st Lt. James H. Field, Company A, 10th Armored Infantry Battalion, the Third U.S. Army's first Medal of Honor recipient.

HILL 318: THURSDAY, 28 SEPTEMBER

Manteuffel's orders for the day were blunt: "take Hills 293 and 318, then press farther toward the northwest in the direction of Arracourt." At dawn on 28 September, the 51st Armored Infantry Battalion retook the forward slope of Hill 318 from Kampfgruppe Hammon, but the fighting surged across the crest throughout the day.

There were 107 fighter-bomber sorties during the fighting, with the P-47s leveling the village of Bures and badly disrupting the concentration of German reinforcements there. After pushing back three more German attacks, the GIs of the 51st Armored Infantry Battalion again retook Hill 318 around noon. The German grenadiers had received little artillery support as the batteries had moved during the night to new positions, and their forward observers were not in place until later in the day. A final German daylight attack was broken up by American artillery fire before it could reach its objective. After dark, the Germans sent in another assault force supported by tanks that secured the south face of Hill 318. The 51st Armored Infantry Battalion withdrew over the north slope but were hit by a heavy German artillery barrage. The 4th Armored Division responded with a fire strike against the south slope by four artillery battalions,

followed by a 51st Armored Infantry Battalion counterattack that secured the southern high ground around midnight. Sporadic fighting on Hill 318 continued throughout the night of 28–29 September.

The fighting on neighboring Hill 265 was nearly as intense. At 19:00 hours, a German infantry attack against Company A, 10th Armored Infantry Battalion forced one of its platoons to pull back, but the attackers were brought under intense American artillery fire. Wietersheim requested to Manteuffel that his troops be allowed to break off the attacks to get some rest or they would simply lose their combat effectiveness. Due to intense pressure from Berlin, Manteuffel refused and insisted that the attacks must continue.

The German attack around Réchicourt and Hill 265 faltered for a variety of reasons. The attacks against Réchicourt by Panzergrenadier-Regiment.111 received less artillery support than anticipated since the majority of the divisional artillery was out of range. The plan to reinforce the attack on Réchicourt with Kampfgruppe Hammon from Panzer-Brigade.113 and the 11.Panzer-Division's reconnaissance battalion stalled in Coincourt for unexplained reasons.[178]

The organic firepower in the armored infantry battalions included a mortar platoon with three half-track M4 81mm mortar carriers. As in many other units, the 4th Armored Division often modified these so that the 81mm mortar pointed over the front end of the half-track instead of the rear.

The Germans attempted to conduct vigorous night patrols to make penetrations into the American lines or to discover weak points. "The enemy's effort to break through our lines with night patrols have been repulsed by the 25th Cavalry Group which is screening our front performing both reconnaissance and counter-reconnaissance missions"[179]

On the American side, the relentless fighting had led to a sharp rise in the number of combat exhaustion cases, especially among the riflemen of the armored infantry battalions, who were bearing the brunt of the fighting. "This trend is due to numerous causes, among which are: length of time in combat, extensive rain, little rest, lack of hot food, and a feeling that they are not fitted for a holding mission."

A FINAL PUSH: FRIDAY, 29 SEPTEMBER

By dawn of 29 September, the 11.Panzer-Division had reinforced its units opposite the CCB positions on Hills 265 and 318 from other sectors. Massing near the smoldering ruins of Bures, its forces included the reconnaissance regiment of the 11.Panzer-Division, a battalion from Panzergrenadier-Regiment.110, an armored engineer company, and the remaining tanks of Panzer-Brigade.111 and 113. The armored strength in the sector included eighteen PzKpfw IV, twenty Panthers, and eleven Flakpanzer IVs, although only a fraction of these were actually operational.

In the predawn hours, Capt. Eugene Bush, commander of Company C, 8th Tank Battalion, reported that "it sounded as if enemy vehicles were coming right into his area." The dense fog and darkness limited visibility to a few dozen yards. The initial German attack on Hill 318 in the early morning hours pushed the 51st Armored Infantry Battalion back about 500 yards, and the Germans controlled the forward crest of Hill 318 by 10:15 hours. Given the heavy casualties suffered by the 51st Armored Infantry Battalion, Colonel Dager ordered the 8th Tank Battalion to send two companies of tanks to provide direct fire support. The fog was still so dense that movement of the tanks proved difficult. Dager told the tank company commanders to wait until the fog lifted before moving over the crest. The tanks of Company A were unable to reach the crest due to stiff German resistance. When the fog lifted around 11:00 hours, the tanks of Company C discovered they were already on the crest, and they immediately came under intense German mortar fire. Captain Bush requested air support.

A tactical air liaison officer with the group directed P-47 Thunderbolt strikes on the panzers in the field below, where they were massing for another attack. Without the fog for protection, the German troops were exposed. The initial air attacks were ineffective as the fighter-bombers had been diverted from a planned mission over Metz with propaganda leaflets. But during the course of the day, the 405th Fighter Group carried out several low-altitude air strikes against the German forces preparing to reinforce their positions on Hill 318. Besides knocking out tanks with bombs and rocket fire, the air strikes managed to drive a number of German tanks out of the cover of woods, where they were then exposed and struck by artillery fire. Bush later remarked that "the Air Corps really did the trick!"[180] The tanks of Company C began firing on the German tanks at the base of the hill, claiming six during the day's fighting. The 11.Panzer-Division commander later recalled:

In a few minutes, eighteen of our tanks and several armored personnel carriers were burning! Our own infantry retreated, strangely enough not pursued by the enemy. . . . As a result, any chance of winning our final objective had been frustrated. We had suffered losses that could have been pre-vented if only we had been satisfied with the line already gained which was suitable for the defense.[181]

By the middle of the afternoon on 29 September, the German troops were in full retreat. After three days of intense fighting, with little sleep and heavy casualties, many of the German units disintegrated. The commander of Kampfgruppe Bode suffered a nervous breakdown. The German staging area at the base of the plateau had the Marne canal at its back, and many of the troops feared that the Americans might charge down off the plateau and trap them against the water obstacle. The 15.Panzergrenadier-Division was forced to set up a straggler line with tanks near Parroy in an attempt to restore some order. The surviving flakpanzers were positioned in Parroy and Bures in an attempt to ward off the continuing air attacks, but they were almost completely ineffective. The corps commander's report to Manteuffel was blunt: "Hill triangle lost. Troops exhausted, need rest." A total of twenty-three tanks and several armored half-tracks were knocked out according to German accounts of the fighting. Only four tanks remained operational by the end of the day, though stragglers continued to filter back to German lines over the next day. Tanks that had been abandoned were attacked and burned out by P-47 fighter-bombers.

The fighting against the neighboring 10th Armored Infantry Battalion was mainly directed against the right flank held by Company A, 10th Armored Infantry Battalion near Réchicourt and Company C on Hill 265. The GIs were finally pushed back to the reverse slope of the hill, but they held their positions at nightfall. Exhausted, the German infantry withdrew into the town of Bézange below. Some German units remained trapped on the hills between Hill 265 and 318 but escaped under the cover of darkness when it became apparent that the other battle groups were withdrawing.

The 29 September attack represented the last major attempt by the 5.Panzer-Armee to cut off Patton's Third U.S. Army's spearhead near Arracourt. The last four days of attacks on CCA, 4th Armored Division had already cost the 5.Panzer-Armee about 700 killed and 300 wounded as well as 14 PzKpfw IV and 22 Panther tanks.

On 29 September, while the fighting was still raging on the hills east of Arracourt, General Balck visited the western-front commander, von Rundstedt, at his headquarters in Bad Kreuznach. Balck told the field marshal that if his forces did not receive reinforcements with at least 140 tanks and more artillery, it would be impossible to continue any offensive actions. Rundstedt replied that any reinforcements were out of the question, and he tacitly accepted that the Lorraine panzer offensive would come to an end without fulfilling Hitler's objective. At 23:00 hours, Balck informed Manteuffel to call off the attack. The battered 11.Panzer-Division was to be pulled out of the line and defensive positions secured.

By the end of September, the Lorraine fighting had ended in stalemate. Deprived of units and supplies, Patton's Third U.S. Army was in no position to plan further offensives. Army Group G's modest panzer force was exhausted and incapable of taking further offensive action against the Third U.S. Army. Hitler, preoccupied with the airborne assault at Arnhem and the penetrations of the Westwall near Aachen, ignored yet another defeat of his ill-conceived schemes.

Crews from the 25th Cavalry Squadron posing on an M8 75mm HMC in the hills above Parroy in early October 1944 after the fighting for Arracourt had died down.

A burned-out Panther Ausf. A of the 2nd Battalion of Panzer-Regiment.15, 11.Panzer-Division photographed in early 1945 in the northern sector of the Arracourt battlefield.

A group portrait of the same officers at the 4th Armored Division headquarters near Château-Salins, from left to right: Bradley, Wood, Patton, Dager, and Eddy. Patton relieved Wood of divisional command on the insistence of Eddy a few weeks later due to continued disagreements.

A wrecked M4A3 (76mm) named "Crescent City Kid" photographed near Réchicourt-la-Petite in 1945. This was probably from Company C, 8th Tank Battalion, which supported the 51st Armored Infantry Battalion in this sector. There were only about twenty of these newer tanks in the 4th Armored Division at the time of the Arracourt fighting, and the 37th Tank Battalion had none of them.

The senior U.S. Army commanders discuss planned operations in Lorraine on 13 November 1944 near Château-Salins. From left to right are Brig. Gen. Holmes Dager (CCB, 4th Armored Division); Gen. Omar Bradley (12th Army Group); Maj. Gen. John "P" Wood (4th Armored Division); Lt. Gen. George Patton (Third U.S. Army); and Maj. Gen. Manton Eddy (XII Corps).

CHAPTER 13

After-Action Assessment

THE SIGNIFICANCE OF THE Vosges Panzer Offensive is largely absent from most English-language accounts of the September 1944 fighting in the ETO. Most histories are dominated by the controversies swirling around Eisenhower, Montgomery, and Bradley over Market-Garden and the September supply crisis. The German perspective of the September campaign in the west has been largely ignored. One reason the Lorraine offensive has been so little appreciated was that Patton thoroughly disrupted the Vosges Panzer Offensive and it never coalesced into a single mass panzer attack as Hitler had originally intended. By keeping Army Group G off balance, Patton frustrated the German attempts to concentrate a panzer force of sufficient size to have any consequence on the battlefield.

Hitler viewed the battlefield dynamics in September much differently from Eisenhower or Montgomery. Patton's fast-paced attacks towards the Saar, combined with the weakness of Army Group G, made the Vosges sector especially vulnerable. This can be seen in the relative balance of resources thrown into the various sectors. German tank strength in September 1944 was very low due to the crippling losses suffered in Normandy. For the German army in World War II, the panzer force was the fulcrum of combat power whether on offense or defense, so panzer strength is a useful measure in assessing the German perspective of the threats in the key sectors. Of the seven panzer brigades diverted from the Russian front to the west, one was committed against Operation Market-Garden, two were committed against the U.S. Army thrust around Aachen, and four were committed in Lorraine again Patton. Of the armored reinforcements from the

Type	Panther	PzKpfw IV	StuG	JgPz	Total
OPERATIONAL GERMAN TANK AND AFV STRENGTH IN THE WEST, MID-SEPTEMBER 1944[182]					
Arnhem Sector	52	2	14	46	**114**
Aachen Sector	83	20	37	27	**167**
Lorraine Sector	202	142	35	11	**390**

Italian theater, both of these panzergrenadier divisions were committed against Patton. As can be seen in the chart above, more than half of the German tank strength in the west was concentrated against Patton in mid-September 1944.

To understand the importance of Patton's actions in Lorraine in September 1944, a counterfactual history can be illuminating. Imagine for a moment that the Third U.S. Army had halted at Verdun at the beginning of September 1944 as proposed by Montgomery. What would have been the consequences?

Without Patton's relentless pressure along the Moselle, the forces for Hitler's Vosges Panzer Offensive would have coalesced unhindered. By mid-September, Army Group G would have built up a panzer force of more than 600 tanks and assault guns, the greatest mass of panzer strength concentrated up to that point in the ETO. This was about four times the strength of the failed Operation Lüttich panzer offensive at Mortain in August 1944. Could this force have had a decisive influence on the autumn 1944 fighting?

Patton and XII Corps commander Manton Eddy conduct a battlefield tour on 8 October 1944 near Arracourt.

The consequence of a full-strength Vosges Panzer Offensive depended largely on the battlefield scenario. Hitler envisioned at least two major options—a northward attack against Patton's Third U.S. Army or a southward attack against Patch's Seventh U.S. Army. An attack against Patton in mid-September would have faced three to four armored divisions, while an attack against Patch's Seventh U.S. Army would have faced a number of separate tank and tank destroyer battalions, but no armored divisions unless the neighboring First French Army intervened.

An attack against Patch's Seventh U.S. Army might have had the most dramatic results, and it could have resembled the first weeks of the Ardennes offensive with a great deal of mayhem and chaos engulfing the Alsace sector. Under a best-case scenario, the offensive might have cut off one or more U.S. infantry divisions, resulting in a repeat of the Kasserine Pass debacle of February 1943 and triggering a temporary crisis in the ETO. However, the ultimate outcome would have likely paralleled the Ardennes. Once the Vosges Panzer Offensive began, Patton would have been in a position to strike its exposed flanks. Furthermore, the Wehrmacht would have faced similar logistics problems to those encountered in the Ardennes since there were widespread shortages of fuel and ammunition in Army Group G. While a best-case scenario for the Vosges Panzer Offensive cannot be ruled out, other scenarios were more likely given the disorganization of the Wehrmacht in September 1944, the leadership crisis, and the weak offensive capability of the Wehrmacht at this stage of the war.

The failed Vosges Panzer Offensive was the ancestor of the eventual Ardennes offensive. The German army historian Joachim Ludewig of the Militärgeschichtliches Forschungsamt (Military History Research Institute) in Potsdam had this to say about the Vosges Panzer Offensive:

> Looking at it in retrospect, it becomes even clearer how important [the Vosges Panzer Offensive] was in Hitler's strategy. Its execution would have resulted in the heaviest concentration of German Panzers in the West to that point. The failure of the attempt to shift from the retreat movement directly into a flanking offensive was a major factor in Hitler's decision to launch the Ardennes Offensive later, in both in terms of timing and force structure.[183]

Hitler gained several key "lessons learned" from the experience that shaped his planning of the Ardennes offensive. Against his explicit instructions, the September offensive had been frittered away by the piecemeal commitment of the panzer force in a succession of weak local counterattacks. To avoid a repetition of this experience, the Ardennes force was taken out of the hands of the field commanders and the panzer force was kept back in Germany until the time came for the attack. Resupply of tanks to the panzer divisions still in the field was kept to a minimum, and all of the elite Waffen-SS panzer divisions were pulled off the field and kept in reserve until the Ardennes attack. The amount of force available for the Vosges Panzer Offensive was never sufficient to overwhelm the Allied forces. Hitler realized that he had to exercise more patience and give the Replacement Army sufficient time to rebuild the shattered panzer force. This was estimated to require two months of panzer production if the majority of new tanks were directed to the west, not to the east. This represented a strategic shift in Hitler's planning, summarized by the new slogan "Attack in the West—Defend in the East." This shift is very evident in the balance between east and west in the supply of new tanks in the final months of 1944. No longer underestimating the U.S. Army, he planned a surprise breakthrough operation by twenty-six German divisions against four American divisions.

German commanders in Lorraine had continually blamed Allied airpower for the defeat of the local panzer attacks. From a detailed look at the battles, this assessment is not entirely convincing. Airpower became an excuse for the poor performance of the panzer brigades and was only a contributory factor in their defeat. Berlin did not have a detailed after-action report of the battles, and their assessment was based on anecdotal accounts that tended to exaggerate the impact of airpower. Regardless of

DELIVERY OF GERMAN REPLACEMENT AFVs BY THEATER					
	Nov 44	Percent	Dec 44	Percent	Jan 45	Percent
West	1,345	82.4	952	60.1	343	21.3
East	288	17.6	631	39.9	1,264	78.7
Total	1,633		1,583		1,607	

the decisiveness of tactical airpower in influencing the battlefield outcome, it strongly shaped Hitler's plans for the Ardennes offensive. Hitler insisted that the offensive be postponed until November or December because the weather was likely to be poor enough to limit the intervention of Allied airpower.

From the U.S. perspective, there were no significant lessons learned from the defeat of the Vosges Panzer Offensive, and indeed there was one overarching failure. The Allies never understood that Germany had attempted a major counteroffensive in Lorraine. The success of the Ultra decrypts of German's Enigma coding system led to overconfidence in the omniscience of this source of intelligence. The timely decryption of warnings of the Operation Lüttich offensive at Mortain in August 1944 created the impression that major German offensive plans would be discovered. In the case of the Lorraine offensive, there was never any decryption of Hitler's intentions for the Vosges Panzer Offensive, and so no appreciation that these plans had been foiled. As the Wehrmacht began to fall back into Germany, communications usually relied on telephone and teletype, which were not vulnerable to interception by Allied signals intelligence. The failure to recognize the declining vulnerability of German tactical communications to interception would have important consequences in December 1944 when the Allies placed too much emphasis on Ultra decryption to predict German intentions prior to the Ardennes offensive.

The Allies were fully aware of the substantial buildup of the panzer force in the Eifel region opposite the Ardennes in December 1944 from both signals intelligence and other means. What they failed to realize was its intent. Since there had been no Ultra decrypts regarding a December offensive, the presumption was that the Eifel buildup was intended to be a counterattack force once the Allies attempted to breach the Roer and the Rhine in early 1945. If the Allies had appreciated the full extent of Hitler's plans for the Vosges Panzer Offensive, they may have been more attuned to the possibility of similar desperate ventures.

Patton remained adamant that he could have pushed on to the German border in September 1944 if given enough fuel and ammunition. The delays in late August and early September were the most galling, since at the time, Army Group G was in total disarray and unready for any bold venture by Patton. Nevertheless, the shortage of supplies for the Third U.S. Army in early September was less dependent on Eisenhower's decisions, and more dependent on geography. Patton's Third U.S. Army was the farthest of any of the field armies from the main ports of supply. It consumed inordinate amounts of fuel to ship supplies to the Third U.S. Army from Cherbourg or the other Channel ports. This would remain a problem until the Allies repaired the French railways and finally opened the port of Antwerp. Patton's prospects in late September would have required a similar logistics miracle, and by this stage of the campaign, the German defenses had finally begun to harden. A largely unexplored issue is whether it would have made sense to detach Patton's Third U.S. Army from Bradley's 12th Army Group and attach it to Devers' 6th Army Group. The main attraction in this case might have been the ability of the 6th Army Group to supply Patton via the Mediterranean ports, especially Marseilles. However, it is by no means certain that the logistics train in this sector would have been sufficient in late September to support the offensive potential of the Third U.S. Army. There were strong political reasons for avoiding this solution, centered mainly around Eisenhower's and Bradley's disdain for Devers. In any event, this intriguing possibility is largely outside the scope of this short book.

TACTICAL ASSESSMENT

Patton's Third U.S. Army thoroughly defeated the Vosges Panzer Offensive. This had not been accomplished in a single battle. Rather, Patton's relentless offensive actions in early September forced Army Group G to prematurely commit two of its four panzer brigades, and so they were destroyed piecemeal. Their loss provided no real tactical benefit to the Army Group G defense. In addition, Army Group G's two strongest divisions, the 3.Panzergrenadier-Division and 15.Panzergrenadier-Division, suffered crippling attrition in the first weeks of September in their attempts to restrain the Third U.S. Army's attempts to breach the Moselle Line. The loss of these forces, in addition to the capture of the Langres Plateau, scuttled the original version of the Vosges Panzer Offensive. Patton's advance past Nancy in mid-September forced Army Group G to prematurely start the Vosges Panzer Offensive on the east bank of the Moselle River with the two other panzer brigades before they could concentrate with the panzer divisions. They were defeated in detail, first at Lunéville on 18 September, and again around Arracourt over the next few days.

From Hitler's strategic perspective, the Vosges Panzer Offensive was a complete failure. It never managed to trap any of Patton's forces; Army Group G suffered disproportionate casualties in the battles. Yet from the tactical perspective of Army Group G, the panzer attacks had important and positive benefits. The panzer attacks helped Army Group G stabilize the front in Lorraine. They were not the only factor, and indeed the defense of the Moselle forts, especially around Metz, had a substantial role. It must be recalled that at the beginning of September, Army Group G was still in retreat and had no coherent defense line in Lorraine. By the end of September, Army Group G had established a coherent defense line in both the 1.Armee and 19.Armee sectors. German commanders were not aware that it was supply issues that had forced Patton to halt his offensive in the third week of September, and so the fighting around Arracourt seemed to have played a significant role in halting Patton's attack. A staff officer of Army Group G later summarized this viewpoint:

> The enemy had been prevented from tearing the front to pieces. Even if there were many weak points, it had been possible to re-establish a cohesive, firm Army Group frontline.[184]

Commanders such as Blaskowitz seldom attract the attention of the more flamboyant leaders such as Model and Manteuffel, but their skilled and patient efforts were instrumental in re-establishing a firm German defensive line in front of the Westwall. While these actions reaffirmed the reputation of the Wehrmacht for its tenacity in adversity, the strategic consequences for Germany were tragic, ensuring a further seven months of war and millions of additional civilian casualties in Germany itself.

COMBAT CASUALTIES IN LORRAINE, SEPTEMBER 1944		
	U.S.	German
Dead, wounded, missing	18,537	38,000
POW	n/a	40,456

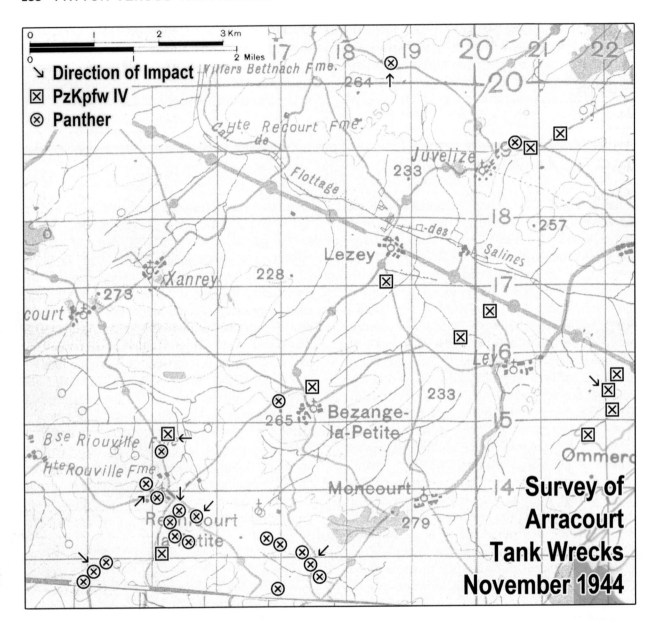

TECHNICAL ASSESSMENT

The Lorraine tank battles in September 1944 were the most sustained tank-vs.-tank battles fought by the U.S. Army in the ETO until the Ardennes offensive. A detailed look at tank casualties on both sides provides some useful insights into the relative combat power of both sides in the autumn 1944 fighting. Although the Wehrmacht had important technical advantages in their tanks, especially the Panther, the poor quality of the new tank crews significantly degraded their battlefield effectiveness.

OPERATIONAL TANK STRENGTH, 4TH ARMORED DIVISION, LATE SEPTEMBER 1944[185]

September	18	19	20	21	22	24	25	26	27	28	29	30
M4 (75mm)	138	138	137	137	134	123	111	119	119	109	109	108
M4A3 (76mm)	20	20	16	16	14	14	14	14	14	13	13	13
M4 (105mm)	18	18	18	18	18	18	18	18	18	18	18	18
M5A1	81	81	79	79	75	74	76	76	76	76	76	76
M8 75mm	17	17	17	17	17	17	16	16	16	16	16	15
M4 dozer	3	3	3	3	3	3	3	3	3	3	3	2
Total	277	277	270	270	261	249	238	246	246	235	235	232

THIRD U.S. ARMY TANK COMBAT LOSSES, SEPTEMBER 1944

	3–9 Sep	10–16 Sep	17–23 Sep	24–30 Sep	Total
M5A1 Light	7	7	15	8	37
M4 medium	1				1
M4 (105mm)	2				2
M4A1	1	17	7	13	38
M4A1 (76mm)			1		1
M4A3	21	5	30	4	60
M4A3 (76mm)			5	4	9
Total	32	29	58	29	148

Total Third U.S. Army armored vehicle losses in September included 49 light tanks and 151 medium tanks and tank destroyers. A total of 392 replacement tanks were issued in September, so by the end of the month, the Third U.S. Army had more than replaced all of its losses.

Of the 616 Panzers and AFVs of the Wehrmacht committed to the Lorraine fighting in September 1944, by 1 October, there were only 127 operational. Total losses had amounted to 341 tanks and AFVs—assault guns and tank destroyers. A further 148 armored vehicles were battle damaged or in need of repair and most would never see action again. As a result, actual losses were about 480 tanks and AFVs. German losses in men and equipment in Lorraine were higher than the American losses, and far more difficult to replace. The overall loss ratio of tanks and AFVs in the Lorraine fighting was about 2.4:1 in favor of the U.S. Army.

OPERATIONAL TANK STRENGTH OF PANZER BRIGADES IN ARRACOURT BATTLES, SEPTEMBER 1944*

	17 Sep	20 Sep	21 Sep	22 Sep	23 Sep	24 Sep	25 Sep
PzBrig 111							
Panther		18	11	3	4	4	n/a
PzKpfw IV		13	11	4	6	6	n/a
PzBrig 113							
Panther	24	4	6	5	10	10	3
PzKpfw IV		19	14	14	9	9	0

*Strength is from end-of-day reports

5.PANZER-ARMEE OPERATIONAL TANK AND AFV STRENGTH, 17 SEP–1 OCT 1944[186]

	17	20	21	22	23	24	25	26	27	28	30	1
Panther	24	22	17	9	19	20	18	30	16	44	19	21
PzKpfw IV		32	25	28	23	15	18	21	10	52	16	11
StuG III		15	4	7	6						3	3
Total	24	69	46	44	48	35	36	51	26	96	38	35

GERMAN AFV STATUS IN LORRAINE, SEPTEMBER–OCTOBER 1944

	Panther	PzKpfw III	PzKpfw IV	JagdPz IV	StuG	FlakPz IV	Total
Peak strength in Sep 1944	201	4	194	80	90	47	616
On hand, 1 Oct 1944	83	3	93	63	12	21	275
Operational, 1 Oct 1944	26	2	28	46	6	19	127
Damaged, in repair 1 Oct 1944	57	1	65	17	6	2	148
Total losses in September	118	1	101	17	78	26	341
Third U.S. Army claims	186	421					607

Aside from the scale of tank losses at field army level, it is worth examining the relative losses in the fighting at Arracourt. Clarke's CCA, 4th Armored Division did a tally at the end of the fighting in September comparing CCA losses versus those they claim to have inflicted against various German units. The table below covers the comparative losses during the peak tank fighting on 19–22 September, as well as the overall losses for the entire month. It should be noted that some of these figures were estimates. For example, the estimate of Germans wounded is very suspect in view of the small number listed relative to the number of killed. These figures suggest that the tank loss ratio of the 4th Armored Division against 5.Panzer-Armee was significantly better than the ratio of the Third U.S. Army as a whole, at about 3.9:1 in favor of the U.S. Army.

The popular myth of the superiority of German tanks in combat in northwest Europe is belied by the record of their actual performance. In a meeting engagement of the type seen around Arracourt, with both sides in an offensive posture and neither side enjoying any particular numerical advantage, the panzer units were overcome by superior American training and tactics. German tanks and antitank guns could still exact a painful toll against American tanks when skillfully employed from defensive positions, as would become evident in the remaining months of the war. But the same was true of American tank and tank destroyer units, as was evident in the difficult opening weeks of the Ardennes offensive when the panzer offensive was stopped in its tracks far short of its objectives. Unlike the eastern front, there were very few meeting engagements or offensive panzer operations in the ETO in 1944–1945. Therefore, perceptions of the relative merits of German versus American armored unit performance are skewed by the natural advantages enjoyed by a force fighting almost exclusively on the defensive.

One problem in assessing the performance of U.S. Army tanks versus German panzers is that the statistical data for tank losses on both sides almost always lacks detail on the causes of the losses. Some postwar studies made assessments of the relative balance of losses to guns, antitank rockets, and mines.[188] However, few if any reports were able to disentangle the gunfire casualties between tanks, other AFVs, and towed antitank guns. Furthermore, the percentage of U.S. tanks knocked out by panzers changed through the course of the year depending on the size of the opposing panzer force. So U.S. tank losses to panzers as a percentage of total losses

COMPARATIVE LOSSES IN ARRACOURT BATTLES, SEPTEMBER 1944[187]				
	Wehrmacht 19–22 Sep	CCA, 4th AD 19–22 Sep	Wehrmacht September	CCA, 4th AD September
Killed	610	25	2,247	53
Wounded	8	88	150	395
POW/Missing	161	6	2,070	46
Tanks destroyed	79	21	124	32*
AFVs destroyed		3	30	10
Vehicles destroyed	22	8	515	16
Artillery destroyed	4	n/a	33	n/a
Aircraft destroyed		n/a	13	n/a

*CCA monthly tank losses were twenty-five M4 medium tanks and seven M5A1 light tanks; AFV losses were three M18 tank destroyers, five M8 armored cars, and two M7 105mm HMC.

OPERATIONAL TANKS AND AFVs IN PANZER DIVISIONS, PZ.GREN. DIV., AND PANZER BRIGADES IN THE WEST, OCT–DEC 1944					
	PzKpfw IV	Panther	Panzer IV/70	StuG III	Total
1 Oct 44	22	151	29	13	**215**
1 Nov 44	66	130	36	4	**236**
1 Dec 1944	132	100	60	45	**337**

was presumably higher in the summer when the panzer force was still relatively significant in size, but presumably much lower in the autumn when the panzer force had dwindled. As can be seen from the chart above, the panzer force in the west was quite modest through most of the autumn since Hitler insisted that the refurbished divisions remain in the Führer reserve inside Germany until the Ardennes offensive. This chart does not include AFVs outside the panzer force such as StuG brigades or infantry division panzerjäger companies. These other units would have more than doubled the number of operational German AFVs, but comprehensive data is lacking. By way of comparison, the U.S. Army fielded 4,944 tanks and 1,008 tank destroyers in the ETO in November 1944, for a total of 5,952. This was more than ten times the size of the panzer force operational in the west.

The myth that it cost the U.S. Army five Sherman tanks for every Panther has been around for many decades, and its origins are obscure. The root of this myth most probably can be traced to a conflation of British experience with the Sherman tank and the very different U.S. experience. The British Army in Normandy did in fact lose very large numbers of Sherman tanks to the Wehrmacht. For example, the Guards Armored Division complained that the Allies were losing six tanks for every German tank.[189] Many older histories of World War II tend to assume that the U.S. Army experience in tank warfare in Normandy was the same as the British experience. This was certainly not the case, as is obvious to anyone with a familiarity of U.S. tank operations in 1944.

The chart on page 193 is a compilation of German army tank kill claims versus the Allies. This provides some idea of the different dynamics of the tank fighting in 1944. As is quite evident, British tank losses in the summer months during the Normandy fighting were quite high and far more modest in the late autumn. In contrast, U.S. tank casualties in Normandy in the summer were substantially lower than the British losses, but significantly higher in the late autumn 1944 fighting. The heavy U.S. tank losses in November were the result of the Operation Queen offensive in the Aachen-Stolberg corridor against Army Group B and the Vosges Mountain offensive and Metz offensive against Army Group G. In November 1944, panzer strength was very modest and antitank guns were the primary cause of U.S. tank casualties, not tank-vs.-tank fighting.

The tendency to equate British and American experiences in tank warfare in the ETO was very common in war-gaming circles in the 1960s and 1970s. This myth was popularized and perpetuated by the influential Avalon Hill war game, "Squad Leader," released in 1977. The 5-to-1 ratio was carelessly applied to all Allied tank operations in the ETO in 1944–1945, including U.S. Army operations, even though it had no particular relevance beyond the British experience in Normandy in the summer of 1944. Its numerical specificity gave it a false verisimilitude.

One of the more recent sources cited for the immortal 5-to-1 myth is *Death Traps*, the memoirs of Belton Cooper, a young ordnance lieutenant in the 3rd Armored Division in World War II. He suggested a 5-to-1 technological superiority of

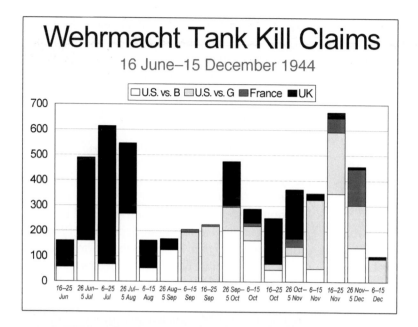

Wehrmacht Tank Kill Claims
16 June–15 December 1944

Legend: □ U.S. vs. B □ U.S. vs. G ■ France ■ UK

This chart provides a graphic representation of the Wehrmacht's kill claims against the Allied armies in 1944. As can be seen, British tank casualties are very pronounced in the early summer months due to the high casualty rate in Normandy. German claims against the U.S. Army are high in November due to offensives against both Army Group B and Army Group G.

WEHRMACHT TANK KILL CLAIMS, 15 JUNE–15 DECEMBER 1944[190]

Date	UK	U.S.	France
16–25 Jun	104	57	
26 Jun–5 Jul	328	161	
16–25 Jul	546	68	
26 Jul–15 Aug	279	268	
6–15 Aug	110	53	
26 Aug–5 Sep	44	125	
6–15 Sep	*	*+194**	12
16–25 Sep	*	*+218	7
26 Sep–5 Oct	174	202+93	6
6–15 Oct	56	163+56	13
16–25 Oct	179	47+23	2
26 Oct–5 Nov	195	104+34	32
6–15 Nov	5	52+272	
16–25 Nov	44	349+243	55
26 Nov–5 Dec	10	135+168	143
6–15 Dec	11	107+91	
Total	**2,085**	**3,283**	**270**

*Army Group B data missing for these dates

**Army Group B claims + Army Group G claims

German tanks over the M4 Sherman.[191] Cooper wrote his memoir four decades after the war and the 5-to-1 ratio myth was probably based on conversations with his younger war-gaming friends, and not his own recollections.[192]

When applied to the U.S. Army experience, the 5-to-1 myth does not survive any serious scrutiny. Cooper's 3rd Armored Division did suffer exceptionally high tank losses, and, in fact, it lost more tanks than any other U.S. armored division in the ETO in 1944–1945: 173 M5A1 light tanks and 632 M4 Sherman tanks.[193] Yet the 3rd Armored Division claimed 1,023 German tanks and 452 AFVs destroyed plus 423 tanks and 307 AFVs destroyed/abandoned by the enemy.[194] This was certainly not a 5-to-1 ratio in favor of the Wehrmacht, but a 2.3:1 ratio in tank losses in favor of the U.S. side. It must be noted that divisional kill claims consist of more than tank-vs.-tank kills, and these claims may very well be exaggerated. Likewise, 3rd Armored Division losses were not solely due to German tanks, and the majority was probably attributable to towed antitank guns, antitank rockets, and mines. Nevertheless, these statistics undermine the 5-to-1 myth. Nor are the 3rd Armored Division statistics an anomaly. In the case of the 4th Armored Division, its own AFV losses in 1944–1945 were 57 light tanks, 216 M4 tanks, and 22 M18 tank destroyers, while the division claimed to have destroyed 847 German tanks and 89 assault guns, a 3:1 ratio in favor of the U.S. side.[195] In the case of a Ballistics Research Laboratory study done after the war looking only at tank-vs.-tank exchanges by the 3rd and 4th Armored Divisions, U.S. losses were 149 versus 158 German tank losses.[196] Eisenhower's headquarters did a survey of U.S. units after the war to tally the number of U.S. tanks and AFVs lost from D-Day to the end of the war. They concluded that 21,179 German tanks and SP guns had been knocked out or abandoned at a cost of 7,688 U.S. tanks and AFVs, a ratio of 2.75:1 in U.S. favor. While the U.S. claims were probably exaggerated, they make it clear that the U.S. Army did not have a perception in World War II that its tank force had suffered disproportionately at German hands.

The purpose of this statistical digression is not to argue one way or the other in favor of or against the Sherman and Panther tanks. Rather, it is to reinforce an argument made earlier in the book against the technological determinism so prevalent in popular discussions of tank performance in combat. Technological factors of tank design, while contributing to tank performance on the battlefield, are not the primary determinant of battlefield success or failure. In terms of firepower and armored protection, the Panther Ausf. G tank of the type used in Lorraine was technically superior to the M4 (75mm) tank used by the 4th Armored Division at Arracourt. Yet the 4th Armored Division prevailed on the battlefield in September 1944 and inflicted much higher losses on the German panzer units than it suffered. Napoleon coined an adage that still applies: "The moral is to the physical as three is to one." Crew training, tactics, and battlefield circumstances play a greater role in the battlefield effectiveness of tanks than do technical factors.

An impromptu conference on the hood of Wood's jeep. The figure to the far left is Gen. Holmes Dager, CCB commander. General Wood is in the center facing the commander and on the right is Maj. Gen. Manton Eddy, XII Corps commander.

Lt. Col. Creighton Abrams officially recognizes the field commissions of four NCOs of the 37th Tank Battalion for their actions in the battles around Arracourt. The soldiers are (left to right) 2nd Lt. Edward Mallon (Co. D), 2nd Lt. Charles Walters (Co. A), 2nd Lt. James Farese (Co. B), and 2nd Lt. Roy Smith (medical platoon). Farese later won the Silver Star but was killed in the battle for Singling in early December 1944.

Creighton Abrams named his tanks "Thunderbolt" after the lightning bolt on the Armored Force insignia. This is his M4A3 (76mm) Thunderbolt VI that he received following the Arracourt tank battles. Abrams was not keen on the new version with the 76mm gun, feeling that it lacked the high-explosive punch of the older 75mm gun. He was persuaded to upgrade to the 76mm version by Bruce Clarke, who argued that if Abrams wouldn't use the new tank, his tank crews would be reluctant to use them.

The town of Arracourt commemorates the September 1944 battles with this tank painted in 37th Tank Battalion markings on the town square. Although the battle damage on this tank might hint it was an actual battlefield survivor, it is in fact a French Army M4A4(T) that was donated to the town for the memorial.

Historical Sources

THIS BOOK WAS PREPARED using both published and unpublished studies. The core of any book on the Lorraine fighting is Hugh Cole's superb official volume in the U.S. Army "Green Book" series. This is an essential account for any readers interested in a broader overview of the Lorraine campaign. Needless to say, there is no comparable German official account of the campaign. Joachim Ludewig from the Militärgeschichtliches Forschungsamt in Potsdam has published an account of German operations in this time frame that provides some essential context for a study of the Vosges Panzer Offensive.

There is a broad range of archival resources on this campaign. Not surprisingly, the U.S. Army records are more detailed than the Wehrmacht records. The U.S. Army after-action reports (AAR), journals, and other documents can be found in Record Group 407 at the U.S. National Archives and Records Administration II in College Park, Maryland. These are organized by major formations at field army, corps, and division level. The divisional records are further subdivided into major subunit records. For example, the 109 archival boxes of the 4th Armored Division start with general division records, then headquarters elements (G-1 personnel, G-2 intelligence, G-3 operations, etc.), combat commands, and the records of component battalions. Beside the main divisional records, the separate "Combat Interviews" collection is an essential reference for anyone wanting a more detailed account of specific battles. U.S. Army historians accompanying the divisions conducted detailed interviews after the main battles to collect more detailed accounts than the administrative records found in the regular divisional files. Patton's personal files are located in the Manuscript Division of the Library of Congress in Washington, DC.

Besides these document collections, there are a large number of U.S. Army internal reports and publications. For example, Patton's Third U.S. Army published a massive two-volume study after the war. Most corps and divisions also published their own accounts after the war, and some have been reprinted by Battery Press over the years. These can be found in some libraries, and one of the best collections is at the U.S. Army Heritage and Education Center (AHEC) at Carlisle Barracks, Pennsylvania.

German records at NARA II can be found in the Record Group 242 microfilm collection. This collection is spotty, with some units having considerable surviving records and other units having few or none. In the case of the Lorraine campaign, the 5.Panzer-Armee records are fairly detailed and there is some useful supplementary data in the records of General Stumpf's General Inspector of the Panzer Troops of OB West, found in the Heeresgruppe D collection. The German records include Tagesmeldungen (daily reports), Kriegstagebuch (KTB: war diaries), and other reports.

As always, the U.S. Army's Foreign Military Studies (FMS) collection contains a good deal of valuable material. This collection of reports was prepared after the war by senior German officers under the sponsorship of the U.S. Army Center of Military History. Since these officers were in many cases still in prisoner-of-war camps, they had little or no access to unit records. They are especially valuable in gaining the officers' impressions rather than in obtaining detailed day-to-day accounts. The FMS reports are available at several federal archives, including NARA II and the U.S. Army AHEC at Carlisle Barracks, Pennsylvania. They are also available on the Internet on the Fold3 and Sturmpanzer websites.

The photos here come primarily from official U.S. sources, especially the collections at NARA II, AHEC, and the former Patton Museum collection at Fort Knox (now in limbo at Fort Benning). I have also included photos from my own personal collection, including photos of the battlefield taken during a 1999 battlefield tour. I have supplemented these with some computer illustrations and maps. The maps have been prepared using period maps from my own collection, as well as captured German army maps found in the NARA II collections. The tactical maps here were based on the map overlays found in the U.S. records, primarily in the divisional G-3 records, combat interviews collection, and unit after-action reports. During the September 1944 fighting, the 4th Armored Division relied on captured German army maps, often based on French maps. These can be found in the divisional records at NARA. I have tried to use these maps when possible as the basis for the maps I have prepared for this book.

ARCHIVAL RECORDS

National Archives and Records Administration II (NARA II), College Park, Maryland

Record Group 165
Combined Services Detailed Interrogation Centre (CSDIC), Boxes 661, 662

Record Group 242 German Military Records (Microfilms)
Tagesmeldungen, OB West, T-78, Roll 313
Generalinspekteur der Panzertruppen, T-78, Rolls 145, 621, 622, 624
Kriegstagebuch des OB West, T-311, Rolls 16, 29
Tätigkeitsbericht, General der Panzertruppe OB West, T-311, Roll 18
Kriegstagebuch, Panzer-AOK.5, T-313, Rolls 421, 481
Kriegstagebuch, 58.Panzer-Korps, T-314, Rolls R-1497,1541

Record Group 338
ETOUSA (European Theater of Operations U.S. Army) HQ, AFV & Weapons Section

Record Group 407, Entry 427: U.S. Army World War II Operations Reports
XV Corps, G-2 Reports
4th Armored Division, After-Action Reports
5th Infantry Division, G-2 Reports
90th Infantry Division, After-Action Reports
712th Tank Battalion, After-Action Reports
37th Tank Battalion, After-Action Reports
704th Tank Destroyer Battalion, After-Action Reports

Record Group 407, Entry 427A: U.S. Army Combat Interviews
2nd French Armored Division
4th Armored Division (inc. 704th Tank Destroyer Battalion)
90th Infantry Division

U.S. ARMY STUDIES AND PUBLICATIONS

After-Action Report, Third U.S. Army 1 August 1944–9 May 1945 (Third U.S. Army, 1945).

Data on WWII Tank Engagements Involving the U.S. Third and Fourth Armored Divisions, Ballistic Research Laboratories Memo Report No. 758, Aberdeen Proving Ground, 1954, p.10.

The Reduction of Fortress Metz: XX Corps Operational Report 1 Sept–6 Dec 1944, XX Corps Headquarters, 1945.

The XX Corps: Its History and Service in World War II, Osaka, Japan: XX Corps Association, 1946.

Maj. Richard Barnes, *Arracourt—September 1944*, Ft. Leavenworth, KS: Command and General Staff College, 1982.

Alvin Coox, *US Armor in the Anti-Tank Role: Korea 1950* (Operations Research Office, July 1952).

Maj. William Jackson et al., *The Employment of Four Tank Destroyer Battalions in the ETO*, Fort Knox, KY: U.S. Army Armored School, 1950.

Capt. Kenneth Koyen, *The Fourth Armored Division: From the Beach to Bavaria*, Munich: Herderdruck, 1946.

Al Lambert and G. B. Layton, *The Ghosts of Patton's Third Army: A History of the Second US Cavalry*, Munich: Munchner Graphische, 1946.

H. W. McDonald et al., *The Employment of Armor in Korea* (Operations Research Office, April 1951).

Vincent McRae and Alvin Coox, *Tank-vs.-Tank Combat in Korea* (Operations Research Office, September 1954).

Lt. Col. Hal Pattison, *The Operations of CCA, 4th Armored Division: From the Normandy Beachhead to the Meuse River—28 July to 31 August 1944*, School of Combined Arms, 1947.

U.S. ARMY FOREIGN MILITARY STUDIES

n.a., *Stellenbesetzung AOK.1 und unterstellte Verbände 10.8–14.9 (1944)*, A-908: 1950.

Col. Gen. Johannes Blaskowitz, *Army Group G: 10 May–22 September 1944*, B-800: 1946.

Gen. Walter Botsch, *Nineteenth Army: June 1943–15 September 1944*, B-515: 1946.

Maj. Gen. Karl Britzmayr, *Operations of the 19. Volksgrenadier-Division during the period from 1 September 1944 to 27 April 1945*, B-527: 1946.

Col. Otto Eckstein, *LXXXIX Corps: 20 Sep–23 Nov 44*, B-760, B-790: 1948.

Col. Kurt von Einem, *Report on the Engagements of the XIII. SS-Korps in Lorraine during the Period from 1 September to 15 November 1944*, B-412.

Col. Albert Emmerich, *The Battles of the 1.Armee in France from 11 Aug to 15 Sep 1944*, B-728: 1946.

Lt. Gen. Heinz von Gyldenfeldt, *Battles of Army Group G: 15–25 September 1944*, B-589: 1947.

Maj. Kurt Hold, *Organization and Composition of the First Army: 11 Aug 44 to 14 Feb 45*, B-732, B-821: 1947.

Lt. Gen. Gustav Höhne, *Commitment of the 11th Panzer Division in Lorraine*, B-364: 1951.

Gen. Otto von Knobelsdorff, *Army Group G on the Western Front: Estimate of the Situation when I Took Command of 1.Armee on 10-9-44*, B-222: 1950.

Lt. Gen. Walter Krause, *Defense of Metz 1–8 Sep 1944*, B-042: 1946.

Gen.derPzTrp. Walter Krüger, *The LVIII.Panzer Korps in the Battles West of the Vosges during the Period from 17 September 1944 to 4 November 1944*, B-548: 1947.

Gen. Hasso von Manteuffel, *Defense of the Vosges Mountains and Commitment of the 5.Panzer-Armee 1944-45*, B-037: 1945.

Gen. Hasso von Manteuffel, *The Commitment of the Fifth Panzer Army west of the Vosges within the framework of Army Group G from about 15 September to 15 October 1944*, B-757: 1947.

Col. Willy Mantey, *First Army: 1 Sep–4 Dec 1944*, B-214, B-751: 1946.

Gen. Maj. Fredrich Wilhelm von Mellenthin, *Army Group G (20 Sep 44–3 Dec 44), Report of the Chief of Staff*, A-999.

Lt. Gen. Kurt Mühlen, 559 VGD, *The Rhineland Campaign: 15 Sep–21 Sep 44*, A-972: 1946.

Maj. Percy Schramm, *OKW War Diary 1 Apr–18 Dec 1944*, B-034: 1947.

Gen. Wend von Wietersheim, *The 11th Panzer Division in Southern France: 15 August–14 September 1944*, A-880: 1947.

Gen. Wend von Wietersheim, *Employment of the 11.Panzerdivision in Lorraine*, B-364, B-416: 1947.

BOOKS

Hanson Baldwin, *Tiger Jack*, Ft. Collins, CO: Old Army Press, 1979.

Hermann Balck, David Zabecki (trans.), *Order in Chaos: The Memoirs of General of Panzer Troops Hermann Balck*, Lexington: University of Kentucky Press, 2015.

Peter Beale, *The Great Mistake: The Battle for Antwerp and the Beveland Peninsula, September 1944*, Throup, UK: Sutton Publishing, 2004.

Martin Blumenson, *The Patton Papers 1940–1945*, New York: Da Capo, 1996–98.

Omar Bradley, *A Soldier's Story*, New York: Henry Holt, 1951.

Donald Brownlow, *Panzer Baron: The Military Exploits of General Hasso von Manteuffel*, North Quincy, MA: Christopher Publishing, 1975.

Friedrich Bruns, *Die Panzerbrigade 106 FHH: Eine Dokumentation uber den Einsatz im Westen vom Juli 1944–Mai 1945*, Traditionsverband der Panzer-Brigade 106 FHH, Celle: 1988.

Richard Buchanan et al., *Men of the 704th: A Pictoral and Spoken History of the 704th Tank Destroyer Battalion in World War II*, Latrobe, PA: St. Vincent College, 1998.

Philippe Burtscher and François Hoff, *Les fortifications allemandes d'Alsace-Lorraine 1870–1918*, Paris: Histoire & Collections, 2008.

John Colby, *War from the Ground Up: The 90th Division in WWII*, Austin, TX: Nortex, 1991.

Hugh Cole, *The Lorraine Campaign*, Washington, DC: U.S. Army Center for Military History, 1981.

Belton Cooper, *Death Traps: The Survival of an American Armored Division in World War II*, Novato, CA: Presidio Press, 1998.

Carlo D'Este, *Patton: A Genius for War*, New York: HarperCollins, 1995.

Frédéric Deprun, *Panzer en Normandie: Histoire des équipages de char de la 116.Panzer-Division*, Louviers, Belgium: Ysec, 2011.

J. Dugdale, *Panzer Divisions, Panzergrenadier Division and Panzer Brigades of the Army and Waffen SS in the West, Autumn 1944–February 1945, Volume 1, Part 1: September 1944 Refitting and Re-equipment*, Milton Keynes, UK: Military Press, 2000.

David Eisenhower, *Eisenhower at War 1943–1945*, New York: Random House, 1986.

William Ellis and Thomas Cunningham, *Clarke of St. Vith: The Sergeant's General*, Cleveland: Dillon/Liederbach, 1974.

Aaron Elson, *Tanks for the Memories: The 712th Tank Battalion during World War II*, Hackensack, NJ: Chi Chi Press, 2001.

Alain Eymard, *2e DB: 1er Août 1944–8 Mai 1945*, Bayeux: Heimdal, 1990.

Rémi Fontbonne, *Les fortifications allemandes de Metz et de Thionville 1871–1918*, Paris: Serpenoise, 2006.

Dominique Forget, *Le Général Leclerc et la 2e DB 1944-45*, Bayeux: Heimdal, 2008.

Don Fox, *Patton's Vanguard: The United States Army 4th Armored Division*, Jefferson, NC: McFarland, 2003.

Eric Freiwald, *The Building and Training of the 4th Armored Division 1941–1944*, Doctoral Dissertation, Philadelphia: Temple University, 2001.

A. Harding Ganz, *Ghost Division: The 11th "Gespenster" Panzer Division and the German Armored Force in World War II*, Mechanicsburg, PA: Stackpole, 2016.

Lonnie Gill, *Code Name Harpoon: The Combat History of the 704th Tank Destroyer Battalion (Self-Propelled)*, La Puente, CA: Baron Publishing, 1982.

Richard Giziowski, *The Enigma of General Blaskowitz*, New York: Hippocrene, 1997.

Ian Gooderson, *Air Power at the Battlefront: Allied Close Air Support in Europe 1943–45*, London: Frank Cass, 1997.

Timm Haasler, *Hold the Westwall or Perish With It: The History of Panzer-Brigade.105—September 1944*, Winnipeg: Federowicz, 2007

F. H. Hinsley et al., *British Intelligence in the Second World War, Volume 3, Part 2*, London: Her Majesty's Stationary Office, 1988.

Tom Ivie, *Patton's Eyes in the Sky: USAAF Combat Reconnaissance Missions NW Europe 1944–45*, Hersham: Ian Allen, 2003.

Thomas Jentz, *Panzertruppen, Vol. 2*, Atglen, PA: Schiffer, 1996.

Oscar Koch, *G-2: Intelligence for Patton*, Atglen, PA: Schiffer, 1999.

Werner Kortenhaus, *The Combat History of the 21.Panzer Division*, Solihull, UK: Helion, 2014.

Paul de Langlade, *En suivant Leclerc d'Alger à Berchtesgaden*, Paris: Laffont, 1964.

Didier Lodieu, *D'Argentan à la Seine: La bataillon de Panther de la 9.Pz.Div. face au XV Corps americain*, Louviers: Ysec, 2003.

Hans von Luck, *Panzer Commander*, New York: Praeger, 1999.

Joachim Ludewig, *Rückzug: The German Retreat from France 1944*, Lexington: University Press of Kentucky, 2012.

Jacques Massu, *Sept ans avec Leclerc*, Paris: Plon, 1974.

Ronald McNair, *Les Panzers en Lorraine*, Bayeux: Heimdal, 1984.

Kurt Mehner, *Die Geheimen Tagesberichte der Deutschen Wehrmachtführung im Zweiten Weltkrieg 1939–1945, Band 11: 1.September 1944–31.Dezember 1944*, Osnabrück: Biblio Verlag, 1984.

F. W. von Mellenthin, *Panzer Battles: A Study of the Employment of Armor in the Second World War*, New York: Ballantine, 1971.

William Moore, *Free France's Lion: The Life of Philippe Leclerc, De Gaulle's Greatest General*, Philadelphia: Casemate, 2011.

Matthew Morton, *Men on Iron Ponies: The Death and Rebirth of the Modern US Cavalry*, DeKalb: Northern Illinois University Press, 2009.

Stephen Napier, *The Armored Campaign in Normandy: June–August 1944*, Philadelphia, Casemate: 2015

Kamen Nevenkin, *Fire Brigades: The Panzer Divisions 1943–1945*, Winnipeg, Federowicz: 2008.

George S. Patton, *War as I Knew It*, Boston: Houghton, Mifflin, 1947.

Henry Phillips, *The Making of a Professional: Manton Eddy*, Westport, CT: Greenwood, 2000.

Nathan Prefer, *Patton's Ghost Corps*, Novato, CA: Presidio, 1998.

Rudi Rolf, *Die Deutsche Panzerfortifikation: Die Panzerfesten von Metz und ihre Vorgeschichte*, Osnabrück: Biblio, 1991.

Ronald Ruppenthal, *Logistical Support of the Armies, Volume II: September 1944–May 1945*, Washington, DC: Chief of Military History, 1959.

Jacques Salbaing, *La victoire de Leclerc à Dompaire 13 septembre 1944*, Issy-les Moulineaux: Editions Muller, 1997.

Alfonso Escuadra Sanchez, *Feldherrnhalle: Forgotten Elite: The Panzerkorps Feldherrnhalle and Antecedent Formations*, Bradford, UK: Shelf Books, 1996.

Wolfgang Schneider, *Tiger in Combat*, Winnipeg: Federowicz, Vol. 1: 1994, Vol. 2: 1998.

David Spires, *Air Power for Patton's Army: The XIX Tactical Air Command in the Second World War*, Washington, DC: U.S. Air Force History and Museums, 2002.

Erich Spiwoks and Hans Stöber, *Endkampf zwischen Mosel und Inn: XIII.SS-Armeekorps*, Osnabrück: Munin, 1976.

H. J. Stöber, *Die eiserne Faust: Bildband und Chronik der 17.SS-Panzergrenadier-Division*, Neckargemünd: Vowinckel, 1966.

Ken Wakefield, *The Fighting Grasshoppers: US Liaison Aircraft Operations in Europe 1942–1945*, Stillwater, MN: Specialty Press, 1990.

Russell Weigley, *Eisenhower's Lieutenants: The Campaigns of France and Germany 1944–45*, Bloomington: Indiana University Press, 1981.

James Wood (ed.), *Army of the West: The Weekly Reports of German Army Group B from Normandy to the West Wall*, Mechanicsburg, PA: Stackpole, 2007.

Steven Zaloga, *Anzio 1944: The Beleaguered Beachhead*, Oxford: Osprey, 2005.

———. *Armored Thunderbolt: The US Army Sherman in World War II*, Mechanicsburg, PA: Stackpole, 2008.

———. *Defense of the Rhine 1944–45*, Oxford: Osprey, 2011.

———. *Gen. George S. Patton*, Oxford: Osprey, 2010.

———. *Kasserine Pass 1943: Rommel's Last Victory*, Oxford: Osprey, 2005.

———. *Liberation of Paris 1944: Patton's Race to the Seine*, Oxford: Osprey, 2008.

———. *Lorraine 1944: Patton vs. Manteuffel*, Oxford: Osprey, 2000.

———. *M10 and M36 Tank Destroyers 1942–53*, Oxford: Osprey, 2002.

———. *M18 Hellcat Tank Destroyer*, Oxford: Osprey, 2004.

———. *M4 (76mm) Tank 1943–1953*, Oxford: Osprey, 2003.

———. *M8 Greyhound Light Armored Car 1941–91*, Oxford: Osprey, 2002.

————. *Metz 1944: Patton's Fortified Nemesis*, Oxford: Osprey, 2012.

————. *Operation Cobra 1944: The Breakout from Normandy*, Oxford: Osprey, 2001.

————. *Operation Dragoon 1944: France's Second D-Day*, Oxford: Osprey, 2009.

————. *Operation Market Garden: The American Airborne Missions*, Oxford: Osprey, 2014.

————. *Panzer IV vs. M4A1 Sherman: France 1944*, Oxford: Osprey, 2014.

————. *Sherman vs. Panther: Battle of the Bulge*, Oxford: Osprey, 2008.

————. *Siegfried Line 1944: Battles on the German Frontier*, Oxford: Osprey, 2007.

————. *US Armored Divisions in the ETO 1944–45*, Oxford: Osprey, 2004.

————. *US Army Tank Crewman in the ETO 1944–45*, Oxford: Osprey, 2004.

————. *US Tank and Tank Destroyer Battalions in the ETO, 1944–45*, Oxford: Osprey, 2005.

Niklas Zetterling, *Normandy 1944: German Military Organization, Combat Power and Organizational Effectiveness*, Winnipeg: Federowicz, 2000.

n/a, *La 2e DB Général Leclerc: Combattants et combats en France*, Paris: Arts et Métiers Graphiques, 1945.

The Commanders

This appendix provides a brief synopsis of the "dramatis personae" of the Arracourt battle in the final months of 1944.

AMERICAN COMMANDERS

Gen. George S. Patton Jr.[197]

Third U.S. Army

Lt. Gen. George S. Patton Jr., commander of the Third U.S. Army.

Lt. Gen. George S. Patton was one of the most famous American commanders of the Second World War both for his military accomplishments and his colorful personality. George Smith Patton Jr. was born on 11 November 1885. He lived a comfortable childhood as the pampered son of a wealthy California land-owning family. Patton's father had hoped to follow in the heroic footsteps of the original Col. George S. Patton, who led the 22nd Virginia during the Battle of the New Market on May 15, 1864, during the Civil War. Colonel Patton was mortally wounded at the age of thirty-one during the fighting near Winchester on September 19, 1864, while leading the Patton Brigade against Gen. Philip Sheridan's Union cavalry. George S. Patton Jr. learned to ride horses on the same saddle on which his grandfather and namesake had been mortally wounded at Winchester, and, not surprisingly, he craved an army career in the cavalry.

He entered West Point in 1904, and after he was commissioned, he was assigned to the cavalry at Fort Sheridan in 1909. In 1912, Patton became the first army officer to represent the United States at the new pentathlon event at the Fifth Olympiad in Stockholm. An offshoot of the Olympics was a brief course in swordsmanship with Adjutant M. Cléry, master of arms and fencing instructor at France's legendary Saumur cavalry school. Patton assisted in the ordnance design of the M-1913 saber, popularly called the Patton sword. In June 1913, the army granted Patton authorization to attend the Saumur cavalry school at his own expense to further study swordsmanship. Patton used the opportunity in the summer of 1913 to travel by auto from the port of Cherbourg through Normandy's bocage country to Saumur in the Loire valley. It was his first contact with the terrain where he would secure his great victories three decades later. On return from France, Patton was assigned to Fort Riley, Kansas, home of the army's Mounted Service School, where he served as "Master of the Sword."

Patton's first combat experience took place along the Mexican border after he volunteered to serve in Gen. John "Black Jack" Pershing's punitive expedition against Pancho Villa. This was also his introduction to mechanized combat. Patton staged a raid to capture the commander of Villa's bodyguards, "General" Julio Cárdenas. Deployed in three Dodge touring cars, Patton's raiding party sped to Cárdenas' suspected hiding place, leading to a chaotic gun battle in which Cárdenas was killed. Patton was celebrated in the press as the "Bandit Killer" even though it was not clear whether Patton had hit or killed any of Villa's men. Regardless of his personal marksmanship, Patton's bravery and initiative had been at the core of the successful raid, and Patton received his first promotion to first lieutenant shortly after.

Due to his contact with Pershing in Mexico, the young officer was stationed with the American Expeditionary Force (AEF) headquarters in France in 1917. After a frustrating spell at a desk job, a sympathetic staff officer told the impatient young Patton that "we want to start a tank school and to get anything out of tanks one must be reckless and to take risks. I think you are the sort of darned fool who will do it." Patton led the formation of the first U.S. Army tank units and led them into combat during the St. Mihiel offensive in September 1918. He was wounded in action during the Meuse-Argonne offensive in late September 1918 as is recounted in more detail in appendix 2.

On returning to the United States after the war, Patton was assigned to the new Tank Corps center at Camp Meade, Maryland. His new neighbor at Camp Meade in 1919 was Lt. Col. Dwight Eisenhower, who had led the tank training center at Camp Colt, Pennsylvania, during the war. Eisenhower was five years younger than Patton, West Point class of 1915, but both were ardent supporters of the tank and students of military doctrine. The friendship established at Camp Meade would have critical consequences two decades later. The U.S. Army was rapidly demobilized after the war and trimmed back to a skeleton force. The Tank Corps was disbanded and absorbed into the infantry. Patton chose to

return to the cavalry and was assigned to Fort Myer and the 3rd Cavalry as a major. He was ambitious, and in spite of his reputation as the army's foremost tank expert, he gave up any visionary role in the Army's mechanization debate, realizing the harm it would cause to his career in the very conservative cavalry branch.

At the start of the war in Europe in September 1939, Patton was again at Fort Myers near Washington with the new army chief of staff, George C. Marshall, temporarily sharing the Patton quarters. Marshall kept a "little black book" to keep track of promising officers who could serve as future army leaders. About Patton, he bluntly noted: "George will take a unit through hell and high water . . . but keep a tight rope around his neck . . . give him an armored corps when one becomes available." The spring maneuvers of 1940 and the defeat of France in May–June 1940 convinced Patton that the days of his beloved horse cavalry were over. When the Armored Force was formed in July 1940, Patton was passed over for divisional command, but he was given his first star and a brigade command in the newly formed 2nd Armored Division at Fort Benning in July 1940. Divisional command of the 2nd Armored Division soon followed. Patton displayed a penchant for bold maneuvers during the November 1941 war games in the Carolinas, and he won praise for his superior leadership. Shortly after America was dragged into the war in December 1941, Patton was again promoted to lead the I Armored Corps at Fort Benning. One of Patton's most important contributions to the U.S. Army was his role in establishing a realistic training regime at the Desert Training Center in the Mojave Desert in California. This facility eventually evolved into the contemporary U.S. Army National Training Center.

While still serving as commander of the I Armored Corps, in the autumn of 1942, Patton was assigned to command the Western Task Force in Operation Torch, leading the amphibious landing near Casablanca. Patton's assignment was due both to Marshall's assessment of him after the Carolina war games as well as his long-standing friendship with Dwight Eisenhower, who had become Marshall's right-hand man. The I Armored Corps in Morocco included the 2nd Armored Division and a number of separate tank battalions. After the landings, Patton's corps was left far from the battlefront in part due to the lack of logistics to support it in Tunisia, and in part due to the need to retain a strategic reserve opposite Gibraltar and Spanish Morocco in case Germany forged an alliance, voluntary or otherwise, with Spain in the wake of occupying the rest of France. There was some concern that Hitler would push his forces along the Spanish coast and then in to Spanish Morocco behind Allied lines as a bold counter to the Allied landings in North Africa. Patton's force was a counterweight to such an adventure. Patton played an important diplomatic role in converting the French army in North Africa into a valuable ally.

While Patton's I Armored Corps was pulling guard duty in Algeria and Morocco, the II Corps was heavily involved in combat farther to the east. The Kasserine Pass debacle in Tunisia in February 1943 was largely attributed to poor senior leadership, and Patton was transferred to lead the dispirited II Corps, helping to rejuvenate the inexperienced and poorly led U.S. forces in the 1943 spring offensives. He helped redeem the honor of the U.S. Army with its first tactical victory against the Wehrmacht at El Guettar in March 1943. Patton led II Corps in the final campaigns in Tunisia and was pulled out of II Corps command shortly before the conclusion of the Tunisian campaign in order to prepare the Seventh U.S. Army for Operation Husky, the amphibious assault on Sicily in July 1943. Even though the U.S. Army was assigned a secondary role in the offensive actions on Sicily, Patton's aggressive determination pushed the U.S. units to Palermo, setting the stage for the concluding capture of Messina after the neighboring British advance bogged down. Patton's fortunes ebbed in late 1943 as the result of his rash behavior when it became public that he had slapped two shell-shocked soldiers. This scandal nearly derailed Patton's career, but Eisenhower valued Patton's talents and saved him from premature retirement. Patton's meteoric rise had come to an end. He was superseded by the younger Omar Bradley, who went on to lead the First U.S. Army in Normandy in June 1944 and the expanded 12th Army Group in August 1944. Patton became trapped at the level of field army commander.

Patton was still a very prominent figure, and so after transfer to Britain, he played a central role in the Allied deception schemes, leading the fictional First Army Group. In spite of the slapping incident on Sicily, Marshall and Eisenhower knew that they needed a bold cavalryman like Patton for tasks ahead in France. His real mission was to command the Third U.S. Army (TUSA). This was the second of the American field armies to enter battle in France in 1944. The first elements of the Third U.S. Army to see combat took part in the opening phase of Operation Cobra, the breakout from Normandy, in late July 1944. Patton formally took command of the Third U.S. Army in France in August 1944.

The Third U.S. Army pushed out of Normandy towards Avranches on the right flank of the First U.S. Army. The Third U.S. Army's mission was part of the original Overlord plans to expand the lodgment area westward towards Brittany. The ultimate objective was to secure additional ports in Brittany, notably in the Quiberon Bay area and the port of Brest, to assist in the Allied logistics buildup. In spite of the spectacular advance, Patton was unsettled by the conduct of the Brittany campaign and began to question its strategic objectives. If Brittany was an irrelevant objective, Patton at the same time sensed the real opportunity. The German 7.Armee was trapped and on the run after Cobra, and there was a void in German defenses on the approaches to the Seine River and Paris. A rapid rush to the Seine River could help bag German forces in a deep envelopment, while at the same time securing the Normandy lodgment area months earlier than anticipated. Patton argued his case with Bradley and Eisenhower and won Montgomery's support as well.

The reorientation east was authorized on August 3. Patton's forces raced eastward against weak German resistance. The tactical situation was a case study for cavalry exploitation, and Patton's bold and risky tactical style was ideally suited to exploit it. Patton urged on his motorized and mechanized spearheads and told them to ignore their flanks. The Wehrmacht attempted to shift elements of the 1.Armee from the Atlantic coast to block Patton, but Patton's forces were simply much faster. The cities west of Paris fell in rapid succession, including the cathedral cities of Chartres and Orleans, and Paris itself beckoned. In spite of the role of Patton's Third U.S. Army in clearing the way to Paris, the task was handed over to the V Corps of the First U.S. Army. Patton's Third U.S. Army headed south of Paris towards the Meuse-Argonne region where he had first led U.S. tanks troops in 1918. This culminated in the campaign on the Moselle and into Lorraine as described previously in this book.

Patton was arguably the most effective field army commander in the U.S. Army in the European Theater of Operations. He was highly regarded by his subordinate commanders. Col. Bruce Clarke, commander of CCA, 4th Armored Division at Arracourt, later described his leadership style:

> Georgie was a character that would take chances. He would command by mission-type orders. If he had confidence in people, he just told them what he wanted to do, and then left them alone. . . . He was an impetuous fellow. His impetuosity got the better of his judgment from time to time, and we who worked for him, used to be able to recognize that and govern ourselves accordingly. . . . But Patton caught the imagination of his people and the imagination of his soldiers, and they all believed in him. You have to believe in a winner.[198]

The popular perception of Patton has largely ignored his battlefield success in Lorraine in September 1944; it is hardly mentioned at all in the popular film *Patton*. The Third U.S. Army was largely inactive in October 1944 due to the supply crisis, and Patton's next offensive did not take place until November 1944. Operation Madison was intended to overcome the fortified region around Metz in the northern sector of the Third U.S. Army and to push forward to the Siegfried Line/Westwall. Patton's campaign in the late autumn of 1944 is often described as his least successful venture. In contrast to the brilliant summer advances, the October, November, and early December fighting was a series of exasperating and brutish skirmishes to finally overcome the Metz fortified zone. However, the campaign barely reached the Westwall

by the time the Ardennes offensive intervened. Patton's frustrations in Lorraine were evident in his jeremiad: "I hope that in the final settlement of the war, the Germans retain Lorraine. I can imagine no greater burden than to be the owner of this nasty country where it rains every day and where the whole wealth of the people consists in assorted manure piles."

Operation Madison began on 8–9 November.[199] Metz did not finally fall until November 22, and the outlying forts held out until December 13, when their defenders faced starvation. Ever the military history buff, Patton reminded his staff that "it was the first time in over four hundred years that the Fortress city [of Metz] had been taken by assault."

The Third U.S. Army claimed to have inflicted 152,000 casualties on Heeresgruppe G in the October–December battles, at a cost of 36,800 of its own casualties. The territorial gains were not particularly impressive compared to the summer battles, with the Third U.S. Army advancing to a depth of about thirty miles (fifty kilometers) in the November–December attacks. The most important consequence of the autumn 1944 fighting was the savage beating that the Third U.S. Army inflicted on the German 1.Armee, as will be explained in a moment.

As Patton's Third U.S. Army began to approach the Saar region of German in mid-December, Patton's intelligence chief, Oscar Koch, noticed the ominous buildup of German forces in the Eifel region north of their objective. Bradley and the other senior commanders dismissed this buildup as a preparation for an eventual counterattack against Allied forces once they reached the Rhine in early 1945. Patton thought this was a foolish presumption and told his planner to create several contingency operations in the event that the Germans attacked in December 1944.

As Patton had predicted, the German buildup was the prelude for the Ardennes offensive, which started on 16 December 1944 against the First U.S. Army. Eisenhower badly needed reinforcements, and at a hasty meeting of senior American commanders at Verdun, Patton exclaimed in his usual colorful fashion that "The Kraut's stuck his head in a meat-grinder and this time I've got a hold of the handle." Patton's optimistic viewpoint was based on two critical factors. The Third U.S. Army had beaten up the 1.Armee so badly that it posed little threat in the Third U.S. Army sector. Secondly, Patton had already shown the foresight to prepare contingency plans to counterattack a German thrust out of the Eifel. Amid the gloom and chill of the Verdun meeting, Patton's boisterous presentation stood out for its brevity and prescience. Eisenhower, who had just been elevated to the rank of General of the Army, remarked to Patton, "Every time I get a new star, I get attacked," to which Patton replied, "And every time you get attacked, I pull you out," a reference to his role in saving Eisenhower's reputation in Tunisia.

Two of Patton's three corps were committed to the Ardennes, and Patch's Seventh U.S. Army to the south was obliged to extend northward to cover Patton's sector in the Saar. As Patton promised Eisenhower, the attacks began in the late afternoon of December 21. The spearhead of the Third U.S. Army drive was Milliken's III Corps. It quickly advanced more than 100 miles, led by Patton's favorite, the 4th Armored Division with the 26th and 80th Infantry Divisions providing the muscle. A task force from Abrams' 37th Tank Battalion, 4th Armored Division pushed into Bastogne on December 26, and it took several more days of intense fighting to create a solid corridor for relief columns to arrive. The remarkable drive by the Third U.S. Army in the Ardennes campaign was its most brilliant moment in the campaign in Europe.

Following the Ardennes fighting, the campaigns along the German border were slow going due to both the weather and the tenacious German defense. Bradley wanted Patton's Third Army on the defensive while the First and Ninth U.S. Armies pushed over the Roer in February 1945. Instead, Patton concocted an "active defense" to take the city of Trier using a minimum of forces. He bitterly noted "I wonder if ever before in the history of war, a winning general had to plead to be allowed to keep on winning." Patton's restless aggressiveness helped the Third U.S. Army exploit the growing weakness of the Wehrmacht. The Third U.S. Army began an offensive to clear the Palatinate on 12 March 1945, as part of a broader Allied offensive

to reach the Rhine. Given the very weak state of the opposing German forces, this culminated in the "Rhine Rat Race." Although the German resistance had been stubborn on the first day of the Third U.S. Army offensive, within a couple of days, both of Patton's corps were advancing against crumbling resistance. The attack built up so much momentum that Eisenhower gave Patton another armored division, the 12th Armored Division from the neighboring Seventh U.S. Army, to bolster the attack. The 4th Armored Division raced forty-eight miles in two days, reaching the banks of the Rhine near Worms, presaging the total collapse of German defense in the Saar-Palatinate triangle in a short one-week campaign.

Patton craved a Rhine crossing of his own, all the better if accomplished before Montgomery's elephantine Operation Plunder/Varsity Rhine River crossing, the largest Allied operation since D-Day. He planned to leap the Rhine on the run without major preparation, crossed near Oppenheim on the night of March 22. Patton phoned Bradley: "Brad, we're across!" A muffled exclamation on the other line, "Across what, George?" "The Rhine . . . and you can tell the world Third Army made it before Monty."

Even in triumph, Patton continued to display a penchant for getting into trouble. In late March, Patton learned that his son-in-law, Lt. Col. John Waters, who had been captured during the 1st Armored Division's disastrous combat actions at Kasserine Pass, was probably in the Oflag XIIIB prisoner camp in Hammelburg, about forty miles behind German lines. Feigning ignorance of Waters presence, Patton ordered the 4th Armored Division to send a task force to liberate the camp. Task Force Baum from the 37th Tank Battalion set off on the night of March 26 and did manage to reach the camp and liberate the prisoners. However, the small task force could only carry about 250 of the 5,000 prisoners, and three Wehrmacht divisions quickly closed in on the small force and crushed it. The survivors were rounded up and put back in the Hammelburg camp. The raid had been a pointless waste of men, and in any event, the camp was liberated hardly a week later by the 14th Armored Division from the neighboring Seventh U.S. Army. Although roundly criticized for the raid, Patton was spared from any official recriminations due to the attention focused on the death of President Franklin Roosevelt on 12 April 1945.

Patton's subsequent advance through southern Germany was so rapid that Eisenhower instructed Patton to continue east. The Third U.S. Army reached the Czech border on May 4, and Patton asked permission to liberate Prague. Eisenhower consented to an advance as far as Plzen (Pilsen), but Bradley had to restrain him from moving any farther east due to previous agreements with the Red Army.

Following the conclusion of the war, the Third U.S. Army was garrisoned in Bavaria, and Patton was assigned the task of military governor. It was a task for which he was ill-suited. His trusted staff gradually faded away as they returned to the United States or to other army assignments. Patton's anti-Soviet attitudes, a string of anti-Semitic remarks relating to the refugees in the displaced-persons camps, and an apparent toleration for Nazis in the local Bavarian government all brought unfavorable press attention. In September 1945, Eisenhower relieved Patton of the Third U.S. Army command, sending him instead to the backwater of Fifteenth U.S. Army in Bad Neuheim. On December 9, 1945, Patton took a short trip with a new driver towards Mannheim, and shortly before noon, his 1939 Cadillac had a collision with an army truck at a speed of about thirty miles per hour. Patton was in the back seat and was thrown forward, causing head injuries and snapping his neck. Patton lingered in the hospital for twelve days before finally dying on December 21, 1945. He was buried alongside other Third U.S. Army soldiers in the Hamm military cemetery near Luxembourg City in the Ardennes on Christmas Eve, a year after the battle that made him so famous.

Maj. Gen. Manton S. Eddy[200]

XII Corps

Maj. Gen. Manton S. Eddy was a considerable contrast to Patton, a cautious infantryman to the bone. He had been commissioned in the army in 1916 from a small military academy and not West Point, served in infantry units in World War I, and after the war served in a variety of posts including as a tactics instructor at the Command and General

Maj. Gen. Manton Eddy, commander of XII Corps.

Staff School. Compared to other corps commanders, he had not been groomed for higher command and had not attended the Army War College.

At the beginning of the war, he was an infantry regiment commander, and during the Tunisia campaign, he commanded the 9th Infantry Division. Although the division got off to a rocky start, Eddy soon developed a reputation as a solid commander and came to Patton's attention for his actions both in Tunisia and Sicily. Eddy was transferred to head XII Corps on 19 August 1944 when Maj. Gen. Gilbert "Doc" Cook was relieved for medical reasons. Under Eddy's command, the corps became known as "the Spearhead of Patton's Third Army." It tended to be an armor-heavy formation, including both the 4th and 6th Armored Divisions, during most of the summer and autumn campaigns. During the explosive breakout from Normandy, it was XII Corps that raced to the Seine. Eddy found Patton's daring tactical style a bit uncomfortable. In Normandy, his infantry division had been bitterly battling their way through the hedgerows yards at a time; a mile a day was good progress. When given command of XII Corps, Patton told him his day's objective was fifty miles behind German lines. He was uneasy about advancing so far, so fast with exposed flanks, but Patton told him to ignore the flanks. Unaccustomed to bold cavalry tactics carried out by armored divisions, Eddy soon came to trust

Patton's judgments and to accommodate himself to the new style of war. Nevertheless, his infantryman's perspective would cause tensions with both Patton and his subordinate armored division commanders, most notably with John "Tiger Jack" Wood of the 4th Armored Division. Eddy was well liked by his troops; the legendary journalist Ernie Pyle dubbed him "Old Shoe."

Maj. Gen. Wade Haislip
XV Corps

Maj. Gen. Wade Haislip, commander of XV Corps.

Wade Haislip was born on 9 July 1889, and he graduated from the U.S. Military Academy at West Point in 1912. He served in the Great War as a young officer, taking part in the battles at St. Mihiel and the Meuse-Argonne. He had a steady rise through the interwar years, attending a variety of staff schools and eventually serving as an instructor at the Command and General Staff School from 1932 to 1936. He was the army's assistant chief of staff for personnel immediately before the U.S. entry into World War II. Following the outbreak of the war, he organized the 85th Infantry Division. He took command of XV Corps in 1943 and led it through Normandy, France, Rhineland, and Central Europe campaigns. He became commander of the Seventh U.S. Army in 1945. He retired from the army in 1951, serving for many years as governor

of the Soldier's Home in Washington, D.C., and he died in 1971.

Maj. Gen. Walton Walker[201]
XX Corps

Maj. Gen. Walton Walker, commander of XX Corps.

Maj. Gen. Walton Walker, commander of XX Corps, was much closer in temperament to Patton. He was nicknamed "Johnnie," as in Johnnie Walker scotch, or "Bulldog," due to his fierce pug appearance. Patton dubbed him "my fightingest son-of-a-bitch." Walker was a graduate of West Point, class of 1912, and served on the Mexican border in 1916. He was decorated with the Silver Star for gallantry as an infantry officer in France in 1918. During the interwar years, he served in a variety of infantry posts, but when the Armored Force was formed in 1940, Walker lobbied Marshall for a transfer to the new branch. He became commander of the 3rd Armored Division in 1942 and later took over the IV Armored Corps, which was redesignated as XX Corps in October 1943. Like Patton, he was an energetic, hands-on commander who could usually be found speeding around the front lines by jeep to prod his divisional commanders forward. The XX Corps became nicknamed "the Ghost Corps" after a German prisoner of war called Walker's corps by that name in an interrogation because the corps had moved so fast and so often that the Wehrmacht had been unable to keep track of them.

Walker commanded the Eighth U.S. Army during the Korean War, and in a curious parallel to Patton, he was killed in a traffic accident on 23 December 1950.

Maj. Gen. Raymond McLain
90th Infantry Division

Maj. Gen. Raymond McLain, commander of the 90th "Tough 'Ombres" Infantry Division.

Maj. Gen. Raymond McLain was a banker and National Guardsman from Oklahoma. He had served in the Mexican expedition against Pancho Villa in 1917 and with the American Expeditionary Force in France in 1918. It was unusual for National Guard officers to receive divisional command in the ETO, and a testament to McLain's previous achievements in the Mediterranean theater, where he commanded the artillery of the 45th Infantry Division. His leadership turned the division around and helped to resurrect the 90th Division's dim reputation. It eventually became one of the best divisions in Patton's Third U.S. Army. McLain's leadership in the autumn 1944 fighting was so superior that he was elevated to command the XIX Corps in October 1944, the only National Guard general to lead a U.S. Army corps in the ETO in World War II.

Maj. Gen. John S. Wood[202]

Maj. Gen. John S. Wood, commander of the 4th Armored Division.

Of the significant U.S. Army commanders of World War II, John "Tiger Jack" Wood has faded into total obscurity. He was regarded at the time as "America's Rommel" and was widely viewed as America's most successful tank commander.

John S. Wood was born in Arkansas on 11 January 1888 and graduated from the University of Arkansas in 1907. He subsequently attended the U.S. Military Academy at West Point, graduating in 1912. Wood received his first nickname, "P" for "professor," at West Point after tutoring many classmates in chemistry, his chosen field. Wood became a second lieutenant in the Coast Artillery on 12 June 1912 and served as an assistant football coach and chemistry instructor at West Point prior to World War I. He served with the 3rd Division and 90th Division in France in 1918, including the battles of Château-Thierry and St. Mihiel. Wood attended the French staff school at Langres, where his classmates included George S. Patton, William Simpson (Ninth U.S. Army), and Alexander Patch (Seventh U.S. Army).

He steadily rose through the ranks during the interwar years, and from September 1939 to 1940, he served as chief of staff of the Third U.S. Army. In April 1941, he took over command of the 2nd Armored Division from George Patton, served as chief of staff of the I Armored Corps under Patton for several months, and took command of the 4th Armored Division in May 1942.

The division deployed to former British army garrisons in Wiltshire near the Avebury and Salisbury plains in early 1944. In February 1944, the division was assigned to Patton's newly formed Third U.S. Army. Under Wood's command, the 4th Armored Division saw its combat debut in late July 1944 during Operation Cobra. The division raced into Brittany with an aim to secure additional ports for the Allies. Wood quickly became convinced that it was a fruitless mission for an armored division. In view of the impending defeat of the German army in France, he convinced Patton to swing the Third U.S. Army around and head for Paris. Patton appreciated the boldness of this scheme, and Eisenhower agreed in early August. As a result, the 4th Armored Division became the spearhead of Patton's Third U.S. Army during the race for the Seine River in August 1944.

Wood had the unhappy fate of being subordinate to Manton Eddy, the commander of XII Corps. Eddy was six years younger than Wood, and Wood was somewhat resentful that he had not been selected for corps command. Three of Wood's classmates at the Langres staff school in 1918 were already field army commanders: Patton, Patch, and Simpson. The gulf that separated Wood and Eddy was not only age, but military temperament. Wood was an aggressive commander, favoring bold attacks. Eddy was a cautious and stodgy infantryman. Patton was often critical of Eddy's slow and deliberate pace, but he had little control over the choice of corps commanders serving under him.

Wood became most frustrated with Eddy during the grim and costly fighting in Lorraine in late November and early December 1944. The exceptionally wet November weather greatly complicated mobile operations. The farm fields became flooded and tanks were forced to travel along the rural roads. The Germans were able to exploit these weather conditions since the limited road network channeled operations in predictable directions. Each crossroad could be defended by a handful of antitank guns, and each little farm village could be converted into an impromptu fortress. The soggy soil created "a front one tank wide." Casualties

quickly mounted, and the 4th Armored Division lost many of its experienced junior officers. Eddy sent both the 4th and the 6th Armored Divisions along narrow axes of attack, euphemistically called "ice-pick" tactics. General Wood felt it was an atrocious misuse of armor. It is interesting to note that the German commanders facing Patton's Third U.S. Army also thought that Eddy's XII Corps was making poor use of its armored divisions.

Wood, bitter and depressed, openly criticized Eddy in the presence of junior officers. Col. Bruce Clarke later recalled an incident during October when he was in Wood's tent when Eddy arrived for a consultation. Eddy reminded Wood that he had asked for his plan for the advance to the Saar. Wood accused him of misusing the division and refused to offer a plan. Clarke was deeply embarrassed by the outburst and helped calm the situation for the time being. However, Clarke was transferred to the 7th Armored Division later in November, and his function as mediator between Wood and Eddy abruptly ended. The final straw came in early December when the commander of the 10th Armored Infantry Battalion, Col. Art West, was badly wounded in combat. In another outburst, Wood blamed Eddy for West's fate due to the poor tactical plan selected by his headquarters. By this stage, Eddy realized he could no longer tolerate this continual insubordination. He explained the situation to Patton: "I don't know what's wrong with 'P' Wood but you've either got to relieve him or me." As in the case of the Patton-Bradley relationship, the older and more experienced tanker did not see eye to eye with the younger and less adventurous infantryman.

Wood was so highly regarded because of the exemplary performance of the 4th Armored Division that Patton spoke with Eisenhower before taking any action. Eisenhower agreed that Wood would have to be relieved, ostensibly for "medical reasons." The 4th Armored Division had been the spearhead of the Third U.S. Army for the summer and autumn, and it was so important that Patton assigned his own executive officer, Maj. Gen. Hugh Gaffey, to take over command of the division at the start of December 1944. For "P" Wood, it was a sad end to a short but spectacular combat career.[203]

Wood returned to the United States and ended his military career in 1946 as the commander of the Armor Replacement Training Center (ARTC) at Fort Knox, Kentucky. After retiring from the army, Wood served as Chief of Mission for the International Refugee Organization in Austria for the United Nations in 1947–1952, and Chief of Mission for the United Nations Reconstruction Administration in Tokyo, South Korea, and Geneva in 1952–1953. He died on 2 July 1966.

Col. Bruce C. Clarke[204]

Combat Command A, 4th Armored Division

Col. Bruce C. Clarke, commander of Combat Command A, 4th Armored Division.

Bruce C. Clarke was born on 29 April 1901 and dropped out of high school to enlist in the army in 1917, serving in the Coast Artillery Corps. He attended the U.S. Military Academy and received his commission in the Corps of Engineers in 1925, also graduating with a civil engineer degree from Cornell University in 1927. He is credited with starting the Non-Commissioned Officers Academy system. After numerous postings in the Engineers in the 1920s and 1930s, he attended the U.S. Army Command and General Staff school at Fort Leavenworth, Kansas, in 1939. After his graduation in 1940, he was assigned to Fort Knox, Kentucky, where he organized and commanded the

16th Engineer Battalion, the army's first armored engineer unit. In December 1940, he was sent to England as a military observer. Upon his return to the United States, Major Clarke was assigned to organize and command the 24th Engineer Battalion of the 4th Armored Division while it was being activated at Pine Camp, New York. He was instrumental in the development of the treadway bridge, widely used by mechanized forces in World War II. On 24 December 1941, he rose to lieutenant colonel, and he became the chief of staff of the 4th Armored Division in early 1942. He was assigned to lead the division's Combat Command A on 1 November 1943.

Like John "P" Wood, Clarke was a very aggressive commander who favored bold mobile operations. Col. Hal Pattison, executive officer of CCA, 4th Armored Division, called Clarke "the greatest tank tactician in the US Army." He was best known in the division for his use of an L-4 Piper Cub liaison aircraft to lead the troops. He liked to fly over the battlefield in the light plane to get a better sense of the terrain.

The superior performance of Combat Command A during the summer campaign convinced Patton that Clarke deserved a general's star. During the lull in the Lorraine fighting in October 1944, Clarke had a conversation with Patton concerning this matter. Patton began in his usual blunt and profane fashion and blurted out "Clarke, you are a damned nobody!" Taken aback by this seeming rebuke, Clarke asked for an explanation. Apparently, Patton had raised the possibility of Clarke's promotion during a meeting with army chief of staff Gen. George C. Marshall during his recent visit to Patton's headquarters in Nancy. Clarke had already been recommended for promotion to brigadier general three times. Marshall admitted that he ignored previous recommendations, since, as an engineer, Clarke had never come to his attention at the infantry school at Fort Benning. Due to Patton's prodding, Marshall looked into the matter and Clarke was promoted to brigadier general at the end of October 1944.

Patton had been very unhappy about the leadership of the 7th Armored Division when it served under the Third U.S. Army around Metz in early September 1944. Bradley agreed, and the newly promoted Clarke was taken from the 4th Armored Division and sent to command Combat Command B of the 7th Armored Division as part of a broader shake-up of its senior leadership. This would prove to be fortuitous a month later when Clarke played the central role in the defense of St. Vith in the opening phase of the Battle of the Bulge, one of the key defensive actions at the start of the Ardennes campaign.

Clarke returned to the 4th Armored Division at the end of the war as its new divisional commander. During the Cold War years, Clarke went on to a series of higher commands at corps, army, and eventually U.S. Army Europe and the Central Army Group of NATO.

Lt. Col. Creighton Abrams[205]

37th Tank Battalion, 4th Armored Division

Lt. Col. Creighton Abrams, commander of the 37th Tank Battalion, 4th Armored Division.

Creighton Abrams was born on 15 September 1914. Abrams won a scholarship to Brown University, but his family's poverty convinced him to apply for a congressional nomination to the U.S. Military Academy at West Point. Abrams graduated in the class of 1936, an exceptional year at West Point that included Bruce Palmer Jr., William C. Westmoreland, and Benjamin Davis Jr.; five men from the class later became four-star generals. Abrams chose the cavalry as his branch of service and served with the 7th Cavalry in Fort Bliss, Texas. Following the formation of the Armored Force in 1940, Abrams followed in the footsteps of other cavalrymen such as Adna Chaffeee and George

Patton, and he was assigned to the embryonic 1st Armored Division. In April 1941, Abrams was transferred as part of a new cadre to create the 4th Armored Division at Pine Camp, New York, and he became the regimental adjutant of the division's 37th Armored Regiment.

Abrams was assigned to command the 3rd Battalion, 37th Armored Regiment in July 1942. His regimental commander later described him as "the best soldier I ever saw. . . . Abe wasn't flashy a bit, but he was damn well impressive. When he said something, he meant it and that was it." When the 37th Armored Regiment disappeared due to the 1943 divisional reorganization, Maj. Creighton Abrams became commander of the reorganized 37th Tank Battalion. Abrams was particularly insistent on gunnery training, and the 37th Tank Battalion was regarded as the best prepared in the division. This would manifest in the Arracourt tank battles.

Abrams led the battalion from his tank, an M4 named "Thunderbolt" after the Armored Force emblem. He was not an officer who led from the rear. He could be seen in the thick of the fight, standing in the hatch of his tank, chomping on a cigar, barking instructions over his radio. One soldier later recalled, "Abrams could inspire aggressiveness in a begonia."

When Bruce Clarke left the 4th Armored Division at the end of October 1944, Clarke recommended that Abrams take over CCA. Clarke understood the importance of the CCA to the division and warned Wood that if he passed over Abrams for one of the redundant colonels in the division, that Wood "would be gone in a month." Wood chose one of his cronies to lead CCA, and Wood was gone by the beginning of December. Abrams remained in command of the 37th Tank Battalion, but he frequently took over temporary command of CCA and CCB. He was formally assigned to the command of CCB on 8 March 1945.

By the end of the war, the thirty-one-year-old Abrams had won the Distinguished Service Cross twice, two Silver Stars, a Bronze Star for valor, and the Legion of Merit. Patton remarked to a divisional commander, "I'm supposed to be the best tank commander in the Army, but I have one peer—Abe Abrams. He's the world's champion." When later told of this, Abrams barked, "He never said that to me—and he had plenty of chances!"

During the Korean War, he served as a corps chief of staff, and on return to the United States, he was appointed chief of staff of the Armor School at Fort Knox. After a tour in the Pentagon, he was promoted to brigadier general in 1959, serving as the assistant commander of the 3rd Armored Division in Germany, and then divisional commander at the time of the 1961 Berlin crisis. Abrams received considerable press attention at this time and, due to his tanker's background, inevitable comparisons to Patton. His former commander, Bruce Clarke, told one reporter that "there's no question that Abrams is smarter, cooler, and more stable than Patton—and equally, fiercely aggressive." He appeared on the cover of *Time* magazine as America's No. 1 soldier. Abrams served as assistant deputy chief of staff for civil affairs in 1962—an especially difficult job due to the army's politically charged role in the government's desegregation programs in the South. He received his third star as V Corps commander in Europe.

In 1967, Abrams became the deputy commander of U.S. forces in Vietnam, the secretary of defense noting that he was an officer who had demonstrated "the capacity for dealing objectively with matters of the broadest significance for national security," and was soon deputy commander of U.S. forces in Vietnam. On 16 October 1972, he was appointed to the army's highest post, becoming army chief of staff. He was a stabilizing force in an army demoralized by the Vietnam War, and, unfortunately for the army, his career was cut short by cancer, with him dying on 4 September 1974 at age sixty. His reputation as one of the U.S. Army's premier tankers led to the decision to name the new M1 main battle tank after him when it was accepted for service in the 1980s.

FRENCH COMMANDERS

Gen. Jacques Leclerc[206]

French 2nd Armored Division
(2e Division Blindée)

Jacques Leclerc was the only foreign general under Patton's command in Lorraine, and one of his most

Commander of the French 2e DB was Gen. Jacques Leclerc. He is seen here on 23 August 1944 when the 2e DB spearheaded the liberation of Paris. Behind him is his aide Captain Girard, and to his side is Lieutenant Colonel Repiton-Préneuf, head of the division's headquarters staff.

remarkable divisional commanders. A detailed look at his career also helps to explain the performance of his "2e DB" at the battle of Dompaire.

Leclerc was not his actual name, but rather his wartime pseudonym. He was born Philippe François Marie, Vicomte de Hautecloque. As his name suggests, he inherited the aristocratic "Viscount" title from his aristocratic family connections. Like many French gentry families, the Hautecloques had a long tradition of military service going back to the Fifth Crusade. Leclerc entered French military service through the elite Saint Cyr academy and Saumur cavalry school, being commissioned as a young cavalry officer in 1925. Like other ambitious young French officers, particularly those who had not served in the Great War, the best path for advancement was combat service. This inevitably meant tours of duty in France's restive North African colonies. In the 1920s, he served in local pacification campaigns in the North African colonies, especially in Morocco. His combat experiences and superior performance in North Africa won him a prestigious teaching post at the Saint Cyr academy, but he quickly tired of the dull routine of peacetime garrison life and during summer vacation in 1933 he returned to the Atlas Mountains in Morocco for what he called "un petite folie"—a little madness. This French colony had been roiled through most of the 1920s by a revolt of the hill tribes. He spent the summer fighting in the mountains and was recommended for the Croix de Guerre for his leadership of an irregular partisan formation during the fighting. The award was delayed by senior officers who did not appreciate his "excessive zeal." In 1938, he was appointed to France's main staff college, the École Supérieure de Guerre. War broke out before he completed his studies.

During the 1940 campaign, he served as a captain on the headquarters staff of the 4e Division d'Infanterie, and he escaped rather than surrender. After hearing one of Gen. Charles De Gaulle's radio broadcasts calling for French patriots to rally to his cause in England, Hautecloque managed to reach London via Spain. He was an odd man out among De Gaulle's officers, who were mostly army reservists. Most professional French officers with aristocratic backgrounds had remained in France and supported Marshal Philippe Petain's collaborationist Vichy government. Hautecloque adopted the wartime pseudonym of Jacques Leclerc to protect his wife and children, who were still in France.

To add political legitimacy to his cause, De Gaulle was attempting to bring the French colonies in equatorial Africa under his Free French movement. He needed brave and adventurous officers to carry out these missions, and Leclerc was selected to stage a coup in Cameroon. His main force was a company of Senegalese colonial troops. Not especially keen to sacrifice their lives for an upstart French officer from London, they deserted before reaching the objective. Nevertheless, Leclerc and two dozen French soldiers managed to reach the capitol of Douala by canoe with British assistance. Leclerc proclaimed himself military governor in the name of De Gaulle's Free French government. The coup succeeded when the commander of the city's garrison, Capt. Louis Dio, sided with him.

Leclerc's next assignment was to seize control of neighboring Gabon, which had opted to side with Petain's government. The military campaign lasted a month and was the culmination of De Gaulle's seizure of the French equatorial African colonies. In view of his remarkable successes with minimal resources, Leclerc received his most difficult assignment from De Gaulle, the seizure of the desert colony of Chad. Unlike the equatorial colonies that were defended by Vichy French forces, Chad was under Italian occupation. The main Italian army garrison was located in the fortress town of Kufra. Leclerc's force consisted of 100 French and 200 African troops and a motley selection of about a hundred trucks and vehicles. On 31 January 1941, the column set off on a journey of nearly 1,000 miles across the Sahara Desert, and it began trickling into the Kufra area on 17 February. After fighting off an Italian motorized company with air support from Bleheim bombers of the Free French Groupe Lorraine, Leclerc laid siege to the fort. The fort finally surrendered on 1 March 1941. For the next year, Leclerc's mobile patrols staged raids against Italian garrisons farther north, culminating in another epic march across the Sahara in December 1942 to overwhelm the Italian garrisons in the Fezzan region of southwest Libya to support Montgomery's El Alamein offensive. After overwhelming several Italian garrisons, Leclerc's force met the British Eighth Army in mid-February 1942. Renamed "L Force," the French detachment fought in Tunisia, distinguishing itself to the extent that Montgomery honored it as the lead formation in the victory parade in Tunis in 1943.

At the end of the North Africa campaign, L Force served as the seed of the new 2e Division Française Libre (2nd Free French Division), what would become the legendary 2e Division Blindée. In view of Leclerc's loyalty and obvious military talents, De Gaulle promoted him to general and assigned him to train the first new French division in Rabat, Morocco.

The U.S. Army's Operation Torch landings in Morocco and Algeria in November 1942 had resulted in the defection of Vichy French units in North Africa to the Allied side. The U.S. government agreed to provide the equipment and training to create a French field army to take part in a future liberation of France. These units were based on French North African colonial regiments, and they eventually formed the French First Army, which landed on the French Mediterranean coast in August 1944 as part of Operation Dragoon.

Leclerc's relations with senior French commanders of the French First Army training in North Africa were strained. Leclerc made no secret of the fact that he viewed them as opportunists who had collaborated with the Germans until November of 1942. He had been fighting against Vichy French forces in equatorial Africa for more than a year. The other French officers had switched to the Allies only after the U.S. Army seized French North Africa; Leclerc had already been fighting on the Allied side for three years. The commanders of the French First Army returned the scorn and viewed him as a troublesome little upstart captain. Leclerc's 2e DB was based around his desert-raiding groups, and the regimental commands went to officers who had served with him in the 1941–1943 fighting.

Leclerc led the 2e DB in the liberation of Paris in August 1944, the crowning glory of the Free French army. At the end of the Paris campaign, Leclerc requested permission to return to Haislip's XV Corps. To participate in the Paris mission, the 2e DB had been transferred to Maj. Gen. Leonard Gerow's V Corps. Gerow and Leclerc came into conflict over many aspects of the Paris mission. Leclerc was under pressure from De Gaulle regarding the details of the Paris campaign, while Gerow expected Leclerc to strictly follow his directions like any other U.S. Army division in spite of the weighty political dimensions of the liberation of Paris. In any event, Eisenhower intervened and agreed to the return of Leclerc to Haislip's command and to Patton's Third U.S. Army.

Leclerc had far more amicable relations with both Haislip and Patton than with Gerow. Like many U.S. Army officers in World War II, they had both served in France during the Great War and deeply admired the French army for its sacrifices in 1914–1918. Much of the equipment and training of the American Expeditionary Force had come from France. Patton's tank brigade in 1918 was equipped with French Renault FT tanks, and Patton had been taught tank tactics and tank operation by the French. Both Haislip and Patton had received advanced military training in France between the wars and spoke French. Haislip attended the École Supérieure de Guerre in 1925–1927; Patton had attended the Saumur cavalry school in 1913. Both American commanders understood Leclerc's dilemma, divided between his responsibilities to the U.S. Army and his loyalties to France. Aside from a more supportive command arrangement, Leclerc also was keen to serve with Patton's Third U.S. Army in Lorraine. The provinces of Alsace-Lorraine had been taken from France by Germany in the wake of the 1870 France-Prussian War, returned to France in 1918, and then re-absorbed into the Third Reich after France's 1940 defeat. Having liberated Paris in August 1944, Leclerc was keen on participating in the liberation of the Alsatian capital of Strasbourg. This took place under his leadership on 23 November 1944.

Leclerc led the 2e DB through the remainder of the war. In May 1945, after the war in Europe, he was assigned command of the French Far East Expeditionary Corps (*Corps expéditionnaire français en Extrême-Orient*, CEFEO), which soon became embroiled in a colonial war for control of Indochina. He urged a political rather than military settlement and was recalled in 1946. He died in an air crash in Algeria in 1947.

GERMAN COMMANDERS
Col. Gen. Johannes Blaskowitz[207]

Army Group G

Although from East Prussia, Blaskowitz was not from a traditional military family; his father was a Lutheran minister. He served as a young officer in the infantry in the Great War, first on the French front, including Verdun, later in Serbia and Russia, and ended the war as a captain with the Iron Cross first and second class. He remained in the Reichswehr after the war, steadily advancing in rank and becoming a major general in October 1932. He was apolitical but strongly nationalistic, so his career continued to advance after the rise of the Nazis. Gen. Günther Blumentritt later recalled that he was "rigorously just and high-minded . . .

Col. Gen. Johannes Blaskowitz, commander of Army Group G through early September 1944.

with a strong spiritual and religious turn of mind." This would not serve him well with the Nazis. Blaskowitz led the 8.Armee during the invasion of Poland, fighting the most intense battle of the campaign during the Polish counterattack on the Bzura River. In the wake of the campaign, he complained about the atrocities against Poles and Jews by the SS, beginning a long feud with Heinrich Himmler. He remained in Poland as Commander-in-Chief-East through the spring of 1940 but ran afoul of Hitler's governor-general, Hans Frank, who had him removed in May 1940. Hitler dismissed his complaints about SS brutality as "childish ideas," and Blaskowitz was sidetracked to occupation duty in France, commanding the 1.Armee on the Bay of Biscay. Although not favored by the Nazis, he had the support of the Army Group B commander in northern France, General Field Marshal Gerd von Rundstedt, and in May 1944, Blaskowitz was placed in command of Army Group G.

Blaskowitz developed the reputation as an excellent organizer and capable commander, and the well-executed withdrawal of Army Group G from the Bay of Biscay and southern France to the Nancy sector was widely regarded as further evidence of his professional ability. Blaskowitz was unpopular at OKW due to his lack of enthusiasm for the Nazi

regime. He ran into trouble again in early September 1944 when he protested an order by Himmler for the creation of a defensive line behind his sector in the Nancy-Belfort sector that was not under his control. Blaskowitz was formally relieved of command on 20 September 1944. His replacement, General Balck, fell out of favor following Patton's capture of Metz, and in December 1944, Blaskowitz returned to the command of Army Group G. He led it again from Christmas Eve 1944 to 28 January 1945, during the Operation Nordwind offensive. At that point, he was transferred to lead Army Group H in the Netherlands. He committed suicide in 1948 rather than stand trial as a war criminal, which he regarded as unjust.

General of Panzer Troops Hermann Balck[208]
Army Group G

General of Panzer Troops Hermann Balck, commander of Army Group G.

Balck was born near Danzig in East Prussia on 7 December 1893 to a Prussian family with a long military tradition. Curiously enough, his great-grandfather had served under the Duke of Wellington in the King's German Legion, and his grandfather served in the British army's Argyll and Sutherland Highlanders. His father was a distinguished general and well-known writer on military matters. In the Great War, the younger Balck served in mountain infantry units on the French, Russian, Italian, and Balkans fronts and ended the war as a company commander. He had been wounded seven times and was awarded the Iron Cross First Class.

Balck remained in the Reichwehr in the interwar years, preferring to serve in line units than on the General Staff. Balck commanded a motorized infantry regiment of the 1.Panzer-Division in the 1940 campaign in France and Panzer-Regiment.3 in the campaign in Greece in 1941. Balck led the 11.Panzer-Division on the Russian front starting in May 1942. His superior performance on the Russian front led to his award of the Knight's Cross with Oak Leaves, Swords, and Diamonds, one of only twenty-seven officers up to that point to have received the distinction. He was subsequently transferred to command the elite Panzergrenadier Division Grossdeutschland, and then he had a succession of corps commands, including 14.Panzer-Korps in Italy and 48.Panzer-Korps on the Russian front. He led the 48.Panzer-Korps during its defeat in the Soviet Lvov-Sandomierz offensive in Poland in the summer of 1944 and was transferred to the 4.Panzer-Armee in August 1944. Hitler regarded him as one of his best commanders and selected him to lead Army Group G in mid-September 1944, a meteoric career rise from corps commander to army commander to army group commander in the span of barely two months.

Balck was personally briefed by Hitler in September 1944 and warned that the command of Army Group G would be a thankless task since he would get no significant reinforcements. All reserves would be husbanded for the planned Ardennes offensive. When the Allied supply network was rejuvenated in early November 1944, Balck was confronted by a series of successive offensives by Patton's Third U.S. Army around Metz, Patch's Seventh U.S. Army in the Saverne Gap, and de Lattre's First French Army in the Belfort Gap. Army Group G was overwhelmed in all these sectors, and Balck was sacked shortly before Christmas by an ungrateful Führer. After the war, Balck was arrested in 1948 for murder for the execution of artillery commander Lt. Col. Johann Schottke, who had been found drunk while on duty in late November 1944. He was found guilty and sentenced to three years, serving half of this sentence.

General of Panzer Troops Otto von Knobelsdorff
1.Armee

General of Panzer Troops Otto von Knobelsdorf, commander of 1.Armee.

Otto von Knobelsdorff was born on 31 March 1886 and was a lieutenant at the time of the outbreak of the Great War. He was seriously wounded in October 1918 and was decorated with the Iron Cross twice during the war. He served in the Reichswehr after the war, commanding an infantry regiment in 1935 and serving as chief of staff of 33.Armee-Korps in the Polish campaign at the start of World War II. Knobelsdorff commanded the 19.Infanterie Division in the campaign for France in 1940, fighting against the British Expeditionary Force (BEF) in Belgium. In October 1940, the division was reorganized as the 19.Panzer-Division, and he led this division during the invasion of Russia in 1941. He was decorated with the Knight's Cross on 17 September 1941 for his division's performance in Russia. In May–October 1942, Knobelsdorff served as a corps commander on the northern front in Russia. He was promoted to General der Panzertruppe on 1 August 1942, and he again distinguished himself as a panzer corps commander in the attempts to relieve Stalingrad. He remained a panzer corps commander through September 1944, being decorated again on 12 November 1943 for his leadership of 48.Panzer-Korps during the battle of Kursk with the Knight's

Cross with Oak Leaves, and in September 1944 for his leadership of the 40.Panzer-Korps in the Nikopol bridgehead with Oak Leaves and Sword.

Knoblesdorf was appointed to take command of 1.Armee from Gen. Kurt von der Chevallerie in early September 1944 under murky political circumstances as described earlier in this book. In spite of his exemplary record, there was some concern in Berlin over his appointment to 1.Armee in Lorraine due to the heavy toll on his health from the Russian front battles; he had been temporarily relieved on two occasions in 1942 and 1943 due to serious illnesses. This indeed proved the case, as at the beginning of November, Knobelsdorff's health had deteriorated to the point where he was sent on furlough for several weeks during the height of the Metz battle. He was eventually relieved of command due to these health problems. He died in October 1966.

General of Panzer Troops Hasso von Manteuffel[209]

5.Panzer-Armee

General of Panzer Troops Hasso von Manteuffel, commander of 5.Panzer-Armee.

The most prominent tactical commander in the Lorraine fighting in September 1944 was General der Panzertruppe Hasso von Manteuffel. Manteuffel was another brash young officer like Model and Balck who attracted Hitler's personal attention due to their bravery and tactical skills on the battlefield.

Manteuffel was born in Potsdam near Berlin on 14 January 1897 to a Prussian family with a distinguished military record. Curiously enough, one of his ancestors, Field Marshal Edwin von Manteuffel, led the southern army in the 1870 Franco-Prussian War and later served as governor of Alsace-Lorraine. Manteuffel served as a young cavalry officer in World War I, including duty at Verdun. He remained a junior cavalry officer in the army after the war, switching to the new panzer branch in 1934. He commanded a motorized infantry battalion in Rommel's 7.Panzer-Division in France in 1940, and he took over regimental command in October 1941 during the fighting in the Soviet Union. He was awarded the Knights Cross for his action in seizing a bridgehead during the Moscow fighting in November 1941. He commanded a brigade in the North Africa campaign and, while still a colonel, formed an improvised division in Tunisia. His commander, General von Arnim, described him as one of his best divisional commanders in Tunisia. Hitler personally assigned him command of the 7.Panzer-Division in June 1943. Following in Balck's footsteps, he was assigned to lead the elite Panzergrenadier Division Grossdeutchland later in 1943 after being decorated with the Oak Leaves for the Knight's Cross. Manteuffel's growing battlefield reputation and personal contacts with Hitler led to his steady advancement. On 1 September 1944, he was called to the Führer's headquarters and ordered to take command of the 5.Panzer-Armee, leapfrogging to army commander in a single step, and bypassing the usual stage as a panzer corps commander. Manteuffel did not have the training or experience for the position, and he would be further handicapped by the awkward deployment of the 5.Panzer-Armee in sectors of the 1.Armee and 19.Armee.

On 12 October 1944, following the Lorraine campaign, Manteuffel's 5.Panzer-Armee head-quarters was pulled back into Germany to refit prior to the Ardennes offensive. The Battle of the Bulge was Manteuffel's moment in the spotlight. By December, he had matured as a field army commander, with a better grasp of the tools of higher command. As German commanders put it, he had an intuitive "finger-feel" for the battlefield based on a sharp intellect and experience. Contrary to Hitler's orders, he permitted scouting along his front, and after donning a colonel's uniform, he scouted the front lines himself in the days before the offensive. This convinced him that there was a major gap in the American lines in the Losheim area. He also determined that American patrols were very active at night, but that they returned to base before dawn and did not resume patrols until mid-morning. Manteuffel was convinced that the artillery preparation planned by Berlin would do little good against the forward American trenches and would only serve to alert the Americans. Since Hitler would not agree to an abandonment of the barrage, he won approval for an initial infiltration of American lines by assault groups followed by the artillery. In contrast, Sepp Dietrich of the neighboring 6.Panzer-Armee paid little attention to the details of his sector and remained convinced that an initial barrage would soften the American defenses and make them easy to overrun. He had no appreciation for the challenges posed by the wooded areas that had to be breached on the first day of the Ardennes offensive.

The contrast in command styles became immediately evident once the Ardennes offensive began. Dietrich's 6.Panzer-Armee was considered the Schwerpunkt (focal point) of the offensive and was allotted the elite Waffen-SS panzer divisions. However, Dietrich's unimaginative tactics led to a complete failure of his army to penetrate the U.S. defense lines in the north to an operational depth, the major reason for the failure of the Ardennes attack. Manteuffel's more effective tactics collapsed two U.S. infantry divisions, cracked open the American defense line, and led to a panzer charge past Bastogne. However, Manteuffel's sector had far less potential to obtain the necessary strategic penetration to Antwerp, and his spearheads were crushed by the 2nd Armored Division in an encirclement battle west of Bastogne in the days after Christmas.

In March 1945, Manteuffel returned to the Russian front in command of the 3.Panzer-Armee north of Berlin in the final doomed battles of World War II. He became a prominent politician after the war.

General of Panzer Troops Walter Krüger

58.Panzer-Korps

General of Panzer Troops Walter Krüger, commander of 58.Panzer-Korps.

Eugen Walter Krüger was born on 23 March 1892 and was commissioned as a young officer in the Royal Army of Saxony shortly before the Great War. He served in the Saxon cavalry during the Great War and was awarded the Iron Cross on two occasions. After the war, he remained a cavalry officer in the Reichswehr, commanding Kavallerie-Regiment.10 in 1937. Like many cavalry officers, he transferred to the motorized infantry of the panzer force, serving as the commander of the 1.Schutzen-Brigade during the 1940 campaigns. He was awarded the Knight's Cross of the Iron Cross on 11 July 1941 for his leadership of the brigade during the opening phase of the campaign in Russia. He subsequently was appointed commander of the 1.Panzer-Division, and on 27 August 1942, he was awarded the German Cross in Gold. He was transferred to France in January 1944 to lead the 58.Panzer-Korps and remained in command of this headquarters during the Lorraine fighting. This corps remained under Manteuffel's 5.Panzer-Armee in the Ardennes and included the 116.Panzer-Division. He served in staff positions after March 1945.

General of Panzer Troops Heinrich von Lüttwitz
47.Panzer-Korps

General of Panzer Troops Heinrich von Lüttwitz, commander of 47.Panzer-Korps.

Heinrich Freiherr von Lüttwitz resembled the Hollywood caricature of a German general—fat, monocled, and arrogant. Yet he was a seasoned, dynamic panzer commander. He was born on 6 December 1896 and served as a young cavalry officer in the Great War. In the interwar years, he served in a variety of Reichswehr cavalry units. As was the case with Krüger, his cavalry affiliation began to shift towards the panzer force in the late 1930s, starting as a reconnaissance battalion commander. He was severely wounded during the Polish campaign in September 1939, and after his recovery, he was appointed to command Schutzen-Regiment.59. He was decorated with the Knight's Cross for the leadership of this regiment on the Russian front on 27 May 1942, and subsequently appointed to command Schützen-Brigade.20. He became commander of the 20.Panzer-Division on 1 October 1942 and served on the Russian front until May 1943. After a short stint at staff work, he was sent to France to command the 2.Panzer-Division, which he led during the Normandy campaign. He received the Oak Leaves on 3 September 1944 shortly before his appointment to lead the 47.Panzer.Korps in Lorraine. His corps took part in the initial fighting against Patton in Lorraine but played a peripheral role in the Lunéville sector during the fighting around Arracourt. He remained in corps command during the Ardennes offensive. His corps made the deepest penetrations of any German unit in the Ardennes, reaching the Meuse River beyond Bastogne around Christmas before finally being trapped and decimated in the Celles pocket in the last week of December 1944. Lüttwitz sent the famous letter demanding the surrender of Bastogne to Gen. Anthony McAuliffe in Bastogne. McAuliffe responded "Nuts," earning lasting fame; Lüttwitz has faded into obscurity.

Col. Franz Bäke
Panzer-Brigade.106 Feldherrnhalle

Col. Franz Bäke, commander of Panzer-Brigade.106 Feldherrnhalle.

Bäke won the Iron Cross First and Second Class as an infantryman in World War I, and he became a dentist after the war. Rejoining the army, he commanded a PzKpfw 35 (t) company in France in 1940. He led a panzer battalion of the 6.Panzer-Division in the climactic tank encounter at Prokhorovka during the 1943 Kursk battles, and he subsequently led the Heavy Panzer Regiment Bäke on the eastern front in 1944. It was equipped with both Tiger and Panther tanks and intended as a "fire brigade" to respond to tactical emergencies on the Russian front. This regiment was credited with the destruction of hundreds of Soviet tanks in early 1944 with the loss of only five of its own tanks. This heavy panzer regiment was in many ways a precursor of the later panzer brigades. Bäke was decorated with the Knight's Cross in January 1943 and the Oak Leaves in August 1943, and he was only the forty-ninth German soldier of the war to receive the Swords to the Knight's Cross in February 1944. Bäke was appointed to lead one of the new panzer brigades during the summer of 1944. In spite of its crushing defeat at Mairy, the brigade was allowed to remain as an independent formation, and it remained engaged on the western front through 1945, taking part in the battle for Cologne. He was replaced as brigade commander in early 1945 for a period of convalescence. He returned to active duty on 10 March 1945, leading the formation of the 13.Panzer-Division, sometimes called Panzer-Division Feldherrnhalle 2. Bäke's division was part of the Panzerkorps Feldherrnhalle that took part in the disastrous retreat through Hungary and Czechoslovakia. He surrendered to U.S. forces in May 1945, and he died in an auto accident in 1978.

Col. Heinrich von Bronsart-Schellendorf

Panzer-Brigade.111

Heinrich von Bronsart-Schellendorf was born in Neustrelitz, north of Berlin, on 21 September 1906. He joined the Reichswehr as a cadet in April 1924 and was commissioned into the cavalry. He commanded Aufklarungs-Batallion.36 (reconnaissance battalion) during the French campaign and was awarded the German Cross in Gold on 24 May 1942 for his leadership on the Russian front. He led Panzergrenadier-Regiment.13 starting in November 1942 and was awarded the Knight's Cross for his leadership during the Battle of Kursk in the summer of 1943. He was again decorated with the Oak Leaves for a heroic rearguard action in January 1944. He was sent to general staff school in March 1944 and then appointed to the staff of 8.Armee prior to his

Col. Heinrich von Bronsart-Schellendorf, commander of Panzer-Brigade.111.

appointment to lead Panzer-Brigade.111. After his death on 22 September 1944 during the Arracourt battles, he was posthumously elevated in rank to major general.

Colonel Horst von Usedom

Panzer-Brigade.112

Horst von Usedom was born on 9 March 1906 near Hanover and came from a long line of Prussian nobility, most closely associated with the Prussian Hussars. He was the son of Maj.

Col. Horst von Usedom, commander of Panzer-Brigade.112.

Gen. Ewald von Usedom, a decorated veteran of the Great War, grandson and great-grandson of Prussian generals. He joined the Reichswehr as a cadet in 1925 and followed the family tradition in the cavalry. Like many Prussian cavalry officers, he made the transition from horse cavalry to motorized rifle units in the late 1930s as Germany's cavalry force was gradually converted into panzer formations. By 1944, he had been decorated with the Iron Cross twice during the campaigns in Poland and France. He received the Knight's Cross in 1941 while leading the motorcycle rifle battalion (Kradschützenbattalion) of the 11.Panzer-Division during the invasion of the Soviet Union. He took command of a panzergrenadier regiment in late 1942, which served in the Italian theater in 1943. His biographies usually omit any mention of his leadership in the disastrous performance of Panzer-Brigade.112 at Dompaire, and on 12 October 1944, he was transferred to the command of Panzergrenadier-Regiment.108 following the absorption of his brigade into the 21.Panzer-Division. He led Panzer-Brigade Kurland in early 1945, winning the German Cross in Gold and the Oak Leaves of the Knight's Cross of the Iron Cross. He took command of the 12.Panzer-Division on 12 April 1945 and fell into Soviet captivity at the end of the war, not returning to Germany until 1955.

Col. Erich Freiherr von Seckendorff

Panzer-Brigade.113

Erich Freiherr (Baron) von Seckendorff was born on 21 June 1897 in Görz, and like many of the Lorraine brigade commanders, he was from the Prussian aristocracy. At the start of the Great War, he served

Col. Erich von Seckendorff, commander of Panzer-Brigade.113.

as a cadet in the Royal Prussian Army and was twice decorated with the Iron Cross. Following the war, he remained a junior officer in the cavalry branch of the Reichswehr. He received the Knight's Cross for his leadership of Kradschützen-Battalion.6, a motor rifle unit, during the French campaign. He subsequently served as a battalion and regimental commander on the Russian front before being assigned to direct the formation of tank units in Germany in 1943–1944. Biographical details on his career are limited, but his 1943–1944 assignment suggests that he had been wounded or suffered serious medical problems in Russia. Following his death on 23 September 1944 during the fighting near Arracourt, he was posthumously elevated in rank to major general.

Patton's Tanks

PATTON WAS THE U.S. ARMY'S top tank commander in World War II. Yet Patton never served in a tank in combat. Furthermore, one of his most skilled subordinates stated after the war that "Patton knew as little about tanks as anybody I ever knew."[210] This paradox warrants a brief digression.

Due to his contact with Pershing in Mexico, Patton was stationed with the American Expeditionary Force (AEF) headquarters in France in 1917. Impatient with staff work, he managed to get a combat posting. On 10 November 1917 he was dispatched to establish the AEF Light Tank School. Patton received a quick orientation from the French on the new Renault FT light tank. Patton subsequently visited British tank expert Col. J. F. C. Fuller to learn the lessons of the first British combat use of the tank and quickly established himself as the AEF's expert on the new weapon. He was a demanding and energetic leader, and the obvious choice to lead the first two tank battalions into combat. While tank training continued at the French camp at Bourg, Patton attended the General Staff School at Langres, where he rubbed shoulders with many of the up-and-coming officers who would be leaders in a subsequent war. George C. Marshall, army chief of staff in World War II, was among his instructors.

Lt. Col. George S. Patton, commander of the 1st/304th Tank Brigade, standing in front of one of his Renault FT light tanks at the Bourg tank school on 15 July 1918.

Patton can be seen here with his back to the camera among the instructors at the Bourg tank school inspecting a group of tankers and their Renault FT tanks on 15 July 1918. The officer to Patton's immediate left is Capt. Ranulf Compton, his chief instructor.

Patton's tank brigade was first committed to action during the St. Mihiel offensive in September 1918, at one point supporting Brig. Gen. Douglas MacArthur's 84th Brigade. The tank brigade had a handful of Char TSF radio tanks for command purposes, but in reality, they were too primitive for the practical control of early tank units in combat. They were mainly intended to link the tank battalions to higher headquarters. It was impractical to command a tank formation from the inside of a Renault FT since there was no means to communicate between tanks. Another reason that Patton may have been reluctant to command from within a Renault tank was his height of six foot, two inches. The interior of the Renault FT was very cramped, and not an easy fit for a big man like Patton. Instead, he came up with the risky expedient of walking behind the tanks during the attack, accompanied by his aide and a few runners. To signal the tanks, he or one of his small party would run up behind a tank, whack at the turret hatch with a walking stick, and then instruct the tank commander.

On 26 September, Patton's tanks again went into action during the Meuse-Argonne offensive. When the attack stalled in a German trench line, Patton made his way forward to prod his unit onward. Of the

seven men who accompanied Patton forward, five were killed, and he suffered a severe wound in the upper left thigh; his batman pulled him to safety and he was later awarded the Distinguished Service Cross for his actions. It was a difficult recuperation and Patton lost thirty pounds in the process. He returned to command the tank school as a full colonel, but his wound kept him from further combat duty.

On returning to the United States after the war, Patton was assigned to the new Tank Corps Center at Camp Meade, Maryland. After the tank corps was disbanded and absorbed into the infantry in 1920, Patton chose to return to the cavalry. He realized that a vocal promotion of the tank in the lean years of the 1920s and 1930s would do little to advance his military career. As a result, advocacy of the tank fell to other U.S. Army officers more willing to buck the tide. Nevertheless, Patton still had the reputation as one of the army's tank experts due to his service in 1918, and he was given his first star and a brigade command in the newly formed 2nd Armored Division at Fort Benning in July 1940. This was one of the few times that Patton actually served from inside a tank. He chose one of the new M1A1 light tanks as his personal command tank. He rode in this tank extensively during unit maneuvers.

The final "combat car" of the U.S. Cavalry was the M2 with its higher turret, trailing idler wheel, and protectoscopes vision devices on the driver's hatch. When this photo was taken in August 1941 during the Tennessee war games, the combat cars had been absorbed into the new Armored Force and redesignated as the M1A1 light tank. This particular vehicle served as the command tank of the new commander of the 2nd Armored Division, Gen. George S. Patton. A local woman from Manchester, Tennessee, takes a good look at the curious contraption parked in front of her house.

Patton's dynamic performance during the 1941 war games kept him in consideration for advancement in spite of his age. He is seen here in his M1A1 command tank talking to an umpire during the advance towards Montrose, Louisiana, during the 1941 Third U.S. Army maneuvers. The multicolored bands around the turret are based on the colored bands differentiating the different regiments in the 2nd Armored Division.

Divisional command of the 2nd Armored Division soon followed. Patton led the division during the November 1941 war games in the Carolinas, winning praise for his superior leadership. In spite of his popular acclaim as one of the army's top tank experts, Patton had little or no contact with the Ordnance Department that actually designed tanks. The mechanics of tanks simply didn't interest him very much. He was much more interested in the tactics of tank units than in the actual hardware.

He was also fond of uniforms and military regalia and proposed a new green uniform for the tank crews, including a football helmet. He received two nicknames at this time. The more popular was the "Green Hornet" due to his proposed uniform and his habit of riding around base in a command car with sirens blazing. The other nickname that would stay with him through the war was "Blood and Guts" after one of the much-used expressions in his lurid and profane pep talks to his soldiers. Shortly after America was dragged into the war in December 1941, Patton was again promoted to lead the I Armored Corps at Fort Benning.

Patton discusses plans with Gen. W. D. Crittenberger, who commanded the 2nd Brigade of Patton's 2nd Armored Division at the time of the Third U.S. Army maneuvers.

Here, the "Green Hornet" is seen in his command half-track in Manchester, Tennessee, on 19 June 1941, wearing the experimental plastic Riddell football helmet he proposed as the new headgear for the Armored Force. One of his staff officers, Lt. Col. Robert Grow, is trying to gather some impromptu intelligence from a local citizen. Grow would later serve as commander of the 6th Armored Division, one of two armored divisions almost continuously under Patton's Third U.S. Army in the 1944–1945 campaigns in the ETO.

Patton was convinced that the U.S. Army would eventually become involved in the war in the North African desert, and he was among the advocates for a more realistic training ground in the wastes of the Mojave Desert in southern California. The Desert Training Center was created under Patton's direction in March 1942 and demonstrated Patton's often overlooked importance in training U.S. troops. Patton used an M3 light tank at the Desert Training Center, the last time he had his own command tank. His use of the M3 light tank may have soured him to the use of tanks as command vehicles. The M3 was the final incarnation of the prewar combat cars and light tanks. The addition of a 37mm gun on the M2A4 and M3 light tanks made the turret space quite cramped compared to the earlier combat cars that had only machine guns in the turrets. Once again, this was uncomfortable and claustrophobic for a big man like Patton. He began to switch to larger vehicles better suited to command functions, including a modified M3 half-track with a special added roof.

Patton strikes a pose shooting an azimuth with his lensatic compass while standing in front of his M3 light tank while commanding the I Armored Corps at the Desert Training Center in the Mojave Desert of California in 1942. He is again seen wearing one of the experimental Riddell plastic football helmets. Note also that he is armed with a .22 cal Woodsman target pistol in a special holster, not his trademark ivory-handled Colt .45 cal Peacemaker revolver.

Another view of Patton's M3 command tank at the Desert Training Center in the Mojave Desert. It carries his two-star pennant and the pennant of the I Armored Corps.

Patton's M3 light tank was not a very suitable command vehicle for a corps commander since it was too small inside to carry a suitable radio fit. Patton had an M3 half-track customized as his command vehicle with an armored roof and a front-mounted .30 cal machine gun. This vehicle is seen here with the command pennants covered. It was cramped and uncomfortable due to the low ceiling, and no doubt like a oven on hot days in the Mojave Desert. There are few images of Patton actually using it at the Desert Training Center.

Patton used a customized M3A1 scout car when in command of the I Armored Corps in North Africa. It had additional machine guns, a hallmark of Patton's customized vehicles, as well as additional armored shields fore and aft.

Another view of Patton's custom M3A1 scout in North Africa. It also had a special radio console fitted inside.

Patton's customized M3A1 scout car is hoisted over the side of an assault transport off the Sicilian coast in July 1943 during Operation Husky. This gives a good view of its additional machine guns.

Patton's customized M3A1 scout car was not especially comfortable or convenient, and as often as not, Patton used a standard Dodge WC-56 ¾-ton command car for transport on Sicily. It carries his three-star pennant as well as the pennant for his command, the Seventh U.S. Army.

By the time of the Sicily operation, Patton's M3A1 scout car was not especially well suited to the needs of a field army command, and Patton generally used a ¾-ton staff car instead. His deputy, Gen. Geoffrey Keyes, often used the M3A1 scout car.

Patton's assignment in the California desert was short-lived as in July he was ordered to Washington, where he was assigned to command the Western Task Force in Operation Torch, leading the amphibious landing near Casablanca. Following his deployment to North Africa, Patton never again relied on a tank as a command vehicle. He used the usual assortment of staff cars, jeeps, and command cars. The one armored vehicle associated with him in North Africa was an M3A1 armored scout car, modified to his specifications with additional machine guns and added armor. He used this through the North African campaign and again on Sicily.

By the time that Patton took command of the Third U.S. Army in France, he had completely given up on the use of tanks as command vehicles. A field army commander seldom needs to appear on the front line, and an armored vehicle was neither convenient nor necessary. By this time, Patton was approaching sixty years old. There is no easy way to climb on to a Sherman tank nor is it particularly easy or safe for an older man to jump off one. Patton showed little apparent interest in adopting a tank as one of his signature command vehicles. On the other hand, Patton was keen on customized command vehicles. All of his jeeps and command cars were modified in some way. They usually had added machine guns, a longtime obsession of Patton. They usually had other flourishes, including customized fenders and windshields to reduce mud splash when traveling on Europe's rough roads.

When assigned to command the Third U.S. Army, Patton had a Dodge WC-57 ¾-ton command car customized with additional armor plate on the floor and a pintle-mounted .50 cal heavy machine gun, as seen here in an ordnance shop in Britain in March 1944.

Patton's preferred mount while commanding the Third U.S. Army was a "peep," the Armored Force nickname for a ¼-truck, instead of the more common "jeep." This photo was taken in the late summer of 1944 when Patton was visiting the 5th Armored Division near Gossicourt. At this stage, the jeep has not yet been heavily customized.

Another view of Patton's command jeep W-20339141, seen here on 8 October 1944 while Patton is loading one of his cameras. This shows the Third U.S. Army command flag. The extra sirens are very evident in this view, as well as the addition to the standard windshield.

This is an interesting view of Patton's command jeep in the early winter of 1945 in use by Eisenhower and Gen. Manton Eddy during a tour of the Third U.S. Army front lines. By this stage, it has had added modifications, including a rebuilt windshield and side doors as well as more extensive mud flaps.

Patton was seldom involved in the technical aspects of tank design during his command of the Third U.S. Army. He was never particularly interested in engineering, but more importantly, he felt that the human element of combat was far more important than the technical. In one of his articles, "The Secrets of Victory," from 1926, he summarized his viewpoint: "It is the cold glitter in the attacker's eye, not the point of the questing bayonet, that breaks the line. It is the fierce determination of the drive to close with the enemy, not the mechanical perfection of the tank, that conquers the trench."[211]

One charge leveled against Patton was that he was responsible for the delays in the U.S. Army's new M26 Pershing tank reaching the hands of U.S. tankers in 1944. This argument was most strenuously made by Lt. Belton Cooper in his 1998 memoirs.[212] He went on further to claim that it was the absence of an improved medium tank like the Pershing that was instrumental in the defeat of Bradley's November 1944 offensive on the German border.[213] This theme has subsequently been taken up in numerous television documentaries, and it is even cited in the Wikipedia entry on the M26 Pershing tank. The problem with this accusation is that it has absolutely no basis in historical evidence. Cooper was too junior an officer in 1944 to have any personal knowledge of this issue, and the source of his animus towards Patton on this issue is unclear. Patton simply did not have any such influence in late 1943 and early 1944 when the critical decisions were being made regarding the fate of the M26 Pershing program. At the time, he was in limbo in Britain waiting for Eisenhower's decision about his future command prospects after his disgrace in Sicily in 1943. Eisenhower had rebuked Patton for the slapping incident on Sicily in November 1943, and after relinquishing command of the Seventh U.S. Army and arriving in Britain, Patton got into trouble again in April 1944 due to another press scandal. This was not a peak period for Patton's influence even if he had any connection with the program. The real problem is that there is no evidence that Patton had any particular interest in the M26 Pershing program at the time, nor is there any evidence in surviving ordnance files of any attempt by him to influence the program.[214]

One of Patton's few attempts to influence the tank designs of the Third U.S. Army took place in the autumn of 1944. As long ago as 1918, Patton had pestered the army's ordnance branch to add more machine guns to tanks. He felt that machine guns were an especially important addition to tanks since a spray of machine-gun fire could intimidate the enemy and bolster the confidence of the tank crew from the sheer noise and visual spectacle of a stream of tracers.

This reverence for the power of machine guns on tanks permeated the Third U.S. Army and became a mantra of many of its senior armored commanders. Gen. Bruce Clarke later explained why: "I told my men that the greatest thing on the tank was a free .50 cal in the hands of the tank commander. We were not able to fight from tanks with the tank commander buttoned up—that has never been successfully done. [Buttoned up] he can't hear or see and so pretty soon he unbuttons. Now if he's got a free .50 cal machine gun, all he has to do is press his thumb and he can pick out a dangerous spot. It may be a bazooka flash or something. He can throw a burst there without even thinking about giving an order."

Patton was convinced by his ordnance officers that sand-bag armor was a bad thing. When the 12th Armored Division was transferred to his command from the Seventh U.S. Army, this caused sparks to fly since most of the tank units of the Seventh U.S. Army had adopted a standardized sand-bag package complete with metal frames and supports. Here, Patton storms back to his staff after having chewed out the hapless crew of an M4A3E8 about this issue.

Patton pestered Ordnance to substitute a rapid-fire aircraft .50 cal heavy machine gun for the usual .30 cal machine gun on the Sherman evident here since it projects beyond the armored mantlet opening. The Third U.S. Army also advocated an additional .30 cal machine gun more conveniently positioned in front of the commander, and movement of the pintle mount for the exterior .50 cal machine gun in front of the loader's hatch.

By late 1944, Patton was senior enough in the command structure that he could get the attention of Ordnance regarding his obsession with tank machine guns. At some point in 1944, he wrote directly to Maj. Gen. Levin H. Campbell, Chief of Ordnance, urging the addition of more machine guns on U.S. tanks. Patton wanted twin coaxial machine guns to replace the single .30 cal machine gun then fitted in the M4 Sherman tank. He preferred high-cyclic-rate machine guns of the type used in U.S. Army Air Force fighters, and he hoped it would be possible to fit one .30 cal and one .50 cal in the turret.

Patton's original letter seems to have vanished, but the subsequent correspondence with Campbell survives in Ordnance files. On 14 November 1944, Campbell offered to send a team of Ordnance officers to the Third U.S. Army to demonstrate potential machine-gun additions to U.S. tanks. In a 29 December letter to General Campbell, Patton apologized for the delay in replying since "we are having a hell of a battle," and accepted that a high-cyclic-rate .30 cal might not be possible. In any event, a young Ordnance officer duly arrived at the Third U.S. Army headquarters in January 1945 with various briefings on tank machine guns. Patton had hoped for a new mounting on the tank, but Ordnance recommended modifying the existing mounting since it would take months before a new mounting could be designed, tested, manufactured, and then shipped to the ETO.[215] Patton agreed that this was "an excellent idea." Patton also solicited the advice of senior officers.

Patton's own chief of staff, Brig. Gen. Hobart Gay, was not keen on switching to the use of rapid-fire aircraft machine guns, arguing on practical grounds that they expended ammunition "too damn fast." Patton's good friend Maj. Gen. Robert Grow, who commanded the 6th Armored Division, was not convinced of the need for any new machine guns.[216] Brig. Gen. Holmes Dager from the 4th Armored Division was not especially interested in the dual coaxial machine-gun idea, but he wanted the roof-mounted antiaircraft machine gun moved forward on the turret so that it could be used more effectively by either the tank commander or loader.

In any event, the whole machine-gun idea became wrapped up in other controversies stemming from the Ardennes fighting. Many tank crews were not happy about the armor on the M4 Sherman tank, especially as German use of the Panzerfaust antitank rocket increased. Many tank units in Bradley's 12th Army Group had adopted an assortment of improvised schemes to defeat the Panzerfaust, most notably the use of sandbags

The Third U.S. Army's Sherman upgrade package impressed Bradley's 12th Army Group headquarters so much that it became the preferred solution to the Sherman's armor problems. This M4A3E8 was used as a model for the upgrade desired for the ETO.

or poured concrete. Patch's Seventh U.S. Army adopted a comprehensive program to fit most of the Shermans with an elaborate sandbag appliqué. Patton's Ordnance officers were very skeptical of sandbags since tests found that they did not provide any real protection against the Panzerfaust while at the same time adding considerable weight that degraded the automotive performance of the tank.

This view was widely shared within the Third U.S. Army. When Gen. Bruce Clarke was transferred from CCA, 4th Armored Division to CCB, 7th Armored Division in November 1944, he discovered that "the well-lubricated, well-painted machines were draped with chicken wire, in turn ornamented with cement blocks and brush." He turned to the battalion commander: "What the hell is that crap hanging on the machines?" The battalion commander replied, "Protection against German Panzerfaust." Clarke then asked, "Colonel, did you ever lose a tank to a Panzerfaust?" The colonel replied, "Not yet sir." Clarke concluded his tirade: "Neither have I! Now I'll be back tomorrow morning. I want all that crap off every machine. I want them clean. I want insignia showing. I'm going to inspect you and all your men and all your tanks. And I want your soldiers looking like soldiers and your tanks looking like tanks and not haystacks. Part of the power of tanks is to scare the hell out of the enemy—when they look like tanks!"[217]

The Third U.S. Army's Ordnance section promoted a fairly obvious solution—welding additional steel armor to the tanks.[218] The source of the armor plate was the large number of destroyed German and American tanks littering the Ardennes. Patton approved the program, and once the supply of tank hulks in the Ardennes was exhausted by March 1945, he asked the neighboring Seventh U.S. Army if his Ordnance troops could cannibalize any wrecks in their sector.

The up-armored tanks also had machine-gun improvements based on Patton's earlier plans. The Third U.S. Army obtained a supply of the aircraft .50 cal heavy machine gun that had a higher rate of fire than the tank version. These were mounted in place of the usual .30 cal machine gun. In addition, .30 cal machine-gun mounts were added on the turrets of Sherman tanks in front of the commander, providing additional fire and reducing the need of the commander to expose himself when firing the machine gun. This package of modifications was considered so successful that Bradley's 12th Army Group headquarters recommended it as a standard fit to the Ordnance department.

A Tanker's View of the Sherman

CONTROVERSIES WILL ALWAYS SURROUND the combat performance of the Sherman tank in World War II since different criteria can be used to judge its relative merits. For an interesting look at the perspective of a tanker who fought during the Lorraine tank battles, here is an essay written by the commander of the 8th Tank Battalion, 4th Armored Division about this issue in 1945 in response to the press complaints about the Sherman tank.[219]

Tank versus Tank
by Lt. Col. Albin Irzyk

"The American tank is not nearly as good as the German tank."

"Next to the German and Russian tanks, the American tanks are the best in the world."

Quotations, opinions, and comments similar to the two above which have been widely publicized and which have caused widespread discussion have been made by various individuals. Because they have, to a certain degree, jumped to hasty conclusions, and because they have helped fashion many erroneous conceptions, I shall attempt in this article to present considerations which they have apparently overlooked and which may change the outlook of many on American tanks.

In making those statements, what standards did the persons involved use? What were the items and factors that they utilized in making their comparisons?

If they used simply the gun, the weight of the tank, and the width of the track and thereby the flotation of the tank as a criterion, as I am sure they did, then I heartily concur with them that the German Tiger tank is unquestionably superior to the American Sherman tank. The German 88 is more powerful than any American tank gun used during the course of most of the war. The German tank *is* much heavier and therefore its armor is much thicker than that of any American tank. The tracks of the former *are* much wider, with perhaps a less vulnerable suspension system than that of the latter. If I stop here, as I am convinced so many have, there is no question but that the German tank is a much better one than our own. In this paragraph there is material, indeed, for sensational headlines in newspapers in the States.

Today, however, let us not stop here. Let us go on! What is the fuel capacity of the German Tiger tank? How long and how far is it able to run on a tank full of gasoline? Does it burn much oil? What is the composition and life of its tracks? How many rounds of ammunition is it able to stow? What is the life (discounting its being hit in action) of a Tiger tank? Is its engine comparatively free of maintenance problems? If maintenance problems occur, are they easy to remedy? How long and how much skill is required to change an engine? Is the German tank able to move for long distances and continuous periods at a steady rate of speed? How is its endurance? Could fifty-three Tiger tanks, for instance, move from the vicinity of Fenetrange, France, in the Saar, to an area near Bastogne, Belgium, a distance of 151 miles, in less than twenty-four hours to answer a fire call as did tanks of the Fourth Armored Division? Could a German Tiger tank be used for weeks of training in England, land in France and fight across the widest part of that country to the German frontier, race back to Belgium, retrace its steps again to the German border, and fight its way well into that country before being replaced? Could the German tank roll for several hours at a speed of twenty-five miles per hour in exploiting a breakthrough?

Did it occur to the critics of the American tank that perhaps questions like those listed above, the answers to which will all heavily favor the American tank, and many others like them should be considered before a decision is reached? Obviously not. I say most emphatically that such factors *must* be included before a thorough, honest, and fair comparison can be made and a sound and intelligent conclusion reached.

In addition to those just cited, items to be remembered, as well, are tactics employed and required respectively by the Germans and Americans, missions involved, and number of tanks on hand for the operations. To create a "true picture"

of the weaknesses and strengths of the tanks being compared, those things take their places in the line of factors necessary to be examined.

On 6 June 1944 and for many days afterward, while the Germans had the Mark V Panther with a 75-mm gun and a Mark VI Tiger with an 88-mm gun, the American Army was equipped with the M4A1 tank, or the Sherman, as it is popularly known. It will be unnecessary in this article to list all the specifications of that tank except to say that it weighed approximately thirty tons and had a 75-mm gun. Its tracks were narrow and consisted of three different types: steel, flat rubber and rubber chevron.

During the initial period in Normandy just after the invasion, when engagements were toe-to-toe slugfests, battles with tanks fighting tanks were common. Soon, however, the deadlock broke and American tanks streaked to and through Avranches and hustled across Brittany. Without stopping for breath, the tanks continued on their way across most of France.

In order to keep rolling over hot roads for long, dusty miles for days on end, a light, mobile tank was needed which the terribly extended supply line could adequately furnish with precious gasoline. To withstand the terrific beating the tank was taking hour after hour, it was necessary for it to

During the September 1944 fighting around Arracourt, most of the 4th Armored Division's Shermans were the standard M4. These were only marginally improved compared to the M4 tanks in use in 1943 in Tunisia and Sicily.

have a simple yet tough and efficient engine and mechanical system. The fact that the American tanks rolled with but few maintenance problems, and those rapidly attended to by the tank crew alone or by company, battalion, or division maintenance, all of which were close enough behind to repair the vehicle rapidly and send it immediately back into action, testifies to the excellence of the tank. Thus, tank units were still at full tank strength and functioning efficiently when they reached as far east as the Meuse River early in September after moving and fighting consistently day after day from the Normandy peninsula. They stopped then only because they had moved too fast and too far and were forced to wait a few days until their supplies could reach them in large enough quantities to send them ahead again. During that phase of operations, a group of tanks had made a forced march of 258 miles in thirty-eight hours and arrived in good enough shape to have continued on had the situation warranted it.

In discussing tanks, many forget that the tank is *not* a vehicle built primarily to fight other tanks. Rather, its mission above all others is to get into the enemy's rear areas, to disorganize him, to destroy supply and communications, and to wreak havoc there. This is done with its 30 caliber machine guns, especially the one mounted co-axially, and with high-explosive fire from the tank cannon. The tank cannon's chief function, however, is to protect the tank while it is disrupting, exploiting, and destroying the enemy. Of course, very, very often a few well placed shots from the tank cannon will be much more effective than the 30 caliber machine guns, and therefore the cannon is used very frequently in offensive action.

The tank served its primary mission gloriously in that dash through France. Its opponent was dazed, disorganized, and on the run. Most of his equipment was "thin skinned," and was "duck soup" for our tanks. The 30-caliber fire and 75-mm high-explosive fire, for good measure, was plenty good enough to leave much of the German Army equipment and personnel strewn by the wayside.

A factor rarely considered, yet on occasion vitally important, is the type of bridge that a Sherman can use to cross a stream or river. Many bridges that are adequate for the American tank would pose a knotty problem for the German tank. The bridge would have to be much wider and much stronger, and would require a great deal of time and more facilities to construct. Many bridges intact and able to accommodate the lighter American tank would deny passage to the heavy, lumbering Tiger.

Hardly a critical word was heard concerning the American tank in those days. The reason obviously

In August, the 4th Armored Division began receiving the new M4A3 (76mm) that had the new 76mm gun and also the improved Ford engine. At the time of the Arracourt fighting, there were only twenty of these in the division. This M4A3 is seen here in Lorraine in November 1944 with the 761st Tank Battalion, a segregated African-American unit attached to Patton's Third U.S. Army.

was that it was plenty good for the task at hand. The tank was accomplishing an ideal tank mission in a superior fashion, and it seemed to have been built for just that kind of job. During the summer and fall of 1944, the Sherman performed to perfection and brought the Allied armies within scent of the German frontier.

It was late in 1944 that the American tank became the target for taunts and criticism. Forgotten quickly were the results it had gained just a month or two before. In October, November, and December the ground became a sticky morass; the war was stabilized and no great advances were being made. The war was bloody and difficult, slow and discouraging. For every yard wrested, from the enemy, tremendous effort had to be exerted.

During this stage of the war, the tanks could not perform as they had earlier. Rather, they were forced to fight tank versus tank. Here the German had a tremendous advantage. He was fighting a defensive warfare. The terrain was admirably suited for him. It was rough, and this enabled him to pick the key terrain features on which to post his men and vehicles. The ground was so muddy that advancing, attacking elements could not maneuver, could not outflank. They had to slug it out toe to toe, face to face. Without a doubt the tank of the Germans was ideally suited for such a fortunate turn in the war

for them. The tank could pick dominating ground, and with its huge gun and thick armor proved to be a roving pillbox par excellence. On many occasions it picked off American tanks as they floundered in the mud in an effort to gain valuable ground and dislodge their adversary. It was during those trying days that many an American tanker and those that observed him began to lose faith in the Sherman. The tanker was forced to move very slowly because of the muck, and very, very often he spotted a German tank, fired first, and scored a hit only to see his 75-mm shot glance off the enemy tank causing absolutely no damage to it. The 75-mm gun proved to be comparatively ineffective during this chapter of the war. At 1,000 yards to 1,500 yards it could be effective, and a single tank has knocked out five Panther tanks with six shots. Yet to get that close to a German tank made the Sherman vulnerable indeed. Many tanks were lost in endeavoring to get in close, which was necessary in order for them to strike a telling blow. The absence of an effective armor-piercing shell proved to be a terrific handicap, as well. Thus, during that siege, the American tank was impotent when running into the German tank head-on. As a result, many a Sherman was lost even after it had shot first and scored the first hit. That was when the seeds of dissatisfaction in the American tank were sown and when much faith was lost.

The definitive version of the Sherman tank in World War II was the M4A3E8, an improvement of the M4A3 (76mm) but with the new horizontal volute spring suspension (HVSS) with 23-inch-wide tracks for better floatation in snow and mud. The 4th Armored Division was one of the first units to receive these around Christmas 1944 during the fighting in the Ardennes.

It must be remembered that the German tank had everything its way. It was fighting a defensive game, the terrain was in its favor, and the wet ground played into its hands. Still, it must not be forgotten that though the cards were stacked against the American tank, it defeated the enemy and gained the desired ground. Though the Shermans were easily bested tank for tank, they could always bank on a numerical superiority, which fact was considered in tactics and strategy employed. By banding together and maneuvering, they were able to dislodge and knock out the heavier German tank. Even during those days, one German tank knocked out for one American tank was its poor score. It was in most cases three to one, four to one, and five to one in favor of our side. One must not forget that the German requirements and our own were totally different. They were fighting a slow war, a defensive war where they picked their spots. They had fewer tanks than we, so their tactics, of necessity, had to be different. We were fighting an offensive war, we were hurrying to get it over with, we wanted to shake loose, and we had many tanks with which to do it. Virtually never did a scrap take place with fifty German tanks against fifty American or twenty against twenty. The proportion was usually five American to one German, even ten to one, rarely if ever less than two to one. So it must be made clear to anyone comparing the tanks of the two nations that, as I said before, throughout the campaigns the requirements and needs were different. We could not use nor did we want a lumbering, heavy, mobile pillbox type of tank, and we could not have done what we did if we were so equipped. Then again we had numbers upon which to fall back, and we considered that in our tactics. Mechanically we had a tank that performed superbly, and after groaning and grunting through heavy, sticky mud for weeks on end, it still was running at the end of this phase.

There is no denying that in those hectic days a tank such as our newest Sherman with a wider track and a more potent gun would have saved many American lives and tanks and would have knocked out more enemy tanks, and more quickly, too. During that period, and that period alone, was the American tank discredited, criticized, and found lacking. The situation was hastily remedied, but for many, it was a little late.

The closing days of 1944 and the early part of 1945 found a new type Sherman joining the ranks of American tanks and replacing its tired brothers. Although it has no additional armor and weighs but a ton or two more, it arrived on the scene with a potent, long-tubed 76mm gun with muzzle brake, and high muzzle velocity that makes it effective at much longer range than the 75mm. As a result, it is not necessary for the new tank to get as close in as the old tank before becoming effective. A new type, high-velocity, armor-piercing shell was added for the gun and gives it far greater penetrating qualities,

The new tank has an engine with a higher horsepower which, in addition to an increase in power, makes it capable of higher speeds. Its track is much wider and has a new type track suspension system which gives it more stability and cross-country mobility with which to combat adverse ground conditions. The tank has the traditional endurance of American tanks and rolls consistently for endless miles. It goes ninety miles and often more on a tankful of gasoline. The tank is characteristically simple, as such equipment goes, and the tank crew alone is able to maintain its vehicle for long periods, New men in tank crews catch on to their jobs quickly, which is one important factor in making our tank crews superior to those of the Germans and explains why our armor operated most of the time at top-notch efficiency. One last advantage, though minor in discussion, was extremely valuable to the tank crew—the turret with two hatches. Also, the new Sherman, like the old, had the potent 50-caliber antiaircraft gun which proved so effective against enemy planes and which played havoc with dug-in Germans.

All in all, the new type Sherman is a marvelous tank. It answered the prayers of the tankers and was on hand to drop the curtain on one of the dirtiest and hardest phases of the European war. It was the new tank with all the advantages of the old one and many new qualities that did the racing in Germany, Austria, and Czechoslovakia, and finished the war in a blaze of glory, Mounted in that tank, no American tanker was afraid to take on any tank that faced him. If only the new type tank could have been produced and brought to the front lines sooner!

Like other units in Patton's Third U.S. Army, the 4th Armored Division improved the protection of its new M4A3E8 tanks with an added layer of armor on the hull and turret front, taken from tank wrecks in the Ardennes.

German tanks, on the other hand, are not what they are cracked up to be. Their heavy armor was a hindrance rather than an asset. The tanks could not carry on the same kind of offensive warfare that our tanks did. With their heavy armor and complicated mechanism they were tank destroyers and not tanks.

Even though the German tanks were much heavier and thicker than ours, their armor was centralized. Most of it was on the front slope plate and turret. Sides and rear were often vulnerable, and how we capitalized on that! The armor on German tanks was generally poor. It often cracked on impact, leaving ragged, gaping holes, whereas the holes in our tanks were clean, circular, and easily repairable. The Germans developed a gun with a high muzzle velocity and an effective armor-piercing projectile. To do this they sacrificed space in the tank, for they had to increase the size of the shell and thus could not stow many rounds. It must be mentioned that once again the Germans lost sight of the purpose and function of a tank and thought primarily of destroying other tanks, Still, though our muzzle velocity was less than theirs, our high-explosive fire was just as effective. Of the two, the high-explosive fire was for us the more important consideration.

Mechanical advantages of the German tank over our own were few. The interiors of their tanks were not nearly as well equipped as ours, and it took altogether too much maintenance to keep a German tank rolling. Still another item often overlooked is that it was necessary for us to carry an adequate basic load of ammunition and gasoline in our tanks, for to replace what we used we had to call upon trucks that had to travel over a long, dangerous supply route. The Germans, on the other hand, sat close in many of their defensive positions to their ammunition and other supply. It might astonish some to know that prisoners of war claimed that some of their large tanks had a running time of a mere two and a half hours on a full vehicular load of gasoline. Thus, the tanks did not have the endurance nor the cruising ranges of our tanks. Therefore, in many instances they had to be transported by rail virtually to the front lines, unloaded, and put into the battle. How far could we have gone with our tanks if we had had to follow a procedure like that?

Not yet mentioned is the power traverse with which American tanks are equipped. It is one of the very important reasons why so many of our tanks bested the German tanks. Of course, it may have been that our gunners and our commanders were superior to the Germans, and that the excellence of our tankers provided us with the upper hand. We agree to that, yet it is felt that of inestimable advantage to our tankers was the distinct handicap under which the German tankers labored because of a lack of a 360° power traverse comparable to ours. Because of that important disadvantage, they were slow firing and in many cases got off one round to our three or four. Instances have occurred where a Tiger tank lay hidden, waited in ambush, and fired the first shot at advancing American tanks and missed! The mistake was fatal, for American tanks maneuvered about it and with their rapid fire destroyed the German tank.

By means of the 360° power turret traverse with which all our tanks are equipped, a tank gunner is able to swing his gun in any direction in a second or a fraction thereof. The average American tank gunner can lay on a German tank, is able to get the first round off, and can usually score the first hit. The power traverse enabled American tanks to move down roads at high speeds shooting from one side of the road to the other. In this manner enemy infantrymen and bazooka teams were killed or pinned down as the tanks rolled by. The power traverse has been such an advantage and of so much importance that it is immeasurable.

At the moment, virtually every tank battalion is nearly completely equipped with the new type Sherman tank technically called the M4A3E8. Of all the tanks operating today, that one, in my estimation, is the best there is. I would choose it above all others. Many, many experienced combat tankers feel exactly as I do. The tank will go faster and will live longer than the German Tiger. The Sherman burns less gas and oil and as a result is able to go much farther on a tank full of gasoline. Its maintenance problems are few and far between and are easily remedied. It is an easy matter to change an engine, which takes little more than four hours and which beats all hollow the best time for the Germans. It has a good gun, and good ammunition for it. It does not take much to tow one of our tanks that is disabled, but a huge vehicle is required for the German Tiger, and often German tanks had to be abandoned because huge vehicles were not available. Yes, considering all factors, I believe that even the most prejudiced or the one most difficult to convince will nod toward the Sherman.

The Sherman must give ground to the Tiger when the size of the gun and the thickness of armor is considered. The tanker knows and takes for granted that if his tank is hit by an 88 it will be penetrated. He also knows that the addition of a few tons of armor will not stop an 88. He respects, and always will, the German gun and the thick armor, but he will never swap his tank for those advantages. To build a tank that would stop an 88 shell would be to lose a tank and gain a lumbering steel pillbox with no mobility left. It has been said, practically speaking, that the only thing that will stop an 88 is "Cease fire." Similarly, to stop our 76 with high-velocity armor-piercing ammunition, the enemy will need a mighty heavy tank, indeed.

Once again, let us not forget that the Americans fought an offensive, fast, deceptive, and *winning* war. We crushed our adversary; therefore the tanks which spearheaded the victories must have been good. Tank for tank, toe to toe, we were outclassed. But that was not our way of fighting. For the person still not convinced I suggest that he tabulate the count of American tanks knocked out by German tanks and vice versa, and I am sure that he will discover, perhaps to his amazement, that the scale will swing heavily in our favor.

Not long before the curtain dropped on hostilities in Europe, the American General Pershing tank made its bow. It has a 90-mm gun, weighs forty-six tons, has a different suspension system, and has a low silhouette. It is said that here is a tank that incorporates all the advantages of the Sherman tank and with its new additions makes it superior to the German Tiger in *every* respect. As far as my personal knowledge goes, I must reserve my opinion until later, for that tank is comparatively untried.

I will say to the persons that have so glibly sold our tank down the river that there is more to it than meets the eye.

The Tiger Tank Myth

I N A BOOK FOCUSED ON U.S. and German tank battles in World War II, it may seem odd that there has not been a single mention of a battle involving a Sherman and Tiger tank. World War II memoirs are full of stories about U.S. tanks fighting the mighty Tiger tank, and the idea has become so fixed in the popular imagination that the recent Hollywood blockbuster *Fury* has a duel between Sherman tanks of the 2nd Armored Division and a Tiger tank as the central episode in the movie.

In reality, there was hardly any fighting between the Sherman tank and the Tiger I heavy tank in the ETO in 1944–1945. GIs in World War II used the name "Tiger" indiscriminately to identify nearly any sort of German tank. Likewise, all German artillery was an "88" even though the 88mm flak gun was in fact fairly uncommon. Part of this was simply the difficulty of distinguishing various tank types in the heat of battle. Tank engagements typically took place at ranges of 500–800 yards, and German tanks as often as not were very well camouflaged.

The reason that I can make the claim that U.S. tanks seldom faced the Tiger is due to the relative rarity of the Tiger tank in the ETO, as well as the ample evidence provided in the numerous histories of the Tiger tank in combat. Here, I am speaking of the classic Tiger I tank as seen in the movie *Fury*. I will discuss the Tiger II, or King Tiger, a bit later. There were only 1,354 Tiger tanks built in 1942–1944 compared to 49,234 M4 Sherman tanks.

INITIAL CONTACTS

The U.S. Army had frequent but small-scale contact with the Tiger I in the North African Theater of Operations and the Mediterranean Theater of Operations. The first known contact between U.S. Army Sherman tanks and the new Tiger I tank was on 14 February 1943 when a small task force under Lt. Col. Louis Hightower attempted to counterattack the German panzer offensive towards Kasserine Pass. Among the forces that fought against Hightower's ill-fated attack was a company of Tiger tanks of s.Pz.Abt.501. There was sporadic contact with this Tiger battalion in the subsequent fighting around Kasserine Pass, but the battalion never numbered more than eighteen Tiger tanks during the entire campaign.[220] Parts of a second Tiger battalion, s.Pz. Abt.504, disembarked in Tunisia in March 1943, and these saw combat with the U.S. Army in late March 1943 in the Maknassy Pass area. This unit also remained small, reaching a peak strength of twenty-one tanks in April 1943 before being wiped out in the final battles. A remaining company of this battalion, 2./s.Pz.Abt.504, served on Sicily in July 1943 at the time of the Operation Husky amphibious landings. This company, numbering seventeen Tiger tanks, counterattacked Patton's Seventh U.S. Army forces at the Gela beachhead on 11 July 1943, losing ten of its seventeen tanks in combat in the first day of fighting. Another Tiger battalion, s.Pz. Abt.508, was deployed to Italy in February 1944 and initially took part in the Operation Fischfang counterattack against the Allied beachhead at Anzio on 12 February 1944. The U.S. Army had sporadic contact with this unit over the next year of fighting in Italy, and all of its Tiger tanks had been lost by February 1945. Although the Tiger I was a formidable tank in combat, it was never available in large enough numbers to have a significant impact on the battlefield in Tunisia or Italy. There were never more than forty tanks in service in these theaters in 1943–1944, and usually far less.

The U.S. Army first encountered the Tiger I in 1943 in Tunisia. This example was captured from s.Pz.Abt.504 and was sent back to the United States. It is seen here on a display in Washington, D.C., in February 1944. The American crew was dressed in Afrika Korps uniforms. This tank later was displayed at Aberdeen Proving Ground and is now at Fort Benning.

The 2nd Company of s.Pz.Abt.504 served on Sicily during the July 1943 fighting. It was decimated in a counterattack against the Gela beachhead. This particular tank was lost on 10 July 1943 when a paratrooper from the 82nd Airborne Division killed the crew with a grenade when they were standing outside the tank.

Another Tiger I of 2./s.Pz-Abt.504 knocked out early in the Sicily campaign in Biscari near Catania and photographed on 16 July 1943.

Following the Sicilian campaign, there were persistent, though small-scale, contacts with Tiger tanks in Italy. This is a Tiger I of s.Pz.Abt.508 lost near Cori, Italy, at the end of May 1944. This Tiger battalion was deployed to Italy in February 1944 to participate in the counterattacks against the Anzio bridgehead and later fought in the battles on the approach to Rome in the late spring of 1944.

TIGER IN THE ETO

U.S. Army encounters with the Tiger I in the European Theater of Operations (ETO) were even less frequent, and there are only a handful of known cases. On 1 June 1944, a few days before D-Day, there were only six Tiger tanks in service in the west. On 1 July 1944 at the height of the Normandy fighting, there were only forty-two in the west after seventeen had been lost during the June 1944 Normandy fighting.[221] At this point in time, there were more than 6,000 Allied tanks in Normandy, the majority of them Shermans. The chart on page 248 summarizes Tiger strength in France in the summer of 1944. The heavy losses listed for September are due to an accounting correction, with the Wehrmacht belatedly writing off the many disabled Tiger tanks abandoned during the retreat from France.

TIGER IN THE WEST, SUMMER 1944[222]				
Strength	**Jun**	**Jul**	**Aug**	**Sep**
Tiger	6	42	84	75
Tiger I (Befels)*	6	3	0	8
Losses	**Jun**	**Jul**	**Aug**	**Sep**
Tiger	17	13	13	91
Tiger II				23
Tiger I (Befels)	2	1	2	2

*Command tank

There was little or no contact between the U.S. Army and Tiger tanks in Normandy in June–August 1944 since both German Tiger battalions, s.SS-Pz. Abt.101 and s.SS-Pz.Abt.102 (Heavy SS Tiger Battalions) both fought in the Caen sector against British and Canadian forces. The combat history of these two battalions have been the subject of numerous books and articles, and their history is amply documented.[223] The first U.S. Army contact with the Tiger I in France occurred as a spin-off of the Caen fighting. Three battle-damaged Tiger I tanks were put on railroad flatcars and sent towards Germany for rebuilding. The train reached as far as Braine, northeast of Paris, where it was intercepted by elements of the 3rd Armored Division. Some M15A1 antiaircraft half-tracks of the 486th AAA Automatic Weapons Battalion spotted the train and saw the tank crews try to get into the stationary Tigers. They swept the crews away from the tanks using the 37mm automatic cannons and .50 cal heavy machine guns. As a result, the damaged tanks were captured before they could engage the American force.

The U.S. Army captured a number of Tiger I tanks that had been abandoned during the Wehrmacht retreat across France. This is a Tiger I of s.SS-Pz. Abt.101 abandoned in Marle, north of Reims, and seen on 30 August 1944 being inspected by U.S. troops of the 3rd Armored Division.

One of the few combat encounters between the U.S. Army and Tiger I tanks occurred on 8 September 1944 at the Braine railway station, northeast of Paris, where a train carrying three damaged Tigers on their way back to Germany were intercepted by M15A1 antiaircraft half-tracks of the 486th AAA Automatic Weapons Battalion. The half-tracks sprayed the tanks with automatic weapons fire to prevent the crews from returning to the tanks, and the train was captured.

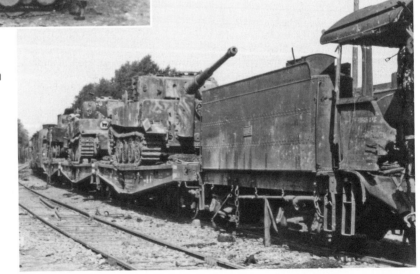

The Tiger I largely disappeared from combat in the U.S. Army sector over the next several months until the Ardennes offensive in December 1944. There was only a single Tiger I company involved in the offensive, Schwere Panzerkompanie (Heavy Tank Company) "Hummel," which was attached to Schwere Panzer-Abteilung.506. At the start of the campaign, Hummel had fourteen Tiger I tanks. They saw limited combat over the next two months until the surviving five Tiger I tanks were dispatched to the 81.Korps in mid-February 1945. A Tiger I from this unit knocked out a T26E3 Pershing named "Fireball" of the 3rd Armored Division on 26 February 1945 near Elsdorf, Germany.

The third instance of combat between the Tiger I and the U.S. Army occurred in April 1945 when an improvised company called Gruppe Fehrmann was created at the Fallingbostel training grounds using six Tiger I tanks and five Panthers. This unit fought for about four days in the area of the Ruhr pocket, mainly against British troops. These tanks had at least one encounter with the U.S. 5th Armored Division on 11 April 1945 before the unit was disbanded. It is entirely possible that there were other sporadic encounters between small numbers of Tigers and U.S. troops in the final weeks of the war, but German records for this period, not surprisingly, are quite scarce.

KING TIGER ENCOUNTERS

Although U.S. Army combat with the classic Tiger I was very uncommon, there was more extensive contact with its larger relative, the Tiger II or King Tiger (Königstiger). The King Tiger began to appear in combat in the summer of 1944. Although it shared a name with the Tiger I, it was a fundamentally new design with thicker armor and a more powerful version of the 88mm gun. Arguably, it was a less successful design than its ancestor since it was excessively heavy and had the usual reliability problems that plagued late-war German heavy-tank designs. For example, on 20 October 1944, s.Pz.Abt.506 reported that of its forty King Tiger tanks, only ten were operational; two were back in Germany being rebuilt, fifteen were under short-term repair, and thirteen were under long-term repair.[224]

The U.S. Army's first encounters with the King Tiger involved one of the more unusual Tiger units, Panzer Kompanie (Funklenk) 316. This was one of two special companies of Tigers that operated the King Tiger as a command tank for Borgward B.IV

One of the first U.S. Army encounters with the King Tiger was the discovery of several abandoned tanks of Panzer Kompanie (Funklenk) 316 near Châteaudun, southwest of Paris, by Patton's Third U.S. Army in August 1944. These were used as command tanks for remote-control demolition vehicles, and they feature the early turret type.

Ladungsträger, a small remote-control demolitions vehicle. This company was deployed near Châteaudun, southwest of Paris, but all of their new King Tiger tanks were abandoned and demolished by their crews. They were found by advancing troops of Patton's Third U.S. Army in August 1944.

The first actual U.S. Army combat encounter with the King Tiger also took place in August 1944 in the Paris area. A company of King Tiger tanks of s.Pz.Abt.503 took part in attacks against the 79th Infantry Division on 22–23 August, part of a broader attempt to crush the Mantes bridgehead over the Seine River. All but two were lost in the fighting, mainly to M10 3-inch GMC tank destroyers.

The number of Tiger and King Tiger tanks assigned to OB West remained small through the autumn of 1944, as shown in the accompanying chart. Most of these tanks were assigned to units that were rebuilding after the Normandy defeat, and few of these saw combat until the Battle of the Bulge in December 1944.

TIGER* STRENGTH ON THE WESTERN FRONT[225]

	Inventory	In Repair	Replacement Tanks
15 Jun 44	46	7	51
4 Oct 44	44	1	0
16 Oct 44	36	18	0
31 Oct 44	43	6	35
15 Nov 44	71	17	0
30 Nov 44	28	34	57
15 Dec 44	79	44	13
30 Dec 44	58	58	7
15 Jan 45	64	46	7

*Includes Tiger I, Tiger I (Befels) command tank, and Tiger II/ King Tiger

The King Tiger was seldom seen in combat again until the Ardennes offensive in December 1944. The peak Tiger strength on the western front was in the days before the start of the Ardennes offensive, with a total of 102 Tigers of all types.[226] To put this in some perspective, the Wehrmacht deployed 724 tanks and 637 AFVs at the start of the Battle of the Bulge, including 14 Tiger I and 52 King Tigers. The King Tiger is probably best known for its use with s.SS-Pz.Abt.101, which served with Kampfgruppe Peiper during the attacks by the 1.SS-Panzer-Division around Stavelot at the start of the Battle of the Bulge. Peiper was not keen on using the King Tiger with his spearhead formation since the tanks were too heavy and clumsy on the rural Belgian roads. Instead, he assigned them mainly in the support role for the accompanying 3.Fallschirmjäger-Division. The battalion started the attack with forty-five tanks, but by 8 January 1945, it was down to fifteen operational tanks and eleven in repair.[227] This fell to only ten operational tanks by mid-January when the unit was finally pulled out of the Ardennes. Many of the King Tigers broke down and were abandoned by their crews. After the Ardennes fighting, the number of King Tiger units in the west declined. For example, on 2 February 1945, there were only forty-two Tigers of all types on the entire western front, including seven Sturmtiger heavy-assault mortar tanks.[228]

The U.S. Army had sporadic contact with King Tiger tanks during the late winter and early spring 1945 campaigns. The most extensive use of the King Tiger in these final campaigns was around its birthplace, the Henschel factory in Kassel. There were a number of skirmishes with King Tiger tanks in this area in April 1945 after the First U.S. Army staged its breakout operation from the Remagen bridgehead. King Tiger strength at this stage of the war was small. For example, on 10 April 1945, there were ten operational King Tigers on the entire western front plus eight more in short-term repair.[229]

I have presented many data tables from German records mainly to show the very small scale of Tiger deployment on the western front in 1944–1945. This helps to explain why combat engagements between U.S. tanks and Tigers were so uncommon.

The s.Pz.Abt.506 lost this King Tiger, tactical number 2-11, near Geronsweiller on 15 December 1944, a day before the start of the Ardennes offensive. It was recovered by the U.S. 129th Ordnance Battalion as seen here and given new markings so that it could be safely driven back through U.S. lines.

The U.S. Army captured a number of the King Tigers of SS-pz.Abt.501 that had been attached to Kampfgruppe Peiper. Number 332 was sent to the First U.S. Army headquarters at Spa, Belgium, and it was displayed near an M4A1 (76mm) to provide a size comparison. This King Tiger was later shipped to the United States and is currently at Fort Benning.

The classic Tiger I had largely disappeared by the time of the Ardennes fighting. At the start of the campaign, there were only fourteen Tiger I tanks of Heavy Tank Company "Hummel" attached to s.Panzer-Abteilung.506. One of these is seen knocked out in Oberwampach, Luxembourg, on 21 January 1945, with a scout patrol of the 358th Infantry, 90th Division using it as an observation post. Only five of these tanks survived the campaign.

In one of the last encounters by the U.S. Army with the Tiger I, a T26E3 Pershing named "Fireball" of the 3rd Armored Division was knocked out on 26 February 1945 by this Tiger of Heavy Tank Company "Hummel" near Elsdorf, Germany. Another Tiger from this unit was knocked out the next day by a Pershing.

There were an increasing number of contacts with King Tiger tanks in April 1945 as the U.S. Army pushed out of the Remagen bridgehead and headed towards Kassel, the production center for this tank type. GIs inspect a King Tiger of s.Pz.Abt.507 knocked out by Task Force Kane, Combat Command A, 3rd Armored Division in front of the Hotel Kaiserhofen in the fighting in Osterode on 10 April 1945.

Endnotes

1. Steven Zaloga, *Panther vs. Sherman: Battle of the Bulge 1944*, Oxford: Osprey, 2008.
2. My earlier book in this series, *Armored Champion*, discusses German tank readiness rates in much more detail.
3. This included 289 tanks and 186 assault guns and tank destroyers. *Panzerlage O.B. Sudwest Stand 31.1.44*, NARA, RG-242, T-78, R-720.
4. Annex No. 2 to Annex 14 "Action Against the Enemy A/ Action Report, Hq. First US Army, 31 August 1944: Days of Combat, Number of Tanks Operative and Losses for Periods 6–30 June and 1–31 July 1944," NARA II, RG 338, ETO AFV & Weapons Section.
5. *Estimated Enemy Tank Casualties Since D-Day, Appendix C to 21 Army Group RAC Liaison Letter No. 2.*
6. Martin Block, John Nelson. "The I.Abteilung/Panzer-Regiment.4 in Italy 1944–45," *AFV Modeler*, Issue 4, May–June 2002, pp. 19–25.
7. For a more detailed description of the clash between the 2nd Armored Division and Panzer-Lehr Division in the opening phase of Operation Cobra, see Steven Zaloga, *Panzer IV vs Sherman: France 1944*, Oxford: Osprey Duel 70, 2015.
8. Frédéric Deprun, *Panzer en Normandie: Histoire des équipages de char de la 116.Panzer-Division*, Louviers, Belgium: Ysec, 2011.
9. Didier Lodieu, *D'Argentan à la Seine: La bataillon de Panther de la 9.Pz.Div. face au XV Corps americain*, Louviers, Belgium: Ysec, 2003.
10. The best of these studies are those of the Operation Research Office of John Hopkins that did a number of studies for the U.S. Army after the Korean War. Alvin Coox, *US Armor in the Anti-Tank Role: Korea 1950* (Operations Research Office, July 1952); H. W. McDonald et al., *The Employment of Armor in Korea* (Operations Research Office, April 1951); Vincent McRae, Alvin Coox, *Tank-vs.-Tank Combat in Korea* (Operations Research Office, September 1954).
11. "Interview with Maj. Gen. Hobbs 30th Division commander and Lt. Col. Hall, division G-2 on 15 August 1944," in Combat Interviews, 30th Infantry Division, NARA II, RG 407 Entry 427A.
12. Bruno Renoult, "Luftwaffe contre Anti-Aircraft: Les combats aériens sur la tête de pont de Mantes- août 1944," *39–45*, No. 193, September 2002, pp.15–33.
13. Deprun, *Panzer en Normandie*, pp. 295–96.
14. One survey of German panzer and AFV strength in Normandy puts the figure at 2,248 tanks and AFVs, but it does not include assorted panzer replacement battalions and other formations. Niklas Zetterling, *Normandy 1944: German Military Organization, Combat Power and Organizational Effectiveness*, Winnipeg: Federowicz, 2000, p. 417.
15. *Final Historical Report*, AFV & Weapons Section, HQ ETOUSA, NARA Record Group 338. British tank strength in June 1944 was 3,033, rising to 3,680 by December 1944.
16. This chart was compiled from several appendices in OKH files that can be found at NARA in RG 242, T-78, R-145, F76029 passim. A more convenient compilation can be found in Norbert Baczyk, "Goracy rok Panzerwaffe," *Poligon*, May–Jun 2009, pp. 22–32. There are small discrepancies between both sources, mainly in regards to subvariants such as command tanks, etc.
17. *Tätigkeitsbericht General der Panzertruppe OB West vom 22.8.44 bis 31.12.1944*, Anlage 33, 12.9.44, NARA II, RG-242, T-311, R-18, F7019858. Aside from the eighty-two tanks and AFVs that were operational, additional tanks were available but battle damaged or broken down. So for example, the 10.SS-Panzer-Division had eight AFVs under repair at Panzer Werkstatt 928 near Krefeld and three more at Panzer Werkstattzug 943 near Düsseldorf with an estimated repair time of eight to fourteen days. (op. cit., F7019868). Researchers should note that the Panzerlage was often coded. "D" indicates Panther, "CL" (or Clg) indicates PzKpfw IV (lang), "F" indicates Befelspanzer (command tank), "L" indicates Flakpanzer IV, "G1" indicates StuG assault gun, "G2" indicates Jagdpanzer IV tank destroyer, and "J" indicates Sturmpanzer IV.

18. Lt. Gen. Heinz von Gyldenfeldt, *Army Group G: May–Sep 1944*, FMS B-488, p. 37.

19. Hugh Cole, *The Lorraine Campaign*, Washington, DC: U.S. Army Center for Military History, 1981, p. 217.

20. Hasso von Manteuffel, *Defense of the Vosges Mountains and Commitment of the 5.Panzer-Armee 1944–45*, FMS B-037, p.14.

21. Joachim Ludewig, *Rückzug: The German Retreat from France 1944*, Lexington: University Press of Kentucky, 2012, pp. 238, 364.

22. Lt. Gen. Heinz von Gyldenfeldt, *Battles of Army Group G: 15–25 September 1944*, Foreign Military Studies B-589, 1947, p. 4.

23. Gen. Hasso von Manteuffel, *The Commitment of the Fifth Panzer Army west of the Vosges within the framework of Army Group G from about 15 September to 15 October 1944*, Foreign Military Studies B-757, 1947, p. 1.

24. "Auszug aus Führer-Weisung für die weitere Kampfführung Ob. West vom 3.9.1944," in *KTB Pz.AOK.5*, NARA Record Group 242, T313,R.481, F.8714273.

25. At the time of the Normandy landings in June 1944, this had originally been called Panzergruppe West. It was commanded by Gen. Heinrich Eberbach until 9 August 1944 and then by SS-Oberstgruppenführer Sepp Dietrich until early September 1944.

26. Manteuffel was forty-seven years old at the time; von Luttwitz of the 47.Panzer-Korps was forty-eight years old; and General Krüger of 58.Panzer-Korps was fifty-two years old.

27. Hans von Luck, *Panzer Commander*, New York: Praeger, 1999, pp. 189–90.

28. Lt. Gen. Courtney Hodge had taken over command of the First U.S. Army in August 1944 when Bradley was elevated to command the new 12th Army Group. The 12th Army Group at the time commanded Hodge's and Patton's field army, expanding soon after with Simpson's Ninth U.S. Army.

29. Steven Zaloga, *Defense of the Rhine 1944–45*, Oxford: Osprey Fortress 102, 2011.

30. George S. Patton, *War as I Knew It*, Boston: Houghton, Mifflin, 1947, p. 115.

31. Martin Blumenson, *The Patton Papers 1940–1945*, New York: De Capo, p. 528; Patton, *War as I Knew It*, p. 117.

32. Brg. Gen. Oscar Koch, *G-2: Intelligence for Patton*, Atglen, PA: Schiffer, 1999, p. 80.

33. Ronald Ruppenthal, *Logistical Support of the Armies, Volume II: September 1944–May 1945*, Washington, DC: Chief of Military History, 1959, pp. 11–17.

34. The 20,000-ton figure is for 1 October 1944, rising to about 23,000 tons by mid-October 1944. Ruppenthal, *Logistical Support of the Armies*, p. 18.

35. Peter Beale, *The Great Mistake: The Battle for Antwerp and the Beveland Peninsula September 1944*, Throup, UK: Sutton, 2004.

36. The Third U.S. Army received an average of 2,285 tons of supplies daily in August 1944, falling to about 1,915 tons per day in September 1944. Among the supplies were 1,400 tons of fuel per day in August, falling to 1,110 tons in September 1944. *After-Action Report, Third U.S. Army, 1 August 1944–9 May 1945*, p. 412.

37. Gen. Karl Thoholte, "A German Reflects Upon Artillery," *Field Artillery Journal*, December 1945, pp. 709–15.

38. J. Dugdale, *Panzer Divisions, Panzergrenadier Division and Panzer Brigades of the Army and Waffen SS in the West, Autumn 1944–February 1945, Volume 1, Part 1: September 1944 Refitting and Re-equipment*, Milton Keynes: Military Press, 2000, p.125.

39. A. Harding Ganz, *Ghost Division: The 11th "Gespenster" Panzer Division and the German Armored Force in World War II*, Mechanicsburg, PA: Stackpole, 2016.

40. Timm Haasler, *Hold the Westwall or Perish with It: The History of Panzer-Brigade.105—September 1944*, Winnipeg: Federowicz, 2007, pp. 5–12.

41. Friedrich Bruns, *Die Panzerbrigade 106 FHH: Eine Dokumentation uber den Einsatz im Westen vom Juli 1944–Mai 1945*, Traditionsverband der Panzer-Brigade 106 FHH, Celle: 1988, p. 37.

42. Hasso von Manteuffel, *The Commitment of the 5th Panzer Army west of the Vosges within the framework of Army Group G from about 15 September to 15 October 1944*, FMS B-757, p. 9.

43. Gen.derPzTrp. Walter Krüger, *The LVIII.Panzer Korps in the Battles West of the Vosges during the Period from 17 September 1944 to 4 November 1944*, Foreign Military Studies B-548, 1947, pp. 4–5.

44. Philippe Burtscher and François Hoff, *Les fortifications allemandes d'Alsace-Lorraine 1870–1918*, Paris: Histoire & Collections, 2008.

45. Steven Zaloga, *US Armored Divisions: The European Theater of Operations 1944–45*, Oxford: Osprey, 2004.

46. Eric Freiwald, *The Building and Training of the 4th Armored Division 1941–1944*, Doctoral Dissertation, Temple University, 2001.

47. Hanson Baldwin, *Tiger Jack*, Ft. Collins, CO: Old Army Press, 1979, p. 18.

48. Interviews by the author with James Leach, commander of Company B, 37th Tank Battalion, in September 1944.

49. Steven Zaloga, *US Tank and Tank Destroyer Battalions in the ETO, 1944–45*, Oxford: Osprey, 2005.

50. Matthew Morton, *Men on Iron Ponies: The Death and Rebirth of the Modern US Cavalry*, DeKalb: Northern Illinois University Press, 2009, p. 156.

51. David Spires, *Air Power for Patton's Army: The XIX Tactical Air Command in the Second World War*, Washington, DC: U.S. Air Force History and Museums, 2002.

52. The controversial issue of close air support is dealt with in some detail in chapter 5, "Allied Fighter-Bombers Versus German Armoured Forces: Myths and Realities," in Ian Gooderson, *Air Power at the Battlefront: Allied Close Air Support in Europe 1943–45*, London: Frank Cass, 1997.

53. Tom Ivie, *Patton's Eyes in the Sky: USAAF Combat Reconnaissance Missions NW Europe 1944–45*, Hersham: Ian Allen, 2003.

54. Ken Wakefield, *The Fighting Grasshoppers: US Liaison Aircraft Operations in Europe 1942–1945*, Stillwater, MN: Specialty Press, 1990.

55. "Letter of Instruction No. 2, HQ Third US Army," 3 April 1944, reprinted in Patton, *War as I Knew It*, p. 413.

56. For a more detailed technical comparison between these two types, see Steven Zaloga, *Panzer IV vs. Sherman: France 1944*, Oxford: Osprey, 2015.

57. "Interview with Capt. Lamison, Co C commander, 37th Tank Battalion: Counter-attacks East of the Moselle from 19 to 25 Sept 1944," *4th Armored Division Combat Interviews*, NARA II, Entry 427A, Box 19077.

58. Interview with Gen. Bruce Clarke by John Albright, Bruce Clarke Papers, Box 9, U.S. Army Military History Insitute, Carlisle Barracks, PA, pp. 64–65.

59. The use of WP ammunition against German tanks was first reported by Armored Force Observers in Memorandum No. 1 of the Armored Section, First U.S. Army Armored Section, 19 June 1944. This tactic was disseminated elsewhere in the 12th Armored Group, and mentioned in interviews with 4th Armored Division veterans with the author.

60. "Einsatzbereite Pz u. Stu.Gesch. Ost in %," Generalinsketeur der Panzertruppen, 3.11.44, NARA II, RG 242, T-78, R-145, F76020.

61. The French army did an evaluation of its stock of captured Panther tanks in 1947: "Le Panther," Groupement Auto-Char, Section Technique de l'Armée, Ministre de Guerre, 1947, repinted in Walter Spielberger, *Panther & Its Variants*, Atglen, PA: Schiffer, 1993, pp.160–61.

62. "Panther Performance Trials," (British Army) Fighting Vehicle Proving Establishment, Automotive Wing, 2 November 1948.

63. Starting on 11 June 1944, the First U.S. Army, and later the 12th Army Group, reported on the daily status of its tanks based on a request from the 21st Army Group. The daily report as of 22:00 hours each day listed in three categories: operational tanks and tanks under short-term (less than twenty-four hours) and long-term repair. *Daily Tank Status*, HQ ETO AFV & W Section, NARA II, Record Group 338.

64. Gen. Otto von Knobelsdorff, *Army Group G on the Western Front: Estimate of the Situation when I Took Command of 1.Armee on 10-9-44*, Foreign Military Studies B-222, 1950, p. 14. For the OKW assessment, see the 4 September 1944 report to Hitler in James Wood (ed.), *Army of the West: The Weekly Reports of German Army Group B from Normandy to the West Wall*, Mechanicsburg, PA: Stackpole, 2007, p. 211 passim.

65. Kriegstagebuch des OB West, 4.9.1944.

66. This was mentioned in the Personalakten (personnel files) of the German army captured by the U.S. Army after the war. Hugh Cole, *The Lorraine Campaign*, Wahington, DC: Historical Division of the U.S. Army, 1981, p. 45.

67. Col. Albert Emmerich, *The Battles of the 1.Armee in France from 11 Aug to 15 Sep 1944*, Foreign Military Studies B-728, 1946, p. 19.

68. Ludewig, *Rückzug*, p. 230.

69. *Stellenbesetzung AOK.1 und unterstellte Verbände 10.8–14.9 (1944)*, Foreign Military Studies A-908, 1950.

70. Kurt Mehner, *Die Geheimen Tagesberichte der Deutschen Wehrmachtführung im Zweiten Weltkrieg 1939–1945, Band 11: 1.September 1944–31.Dezember 1944*, Osnabrück: Biblio Verlag, 1984, p. 15.

71. This was contained in Armeebefehl Nr. 11. Friedrich Bruns, *Die Panzerbrigade 106 FHH: Eine Dokumentation uber den Einsatz im Westen vom Juli 1944–Mai 1945*, Traditionsverband der Panzer-Brigade 106 FHH, Celle, 1988.

72. Knobelsdorff, FMS B-222, op. cit., p. 1.

73. Col. Kurt von Einem, *Report on the Engagements of XIII. SS-Corps in Lorraine during the Period from 1 September to 15 November 1944*, Foreign Military Studies B-412, 1946.

74. *After-Action Report, Third U.S. Army, Quartermaster Section, September 1944 Operations*, p. 4.

75. *The XX Corps: Its History and Service in World War II*, Osaka, Japan: XX Corps Association, 1946, p. 108.

76. Alfonso Escuadra Sanchez, *Feldherrnhalle: Forgotten Elite, the Panzerkorps Feldherrnhalle and Antecedent Formations*, Bradford, UK: Shelf Books, 1996.

77. Dugdale, *Panzer Divisions, Panzergrenadier Division*, pp. 138–39.

78. *Vorläufige Richtlinien für Fuhrung und Kampf der Panzer Brigade*, Generalinspekteuer der Panzertruppen, 26 July 1944.

79. Generalmajor Karl Britzmayr, *Operations of the 19.Volksgrenadier-Division during the period from 1 September 1944 to 27 April 1945*, Foreign Military Studies B-527, 1946, p. 3.

80. Col. Kurt von Einem, *Report on the Engagements of the XIII.SS-Korps in Lorraine during the Period from 1 September to 15 November 1944*, Foreign Military Studies B-412.

81. The figure of twenty-two tanks comes from a report by Minister of Armaments Albert Speer from trips to western Germany in September–December 1944 archived at the Imperial War Museum at Duxford, UK, and provided by Bill Auerbach. Speer Document (Flensburg), *Vier Berichte Über Reisen nach den Westgebieten*. FD. 2690/45 Vol. 8 (G2). This is reinforced by prisoner-of-war interrogations after the battle that indicated that about ten Panther tanks were left behind for repair on 7–8 September 1944.

82. A copy of the attack orders for 7 September 1944 were captured and translated by the 90th Infantry Division, and can be found in their After-Action Reports, Record Group 407, Entry 427, NARA II.

83. John Colby, *War from the Ground Up: The 90th Division in WWII*, Austin, TX: Nortex, 1991, pp. 256–58.

84. Aaron Elson, *Tanks for the Memories: The 712th Tank Battalion during World War II*, Hackensack, NJ: Chi Chi Press, 2001, p. 202.

85. WO Carl Jenkins, "The Battle of the CPs," in *90th Division Combat Interviews*, Record Group 407, Entry 427A, Box 19064, NARA II.

86. Colby, *War from the Ground Up*, p. 260.

87. *After-Action Report, 712th Tank Battalion*, 9 September 1944, NARA, Record Group 407, Entry 407.

88. Major Lytle, in *90th Division Combat Interviews*, op. cit., p. 3.

89. Patton, *War as I Knew It*, p. 128.

90. Cole, *Lorraine Campaign*, op.cit., p. 159. OKH Generalstab des Heeres, Operationsabteilung/II, *"Tagesmeldungen OB West,"* NARA II, RG 242, T-78, Roll 313, 10 September 1944.

91. Data from RG 252 at NARA II via Tom Jentz. The brigade lost one or more Panther tanks in the fighting with the 5th Armored Division in Luxembourg on 9 September 1944.

92. The HQ Battery, Division Artillery lost five dead and twenty-three wounded. *90th Division Combat Interviews*, op. cit.

93. *712th Tank Battalion After-Action Report*, RG 407, Entry 427, NARA II.

94. Ludewig, *Rückzug*, p. 228.

95. Bruns, *Die Panzerbrigade 106 FHH*, p. 81.

96. n.a., *Paths of Armor: The 5th Armored Division in World War II*, Nashville: Battery Press, 1985, pp. 110–11.

97. There are numerous histories of the 2e DB in French. Recent ones include Dominique Forget, *Le Général Leclerc et la 2e DB 1944–45*, Bayeux: Heimdal, 2008; Alain Eymard, *2e DB: 1er Août 1944–8 Mai 1945*, Bayeux: Heimdal, 1990.

98. There are numerous biographies of Leclerc in French and an excellent one in English: William Moore, *Free France's Lion: The Life of Philippe Leclerc, De Gaulle's Greatest General*, Philadelphia: Casemate, 2011.

99. Hubert Pittino, *Combats de la 2e DB en Normandie: Alençon, Carrouges, Écouché*, Issy-les-Moulineaux: Muller, 2002.

100. The brigade was short 209 officers and NCOs, about 16 percent of the authorized strength. Dugdale, *Panzer Divisions, Panzergrenadier Division*, p. 159.

101. G-2, Headquarters, XV Corps, 21 Sep 1944, *Order of Battle Annex No. 17*, NARA II, RG 407, WWII Operations Reports, Entry 427, Box 4127.

102. A rating of "1" meant suitable for offense, "3" meant suitable for defense, and "4" meant limited suitability for defense, the lowest ranking. *Tätigkeitsbericht General der Panzertruppe OB West vom 22.8.44 bis 31.12.1944*, Anlage 54, 16.9.44, NARA II, RG-242, T-311, R-18, F7019903.

103. Gen. Maj. Fredrich Wilhelm von Mellenthin, *Army Group G (20 Sep 44–3 Dec 44) Report of the Chief of Staff*, Foreign Military Studies A-999, p. 7

104. Luck, *Panzer Commander*, p. 193.

105. Ibid.

106. Patton, *War as I Knew It*, p. 130.

107. These were called Sous Groupement (SS/GPMT) in French, and corresponded to task forces in the U.S. Army's armored divisions. They were ad hoc formations, and their internal organization could change on a daily basis depending on the tactical mission.

108. Jacques Massu, *Sept ans avec Leclerc*, Paris: Plon, 1974, p. 164.

109. The most detailed account of the battle is Jacques Salbaing, *La victoire de Leclerc à Dompaire 13 septembre 1944*, Issy-les Moulineaux: Editions Muller, 1997. There are also detailed interviews with several of the participants by U.S. Army historians, including Lt. Edmon Bissirier (G-3, GTL), Maj. Paul Massu, Captain de Parceveau (S-2 Group Minjonnet), and several junior officers of Group Minjonnet. *Combat Interviews, 2nd French Armored Division*, NARA II, RG 407, Entry 427A, Box 19071.

110. Massu, *Sept ans avec Leclerc*, p. 167. The orange and cherry panel he refers to is the standard U.S. Army air identification panels introduced in the summer of 1944 to minimize the risk of Allied aircraft attacking friendly tanks.

111. Luck, *Panzer Commander*, p. 194.

112. Paul de Langlade, *En suivant Leclerc d'Alger à Berchtesgaden*, Paris: Laffont, 1964, pp. 248–49.

113. *Tätigkeitsbericht General der Panzertruppe OB West vom 22.8.44 bis 31.12.1944*, Anlage 65, 16.9.44, NARA II, RG-242, T-311, R-18, F7019918.

114. "September Operations," in *After-Action Report, Third U.S. Army, 1 August 1944–9 May 1945, Vol. 1: The Operations* (Third U.S. Army, 1945), p. 61 passim.

115. Third U.S. Army was also in command of the VIII Corps laying siege to Brest in Brittany, but this command was relinquished in September to permit Patton to concentrate on the Lorraine fighting.

116. Philippe Burtscher and François Hoff, *Les fortifications allemandes d'Alsace-Lorraine 1870–1918*, Paris: Histoire & Collections, 2008; Rémi Fontbonne, *Les fortifications allemandes de Metz et de Thionville 1871–1918*, Paris: Serpenoise, 2006; Rudi Rolf, *Die Deutsche Panzer-fortifikation: Die Panzerfesten von Metz und ihre Vorge-schichte*, Osnabrück: Biblio, 1991.

117. The records of the Metz OCS were destroyed prior to the surrender of Metz. However, one abbreviated history of the Kampfgruppe Stössel survived at the Metz Gestapo headquarters and was secured by XX Corps counterintelligence. Another short history was preserved in the Combat Interviews collection of RG-407, Entry 427A, Box 19071, at NARA II under the tile *German OCS VI: Defense of Metz, 2–24 September 1944*. A considerable amount of detail of the unit can be found in the 5th Infantry Division G-2 records, also in RG-407.

118. *The Reduction of Fortress Metz: XX Corps Operational Report 1-Sept–6 Dec 1944*, XX Corps Headquarters, 1945; *The XX Corps: Its History and Service in World War II*, Osaka: Mainichi Publishing, 1945, pp. 111–21.

119. H. J. Stöber, *Die eiserne Faust: Bildband und Chronik der 11.SS-Panzergrenadier-Division*, Neckargemünd: Vowinckel, 1966, pp. 44–47.

120. Steven Zaloga, *Metz 1944: Patton's Fortified Nemesis*, Oxford: Osprey, 2012.

121. Dugdale, *Panzer Divisions, Panzergrenadier Division*, p. 113.

122. Kamen Nevenkin, *Fire Brigades: The Panzer Divisions 1943–1945*, Winnipeg: Federowicz, 2008, pp. 493–94.

123. *Tätigkeitsbericht General der Panzertruppe OB West vom 22.8.44 bis 31.12.1944*, Anlage 30, 11.9.44, NARA II, RG-242, T-311, R-18, F7019845.

124. *Tätigkeitsbericht General der Panzertruppe OB West vom 22.8.44 bis 31.12.1944*, Anlage 78, 19.9.44, NARA II, RG-242, T-311, R-18, F7019935.

125. Combined Services Detailed Interrogation Centre (CSDIC) report from prisoner of war of 1./Panzer-Abt.2111 captured at Arracourt on 29 September 1944, NARA II, RG 165, Entry 179, Box 661.

126. Combined Services Detailed Interrogation Centre (CSDIC) report from prisoner of war Sr. Lt. Lohmann, executive officer of Pamnzergrenadier-Regiment.2111, captured near Parroy on 22 September 1944, NARA II, RG 165, Entry 179, Box 662.

127. These were called Holzgas-wagen and Anthrazit-wagen and burned wood or coal that fed the heated gas into the engine.

128. *Kriegstagebuch 5.Panzer-AOK*, NARA II, RG 242, T-313, R-421, F8714287.

129. Cole, *Lorraine Campaign*, p. 218.

130. *KTB OB West, 3,00 Uhr, 15.9.44*. NARA II, RG 242, T-311, R-16, F7017365.

131. *KTB 5.Pz.-AOK*, NARA II, RG 242, T-313, R-421, F8714285-86.

132. The list of shipments in September can be found in the records of Stumpf's command: *Tätigkeitsbericht General der Panzertruppe OB West vom 22.8.44 bis 31.12.1944*, Anlage 33, 12.9.44, NARA II, RG-242, T-311, R-18, F7019995-98.

133. Gen. Hermann Balck, David Zabecki (trans.), *Order in Chaos: The Memoirs of General of Panzer Troops Hermann Balck*, Lexington: University of Kentucky Press, 2015, p. 381.

134. The "88" was more likely a 75mm PaK 40 antitank gun. Al Lambert and G. B. Layton, *The Ghosts of Patton's Third Army: A History of the Second US Cavalry*, Munich: Munchner Graphische, 1946, pp. 145–46.

135. *After-Action Report, 4th Armored Division, 17 September 1944*, NARA II, RG 407, Entry 427, Box 12337.

136. There are few surviving records for either the 15.Panzergrenadier-Division from this period or the 47.Panzer-Korps.

137. *Befehl zum Angriff fur den 18.9.44*, in 58.Panzer-Korps KTB, NARA II, T-314, Roll 1541, F000597.

138. Panzer-Brigade.112 had numerous tanks under repair, and once maintenance was accomplished, the brigade could be brought up to a strength of ten Panthers and twenty-five PzKpfw IVs.

139. Interview with 3rd Platoon, Company B commander, 1st Lt. Jerome Sacks, in *4th Armored Division Combat Interviews*, NARA II, RG 407, Entry 427A.

140. Account by Lt. Richard Buss in Richard Buchanan et al., *Men of the 704th: A Pictoral and Spoken History of the 704th Tank Destroyer Battalion in World War II*, Latrobe, PA: St. Vincent College, 1998, p. 43.

141. *HQ XV Corps, G-2 Section, Order of Battle Notes 18, 22 September 1944*, p. 1, NARA II, RG 407, Entry 427.

142. Werner Kortenhaus, *The Combat History of the 21.Panzer Division*, Solihull: Helion, 2014, pp. 310–11.

143. Luck, *Panzer Commander*, p. 195.

144. *KTB 58.Pz.Korps*, NARA II, RG 242, T-314, R-1497, F0478.

145. *Third US Army G-2 Work Map: Situation as of 0300 hours 18 Sep 1944*, Third U.S. Army G-2 records, NARA II, RG 407, Entry 427.

146. For a summary of the Ultra signal intelligence decrypts connected with the Lorrain fighting, see F. H. Hinsley et al., *British Intelligence in the Second World War, Volume 3, Part 2*, London: Her Majesty's Stationary Office, 1988, pp. 391–92.

147. Maj. William Jackson et al., *The Employment of Four Tank Destroyer Battalions in the ETO*, Fort Knox, KY: U.S. Army Armored School, 1950, p. 72.

148. "Interview with Lt. Col. Pattison, Exec Officer CCA: German Tank Counteratttacks on CCA 19–22 Sept at Moselle Bridgehead," *4th Armored Division Combat Interviews*, NARA II, RG 407, Entry 427A, Box 19077.

149. *Battalion Diary, HQ 37th Tank Battalion, 19 September 1944*, NARA, RG 407, Entry 407.

150. Patton, *War as I Saw It*, pp. 134–35.

151. *KTB 55.Pz.Korps 19.9.44*, NARA II, RG-242, T-314, R1497, F623.

152. *KTB 5.Pz.AOK, Morning report, 19.9.44*, NARA II, RG-242, T-313, R-421, F8714326.

153. *KTB OB West, 18.9.44*, NARA II, RG-242, T-311, R29, F7036708.

154. *KTB 58.Panzer-Korps, Day report, 20.9.44*, NARA II, RG-242, T-314, R-1497, F653.

155. Interview with Lt. Col. Hal Pattison, executive officer of CCA, 4th Armored Division, in *4th Armored Division Combat Interviews*, NARA II, RG-407, Entry 427A.

156. Due to the controversy over this incident, Lamison was interviewed a second time by army historians on 27 October 1944 in hopes of clarifying the reports. "Interview with Capt. Lamison, Co. C commander, 37th Tank Battalion (supplementary): Action at Ley and Juvelize 20 and 25 Sep 1944," *4th Armored Division Combat Interviews*, NARA II, Record Group 407, Entry 427A, Box 19077.

157. "Interview with Capt. Thomas MacDonald, 10th Armored Infantry Battalion," *4th Armored Division Combat Interviews*, NARA II, RG-407, Entry 427A.

158. *37th Tank Battalion After-Action Report, 20 September 1944*, NARA II, RG 407, Entry 427.

159. *KTB 5Pz.AOK, mid day report, 21.9.1944*, NARA II, RG-242, T-313, R-421, F8714341; *KTB 58.Pz.Korps, 21.9.1944*, NARA II, T-314, R-1497, F663.

160. The data primarily comes from the daily reports in the *58.Panzer-Korps Kriegstagebuch (war diary)*, NARA II, RG-243, T-314, R1497, various frames.

161. Richard Giziowski, *The Enigma of General Blaskowitz*, New York: Hippocrene, 1997, p. 354.

162. F. W. von Mellenthin, *Panzer Battles: A Study of the Employment of Armor in the Second World War*, New York: Ballantine, 1971, pp. 371–72.

163. Blumenson, *The Patton Papers*, p. 552.

164. Maj. Gen. Friedrich von Mellenthin, *Army Group G, 20 Sep 44– 3 Dec 44: Report of the Chief of Staff*, Foreign Military Studies A-999, 1945, p. 12.

165. Lt. Gen. Gustav Höhne, *Commitment of the 11th Panzer Division in Lorraine*, Foreign Military Studies B-364, 1951, p. 2.

166. Ibid., p. 3.

167. *KTB Panzer-AOK.5, End-of-the-day report 22.9.44*, NARA II, RG-242, T-313, R421, F353.

168. Contemporary maps show this as Hill 242 "le vieux Gué" (the old ford) since the Ruisseau de Névoine (Nevoine stream) passes by the southwest foot of the hill.

169. Jean Paul Pallud, "Panzer Attack in Lorraine," *After the Battle*, Issue #84, 1994, pp. 40–42.

170. "Tagesmuldung der 113.Pz.Brigade v. 23.9.44," in *KTB, 58.Panzer-Korps*, NARA II, RG 242, T-314, R-1497, F717.

171. Gen. Hasso von Manteuffel, *Fifth Panzer Army West of the Vosges: 14 Sep–15 Oct 1944*, Foreign Military Studies B-757, 1947, p. 13.

172. "Eingliederung der Panzer-Brigaden in bestehende Divisionen," *KTB Panzer-AOK.5, 22.9.44*, NARA II, RG-242, T-313, R-421, F347.

173. The term "in the clear" meant that no effort was made to encrypt or disguise the messages. William Ellis and Thomas Cunningham, *Clarke of St. Vith: The Sergeant's General*, Cleveland: Dillon/Liederbach, 1974, p. 76.

174. *KTB, 5.Pz.AOK, 25.9.1944*, NARA II, RG 242, T-313, R-421, F 374.

175. *51st Armored Infantry Battalion, After-Action Report*, 26 September 1944, NARA II, RG 406, Entry 427.

176. *4th Armored Division, After-Action Report, 26 September 1944*, NARA II, RG 407, Entry 427.

177. Interviews with officers of A/10th Armored Infantry Battalion in *4th Armored Division Combat Interviews*, NARA II, RG-407, Entry 427, Box 19077.

178. Lt. Gen. Wend von Wietersheim, *Commitment of the 11th Panzer Division in Lorraine*, FMS B-364, p. 15.

179. *4th Armored Division After-Action Report, 27 September 1944*, NARA II, RG 407, Entry 427.

180. "Action on Hill 318 to the west of Rechicourt, France on 29 Sept 1944 as related by Captian Eugene Bush, Commanding officer of C/8 Tank Bn," *4th Armored Division Combat Interviews*, NARA II, RG 407, Entry 427A, Box 19077.

181. Wietersheim, *Commitment of the 11th Panzer Division in Lorraine*, p. 16.

182. *Tätigkeitsbericht General der Panzertruppe OB West vom 22.8.44 bis 31.12.1944*, Anlage 33, 12.9.44, NARA II, RG-242, T-311, R-18, F7019858, and various Panzerlage already cited from KTB Pz.AOK.5. These figures somewhat overstate German operational strength since two of the brigades, Panzer-Brigade.105 in the Aachen sector and Panzer-Brigade.106 in the Lorraine sector, had already suffered significant casualties. Also, 10.SS-Panzer-Division in the Arnhem sector had a significant fraction of its AFV strength at repair facilities inside Germany.

183. Ludewig, *Rückzug*, p. 251.

184. Lt. Gen. Heinz von Gyldenfeldt, *Battles of Army Group G: 15–25 September 1944*, FMS B-589, p. 18.

185. *Daily Tank Strength Reports, European Theater of Operations US Army Headquarters, AFV & W Section*, NARA II, Records Group 338.

186. This chart was prepared from the KTB of the 5.Pz.AOK and 58.Pz.Korps. The daily reporting was very erratic and incomplete, and this data should be viewed with caution. On some days, the reporting covered only the Panzer brigades; other days it covered all subordinate units. The data for 28 September is probably overall strength rather than operational strength.

187. *After-Action Report, September 1944, Headquarters, CCA, 4th Armored Division*, p. 39, NARA II, RG-407, Entry 427.

188. Alvin Coox and L. Van Loan Naisawald, *Survey of Allied Tank Casualties in World War II (ORO-T-117)*, Operations Research Office, John Hopkins University, March 1951.

189. Stephen Napier, *The Armored Campaign in Normandy: June–August 1944*, Philadelphia: Casemate, 2015, p. 415.

190. Army Group B claims of U.S. tank casualties against First U.S. Army and Ninth U.S. Army; Army Group G claims against Third U.S. Army and Ninth U.S. Army. Data for some periods is missing, notably Army Group B claims against UK and U.S. forces in early September. "Feindverluste im Zeitabschnitt/Monat," OB West, NARA, RG 242, T-311, Roll 17, F7018808-851.

191. Belton Cooper, *Death Traps: The Survival of an American Armored Division in World War II*, Novato, CA: Presidio Press, 1998, p. 308.

192. In telephone conversations I had with Belton Cooper after the book was published, he did not have a clear memory of where many of these details originated. This is not an uncommon issue when dealing with traumatic events from decades past, and it is one of the banes of relying on oral history collected long after the event in question. His friend Michael Benninghof edited and contributed to the manuscript. Benninghof is a well-known war gamer associated with Avalanche Press.

193. The average divisional loss in the ETO was 48 light tanks and 170 medium tanks. *12th Army Group Unit Historical Notes, 3rd Armored Division*, NARA II, Record Group 331, Entry 210, Box 2.

194. Headquarters, 3rd Armored Division G-2, *Subject: Destruction of German Combat Vehicles by US Forces*. This letter was in response to a request from Eisenhower on 17 April 1945 for units to provide a listing of enemy materiel destroyed during the ETO campaign. The responses can be found at the Digital Library portion of the Ike Skelton Combined Arms Research Library at Fort Leavenworth.

195. 4th Armored Division AFV losses from 22 July 1945 letter to G-4 by divisional ordnance section, NARA II, RG 407, Entry 427, 4th Armored Division historical records.

196. *Data on WWII Tank Engagements Involving the US Third and Fourth Armored Divisions*, Ballistic Research Laboratories Memo Report No. 758, Aberdeen Proving Ground, 1954, p. 10.

197. Carlo d'Este, *Patton: A Genius for War*, New York: Harper Collins, 1995.

198. Col. Francis Kish, "Interview with Gen. Bruce C. Clarke," Senior Officers Oral History Program, U.S. Army Military History Institute, Vol. II, 1982, pp. 289–90.

199. Steven Zaloga, *Metz 1944: Patton's Fortified Nemesis*, Oxford: Osprey, 2012.

200. Henry Phillips, *The Making of a Professional: Manton S. Eddy, USA*, Westport, CT: Greenwood, 2000.

201. Wilson Heefner, *Patton's Bulldog: The Life and Service of General Walton H. Walker*, Shippensburg, PA: White Mane Publishing, 2002.

202. Baldwin, *Tiger Jack*.

203. This account is based largely on the recollections of Col. Bruce Clarke. The background of Wood's relief was kept hushed up for many years, but Clarke explained the reasons in an interview with John Albright that is contained in Clarke's papers at the Military History Institute at AHEC in Carlisle Barracks, Pennsylvania.

204. William Ellis and Thomas Cunningham, *Clarke of St. Vith: The Sergeant's General*, Cleveland: Dillon/Liederbach, 1974.

205. Lewis Sorley, *Thunderbolt: General Creighton Abrams and the Army of His Time*, New York: Simon & Schuster, 1992.

206. William Moore, *Free France's Lion: The Life of Philippe Leclerc, De Gaulle's Greatest General*, Havertown, PA: Casemate, 2011.

207. Richard Giziowski, *The Enigma of General Blaskowitz*, London: Leo Cooper, 1997.

208. Herman Balck, *Order in Chaos: The Memoirs of General of Panzer Troops Hermann Balck*, Lexington: University Press of Kansas, 2015.

209. Donald Brownlow, *Panzer Baron: The Military Exploits of General Hasso von Manteuffel*, North Quincy, MA: Christopher Publishing, 1975.

210. John Albright, *Interview with Gen. Bruce Clarke*, Bruce Clarke Papers, U.S. Army Military History Institute, Carlisle Barracks, PA, p. 78.

211. William Woolley, "Patton and the Concept of Mechanized Warfare," *Parameters*, Vol. XV, No. 3, 1985, p. 73.

212. Cooper, *Death Traps*, pp. 26–27.

213. Ibid., pp. 154–55.

214. I should note that I accepted Cooper's viewpoint when I wrote one of my early books on the M26 Pershing in the Osprey Vanguard series in 2000. However, I have subsequently spent considerable time in the archives on this issue, and my more recent research on the subject is reflected in a companion book in this series, *Armored Thunderbolt*, from 2008.

215. The debate over Patton's ideas has been detailed in Nicholas Moran's blog "The Chieftain's Hatch," which appears on the World of Tanks website: http://worldoftanks.com/en/news/21/The_Chieftains_Hatch_Pattons_MGs/.

216. Grow had been Patton's executive officer in the 2nd Armored Division before the war.

217. Ellis and Cunningham, *Clarke of St. Vith*, pp. 82–83.

218. *After-Action Report, Third U.S. Army, 1 August 1944–9 May 1945*, Ordnance Section Report, February 1945.

219. The author found a copy of this report in the 4th Armored Division files at NARA, but it was subsequently printed in *Military Review*, Vol. XXV, No. 10, January 1946. *Military Review* is the journal of the U.S. Army Command and General Staff School. Irzyk later wrote his memoirs in a book entitled *He Rode Up Front for Patton*.

220. Wolfgang Schneider, *Tiger in Combat, Vol. 1*, Winnipeg: Federowicz, 1994, p. 43.

221. *Kraftfahrzeuge (gepanzert)-Heer-Westen 1.8.1944*, KTB Inspector General of the Panzer Troops, NARA II, T-78, R-145.

222. *Kraftfahrzeuge (gepanzert)-Heer-Westen*, KTB Inspector General of the Panzer Troops T-78, R-145, F75880 passim.

223. Wolfgang Schneider, *Tigers in Combat, Volume II*, Winnipeg: Federowicz, 1998.

224. *Tätigkeitsbericht General der Panzertruppe OB West vom 22.8.44 bis 31.12.1944*, Anlage 135, 20.10.44, NARA II, RG-242, T-311, R-18, F7020050.

225. *Panzerlage und Sturmgeschutzlage Stand 15.1.45*, General Inspector of the Panzer Forces, NARA II, T-78, Roll 624, F485 passim.

226. *Panzerlage und Sturmgeschutzlage Stand 15.1.45*, General Inspector of the Panzer Forces, NARA II, T-78, R-145, F75880 passim.

227. *Stärkung 6.Pz.Armee 8.1.45*, General Inspector of the Panzer Forces, NARA II, T-78, Roll 622, F1131.

228. *Panzerlage OB West Stand 5.2.45*, General Inspector of the Panzer Forces, NARA II, T-78, Roll 622, F188.

229. *Panzerlage Zusammenstellung Stand 10.4.45*, General Inspector of the Panzer Forces, NARA II, T-78, Roll 621, F530.

Index